Western Steelhead Fishing Guide

Milt Keizer

Frank Amato Publications • P.O. Box 02112 • Portland, Oregon 97202 • (503) 653-8108

ABOUT THE AUTHOR

Milt Keizer was born in Settler's Township, Iowa and grew up fishing the streams, large gravel pits and Big Sioux River near Hawarden. From there his angling spread across the state and to South Dakota, Minnesota, Michigan and Wisconsin before being interrupted by service with the U.S. Marines during the Korean conflict, University of Iowa schooling, business employment in the U.S. and province of Ontario and a final year of Journalism School at UI. In the late 1960's he and his wife, Joelle, and four children moved to the state of Washington and steelheading became his prime passion for the past 25 years.

Milt is a freelance outdoor article and book writer, has newsaper and magazine reporting, editing and publishing experience, has fished extensively in the western states and province of British Columbia and is a member of the Northwest Outdoor Writers Association and the Outdoor Writers Association of America.

Although this book is dedicated to fishing partners old and new, the author also says, "Without strong family support and encouragement, I would not have had the freedom to fish or time to write, so I feel this book belongs equally to Joelle, Colin, Robin, Lance and Wendy. Thank you, family!"

AUTHOR'S NOTES

Each steelheader is responsible for reading, comprehending and obeying all fishing regulations in effect where they are angling. I have tried to generalize for your convenience fishing rules in effect as this book was written, but cannot guarantee their accuracy. Individuals MUST fully acquaint themselves with, and follow, current departmental, local and emergency fishing regulations.

RIVERS & REFERENCES

You will not find all rivers that hold steelhead listed in the river chapters. Unless a stream consistently produces a number of fish I feel should be "touted" beyond local anglers' endeavors it was purposely omitted. If you prefer fishing these small, unheralded streams you probably already have your favorite spots and would not want them overcrowded with dozens of fishermen, guidebook in hand. Enjoy them in peace... I do.

I'd be remiss in coverage, though, if there were no mention made of how to find untrammelled angling. There are excellent maps available that can guide you to any steelhead waters. The best of these are: 7½ and 15-minute topographical maps which are available from larger book/map stores or from the Branch of Distribution, U.S. Geological Survey, Federal Center, Denver, CO 80225: state atlases (Washington and California now, more later) by DeLorme Mapping Company, P.O. Box 298, Freeport, ME 04032; county maps from bookstores and map shops or from Metsker Maps, 911 Pacific Ave., Metsker Building, P.O. Box 400, Tacoma, WA 98401 and Pittmon Sportsman's Maps, in shops or Oregon Blue Print Company, 930 S.E. Sandy Blvd., Portland, OR 97214.

ACKNOWLEDGEMENTS

Good fishing companions treble and quadruple the enjoyment derived from my angling, past and present. With humble thanks for sharing this most pleasant of pursuits with me I dedicate this book to: Frank Hout, my friend, classmate and first fishing buddy; Ellwood Youngkin, for our after-work fishing forays and the unforgettable Lake of the Woods high school graduation trip; Bob Dias, my willing Ontario bridge, ball and angling accomplice; John Thomas, who initiated me into the steelheading fraternity with a handful of spoons, 10 years of advice and shared fishing and to Chuck Shroeder, my angling partner for 18 years, who has listened patiently to my theories, shared my ethics, cheered my catches more happily than his own and perked my spirit with ever-ebullient good nature. Thanks, friends.

Photo Credits:

Milt Keizer - p. 2, 8, 50, 52, 104
Frank Amato - p. 38, 52, 55, 58, 61, 65, 67, 73, 75, 83, 85, 91, 94, 101, 105, 109, 112, 115, 118, 122, 125, 129, 132
Nick Amato - p. 13, 34, 47, 69, 98, 102, 123
Bill Herzog - p. 70
Marty Sherman - p. 86, 110
Ron Lane - p. 31
Don Roberts - p. 93
Oregon Historical Society - p. 77, 97, 117

Book Design: Joyce Herbst - Typsetting: John F. Michael

Cover Photograph: Dave Vedder - Cover Design: Tony Amato

Printed in Singapore

ISBN: 0-936608-76-5

10 9 8 7 6 5 4 3 2

CONTENTS

Chapter 1

Steelhead Tales and Some Truths

Steelhead fishing is a magnificent malady from which the one in four or five western anglers who tries it never recovers. It runs its course through the receptive cells of an angler's body in strange and unpredictable fashion. The affliction is wildly variable as to effects and length of its stay. Some anglers may fish for as many as five years before landing their first steelhead, while other beginners may catch one or more steelhead on their first trip.

Early settlers along the west coast swiftly discovered that the "little salmon" encountered by explorers George Rogers Clark and Merriwether Lewis and named so by Indians who netted, smoked and traded dried steelhead along with salmon was neither little nor a salmon. By the late 19th century, sport anglers were taking the migratory rainbow trout on hook and line on a wide variety of baits. Efforts to interest steelhead in artificial lures bloomed in the decades from 1910 through 1930 after the conception of the Apple Knocker and Cherry Bobber, two ancestors of the myriad of lures developed since then to deceive wary steelhead into striking.

Steelhead have captured the imagination of anglers as almost no other sportfish has done. Big and wild as the country in which they were found, swift, strong and glittering bright on arrival in natal streams from the ocean, this largest of the rainbow trout *(Salmo gairdneri)* clan has birthed new methods of fishing and created an ultra-dedicated and devoted breed of fishermen. True steelheaders readily admit they would far rather catch just one steelhead than a hundred of their miniscule rainbow, cutthroat, brook and brown trout cousins.

Few other fishing pursuits can persuade otherwise fully sane, adult men and women to spend long hours (and whole days aren't unusual) standing thigh deep in near-frigid, deep, swiftly moving rivers, enduring chilling rain and the stabbing bites of wind piercing the fabric of their clothing, all in the hope of catching one fish.

And then, when the gods and odds of fishing choose to smile on a fortunate fisherman, the sheer shock and sudden surprise of being attached to a rampaging fish a yard or more in length and wildly upset about the situation often causes beginners, and sometimes veteran anglers, to exhibit character quirks that might otherwise qualify them for an extended trip to the local loony bin but are clearly understood, often shared, and readily forgiven by fellow steelheading fraternity members.

Consider the case of the housewife who, in an attempt to understand her husband's fascination with steelheading, purloined his tackle one morning and headed for the nearby Cracker Bar to try this sport. The fishing gear was complete, having been left intact from hubby's last venture, so she found an open area between other patient steelheaders and began casting, allowing the bobber/yarn-bedecked hook to skip and bounce downstream in imitation of the nearby fishermen who, incidentally, had not seen a strike occur in the past hour-and-a-half of angling.

Of course, as you no doubt expected, there was at least one suicidal steelhead in that drift, which launched itself upon her lure and hook so savagely it firmly impaled the hook past the barb. She pulled. The steelhead pulled harder, leaping and rolling on the surface to further distract the now-thunderstruck young lady. With a wild shriek of, "I've got one!" the thoroughly unnerved heroine turned her back to the river, propped the rod over her shoulder and, firmly clenching the rod handle, dashed across the bar until about 45 feet away from the river. Reaching a steep gully and heavy growth of brush, she halted and wheeled around.

"Is my fish still on?" she implored of the startled anglers who had spun to observe her flight.

An elderly and amused oldtimer she'd nearly run over 10 feet back from the water by a warming bonfire took it upon himself to give her an answer.

"Well, Ma'am," he dryly confirmed,"It was... when it went bouncing past me!"

In all fairness, lifelong fishermen also can take temporary leave of their fishing acumen when they fall under the spell of steelhead...even those who have caught them for 45 years, as has my fishing partner, who may X me from his companion list after I relate one particular incident. The pool we fished deepened greatly after a sudden drop from a riffle and ran between a ledge on the far side and a huge boulder near us. At our feet was a slow eddy only four to five feet deep. He dropped a too-short cast into the eddy and began picking a slight involuntary overrun from his reel while watching the large ball of cluster eggs he'd baited on his hook roll around bottom in the swirling, clear water. I too, noted with great interest the softly tumbling eggs AND the large, bright, buck steelhead that slid out of the current, timed perfectly the next bouncing roll of the bait and matter-of-factly engulfed it.

"Strike!...hit it!" I screamed, waking my bemused partner from his wide-eyed trance. He belatedly splashed backward several feet, cranking on his reel and sawing at the air with his rod, trying to get enough slack out of his line to set the hook...gone! Patiently, I explained to my partner (who's caught as many steelhead as I have seen) that the purpose of the day's venture was to put the little, bent, pointy things on the end of our lines in the fishes' mouths and then pull hard on them so as to coax one or more said fish to climb up on the bank for a nap, and not to watch them dine uninterrupted. "I know you saw it too," I said. "Why didn't you strike?"

"I saw it," he readily admitted "but I didn't BELIEVE it." The confident approach and calm, unhurried, mouth opening-mouth closing action of the fish had enthralled him so deeply that, as a clinical observer, he'd completely forgotten the baited eggs were HIS!

Even regularly catching huge steelhead cannot provide steelheaders with an anti-toxin against this insidiously enjoyable fishing fever. The 32-pound, 10-ounce winter steelhead that held sway as Washington's record fish in the early 1970s was only one of several giant steelhead caught by Clifford Aynes, who in that era fished the Cowlitz River regularly and was acclaimed as a near-expert. When he later helped net a mid-20s steelhead for his fishing companion, Buddy Rogers, though, the steelhead fever blazed bright and, had we watchers on the far bank recorded the action on video, the tape sales (or hush money) would have made us rich!

Oops!...SPLASH! Unstrapped hip boots awash with full loads of water after slipping on the rocks and missing the fish on his first netting attempt, Cliff sloshed deeper over the slick bottom, making a second pass with the net at the rolling, thrashing fish. Down he went again in a welter of spray. But he had pinned the fish between the net and his leg and was able to inch, crablike, successfully to the bank as all hands raised a rousing cheer!

Steelheading has evoked both the epitome of praise for a gamefish and creation of some of the best prose ever written by America's sportswriters. The mystique of challenging broad rivers rolling beneath majestic evergreens and through untrammelled wilderness to yield silver-bright steelhead giants has been extolled by some of the finest sportsmen ever to take rod and pen in hand. Legendary Joe Brooks, a supreme fly-rod angler who lovingly and thoroughly roamed the known fishing universe, once said of steelhead fishing on the Thompson River simply that, "Heaven is a steelhead." The incomparable writer and angler Zane Grey was so enthralled by steelheading that he would abstain from his beloved saltwater angling for months at a time to haunt the banks of the Rogue River, where he was one of the earliest practitioners of fly-fishing for steelhead. Roderick Haig-Brown adopted British Columbia's Campbell River as his home stream to study, cherish, protect and fish and became famous for his detailed biologic knowledge, strength, color and clarity of writing and his angling skill. Eastern trout angling luminary Ray Bergman of fly-fishing fame came west to know with intimate passion steelheading streams and some particularly memorable spots, such as the Sawtooth Pool on the North Umpqua in Oregon.

Having absorbed by osmosis the steelhead virus via the captivating, superlative writing of these outdoor titans, what would-be fisherman would not want to angle the same waters, catch or lose the same breed of battling fish and drink the same wine of wilderness experiences? These gurus of sportfishing and outdoor writing were the heroes of my midwestern boyhood and they could magically transport me from the panfish ponds and streams that I could touch to the banks of deep, green, cold and rushing rivers about which I could dream. One distant day the dream ripened into reality and I was in their world, catching the great, silver-clad giants about which they had written. On the bank of a cool and liquid, emerald river there finally came the day of the big fish that is and forever will be indelibly etched in the window of my mind.

"Oh God!...It's huge!" Nothing about the strike or first few runs and shakes of the steelhead had alerted me that the fish I had hooked was more than a good, large one. But long minutes later it finned a few feet below the surface at the center of the river, clearly visible in the translucent water, gleaming silver bright, longer than my leg and as deep as a quart vacuum bottle. Huge? It was colossal! Through my mind flashed the dozens of ways sadly learned of how to lose a big steelhead, the fear my leader and bobber/yarn rig might have incurred slight damage from yesterday's six-pounder, and despair there was no one else on the steep and lonely streambank to see the fish before it broke off or to help me land it.

One on one, we tested each other and the fabric of dreams, the fish and I. Again and again, the deep-bellied hen steelhead determinedly drove for upriver and downriver distance, yielding reluctantly to the insistent urging of my long rod, until the mother fish of all fishes lay on her side, gasping, at my feet. The sharp point of the tiny gaff slid faultlessly into her tough pectoral area and I went up the 50-degree riprapped bank like a scalded cat, not stopping until reaching level ground 20 feet above me. (My angling partner later told me he could point out the exact place where I'd taken that whopper. "You left a blood trail through that brush like a mountain lion dragging a stolen pig!" he advised.)

That fish made my whole day, even though our state allows an angler to take a daily limit of two. One of that size was enough. One big steelhead can fill all my personal needs for a long, long time and, given the opportunity, many other steelheaders also will stop at one or release all other steelhead caught.

Once, sitting by a warming campfire and sipping a hot cup of coffee to take the day's chill from my body, I was startled from behind by the quiet approach of a small, very tired elderly man returning from far downstream.

"Any luck?" I asked as he eased onto a big rock close to my fire. In response, he slid a cord from his shoulder and allowed a giant, newly-minted female steelhead to swing into view and to the gravel bar.

"This one," he sighed. "It took me 25 minutes to catch it...wouldn't stop fighting, and my double hook almost pulled clear through her lower jaw... see there?" and his finger traced the long slit from the middle of the over-20-pound hen's mouth to a bare 1/8-inch of unbroken lip through which his silver Sammy Special's hook had not cut. He continued,"I'm not going to fish anymore today...I've had all the luck I could hope for."

Luck perhaps attends the first catches of budding steelhead fishermen, but acquired skills certainly can influence the success rate of anglers who continue to catch dozens of these sportfish each year. Sure knowledge of the tackle needed, how to rig in a variety of ways for a day's fishing, lures and baits that appeal to steelhead, and knowing when and how to fish particular rivers all pay handsome dividends too.

Steelhead can be caught by the book if the book is a log or record of your and your fishing companions' trips, water levels and conditions, weather and temperature and the lures or baits you were using. In addition to these records, dedicated steelheaders will obtain from their fish/wildlife agency all the information available to the public on steelhead hatchery plants and wild fish programs, plus monthly catch summaries on individual rivers or estimates from previous seasons. Knowing when steelhead are most likely to be in certain rivers and then fishing the streams with greatest potential returns at the peak of timing for maximum numbers will help you take steelhead.

Other informational aids are newspapers, which often provide fishermen with data on river levels and flow changes, as well as weather reports and up-to-date angling news. Steelhead guide and how-to books can illustrate the basics for beginners and perhaps expand the angling repertoires of experienced fishermen. Reading fishing and general outdoor magazines (especially periodicals that show maps of the stream areas), too, can provide valuable how-to and where-to tips on where to find steelhead. Best steelheading success often comes to the anglers who learn all they can about the species, its habitat and life cycle.

Fishing for winter steelhead on Washington's Cowlitz River.

Chapter 2

Life and Style of West Coast Steelhead

Steelhead are bright, glistening proof that Nature's rule of survival of the fittest produces hardy, hard-fighting specimens of this native American migratory rainbow trout. Strong, often wildly active, acrobatic and stubborn battlers, individual *Salmo gairdneri* may weigh from 5 to 40 pounds and are hard to visualize as the almost insignificant squiggles that began life squeezing from between grains of gravel on our west coast river bottoms.

Tiny, nearly transparent, and carrying a bulging, nutrient-filled yoke sac, steelhead *alevin* start their adventurous life in late February through early June. Hatched from 1,600 to 3,500 eggs laid in a redd or redds by one spawning female in December to May, the eggs mature in 40 to 50 days, depending on water temperature, and the alevin timidly emerge from their sand and gravel nests into a world that's ready to accept them with open jaws! It's a real jungle out there, and sculpin, squawfish, minnows, whitefish, crayfish, hellgrammites, larger trout and salmon cousins, mergansers and other ducks, mink, raccoons, herons, kingfishers and many other predators feed with gusto on the slowest, unluckiest and least alert of the young steelhead.

Thanks to man, hatcheries circumvent many of the survival hazards of immature steelhead. Eggs are taken from ripe female steelhead and sperm from males much like milking cows...hand pressure down the fishes' bellies and flanks (called stripping) causes the steelhead to release their burden into buckets where the egg/sperm mix is stirred by hand, then the fertilized eggs are placed in shallow trays to eye and ripen. The eye is a dark spot that signifies the egg is forming an embryo. Water temperature is held at 44 to 50 degrees and the eggs will hatch in approximately 45 days. The hatched steelhead then are placed in rearing pools, where they will stay through the alevin and fry stage, in which millions of the wee, 2- to 3-inch ever-hungry youngsters swiftly learn how to grab dinner and whisk it away from their kin. Successful fry graduate in about 10 months to become smolt (also called *parr*) measuring about five to seven inches, at which time the 85 to 90 percent survivors of the original hatch are ready to be released into streams to join their wild brethren. Many rearing ponds are concrete, and hatchery fish often can be identified from steelhead born in the wild by damage to the rays in their dorsal or anal fins...broken by the young fish bumping and rubbing on the harsh concrete.

Steelhead produced by natural reproduction in streams take longer to grow to the smolt stage – from little more than one year to more than four years, but averaging about two years – at which time they are sufficiently mature to forge downstream to larger waters and eventually the Pacific Ocean. Mortality is high on young fish hatched in the wild. Naturally spawned steelhead are avidly gobbled by every streamside creature seeking to satisfy its hunger. In addition, the kind and benevolent Mother Nature portrayed in children's cartoons sometimes turns into a harsh and deadly myth...steelhead fry wandering into a side channel or quiet pool may be stranded by the thousands to die as water levels drop, or heavy rains can fill their stream with so much silt the tiny fishes' gills clog and they suffocate. A large gray heron, merganser brood or hungry cutthroat trout taking up residence in a given stretch of stream where juvenile steelhead hide can decimate the school of newly-born fry.

Both wild and hatchery steelhead will display the same characteristics when they are ready to begin their sojourn to the sea. They undergo a change in hue, scales become bright silver and easily flake off, and the smolts are seized with a relentless itch to travel that causes them to group together in a compact ball of bodies, constantly moving, and dozens of the brash young steelhead simultaneously and repeatedly leap upstream of any obstruction to their downriver passage. When they surmount the obstacle, or are released from a hatchery pond, they immediately and aggressively move toward salt water, voraciously feeding as they travel.

High water flows in spring speed them on their way, but low stream levels often cause them to linger undecidedly at the mouths of native streams or in deep pools and runs of larger rivers. There is everpresent danger for the inexperienced juvenile fish, both from natural predators and from man. Their increased size makes them tasty tidbits for mink, bears, eagles, ospreys and other big creatures with big appetites. Accustomed to regular and readily eaten meals, hatchery smolts are especially overeager victims of bait, flies, tiny bobber/yarn rigs, small spoons and spinners...so gullible that some fish management agencies specify closed spring seasons and/or bait, hook barb or minimum size restrictions to protect migrating steelhead. New and greatly improved hatchery foods and increasingly knowledgable rearing procedures often can produce large and sturdy smolts that do not have the street smarts of naturally spawned fish, however, and the unknowing May or early June fisherman who rejoices over taking a limit of fat trout might unwittingly be killing 8- to 10-inch migrants that could return in two years' time as brawny, brawling 8-pound steelhead.

"Hey, Ho! And a nonny, nonny, it's off to the open sea they go." Where do they disappear to after slipping from river mouths onto the continental shelf? Marine fish biologists only now are beginning to piece together the wandering travels of these bold underwater voyagers. Beset by otters, seals, sea lions, sharks and many saltwater fish species as soon as they sniff their way into the briny deep, steelhead pull a vanishing act for two or more years before appearing once more off their home streams as fat, bright veterans of far-flung feeding forays on schools of shrimp, krill and young greenlings. Growing steelhead have been caught offshore by hook and net from mid-California to nearly the Arctic and by Japanese long-line fisheries within a few hundred miles of their homeland. Still, the mystery remains...no person knows the exact location of the major ocean feeding range of steelhead, and perhaps that is beneficially conducive to their ocean survival (unlike the havoc wreaked upon the Atlantic salmon population when netting efforts converged on their ocean pastures off Greenland!).

Most steelhead will remain at sea two, and sometimes three, years, feeding lustily and growing in size to 5, 7 or 10 pounds. A three-salt steelhead might return as a belligerent 14-pounder, and truly huge fish that continue for more years to ignore the reproductive urge in favor of gorging themselves to the hilt can tilt scales into the 30-pound range or even higher. Invariably, the largest of the steelhead clan will be the male, with hen steelhead smaller in scale. In retribution, the female of the species gets the good

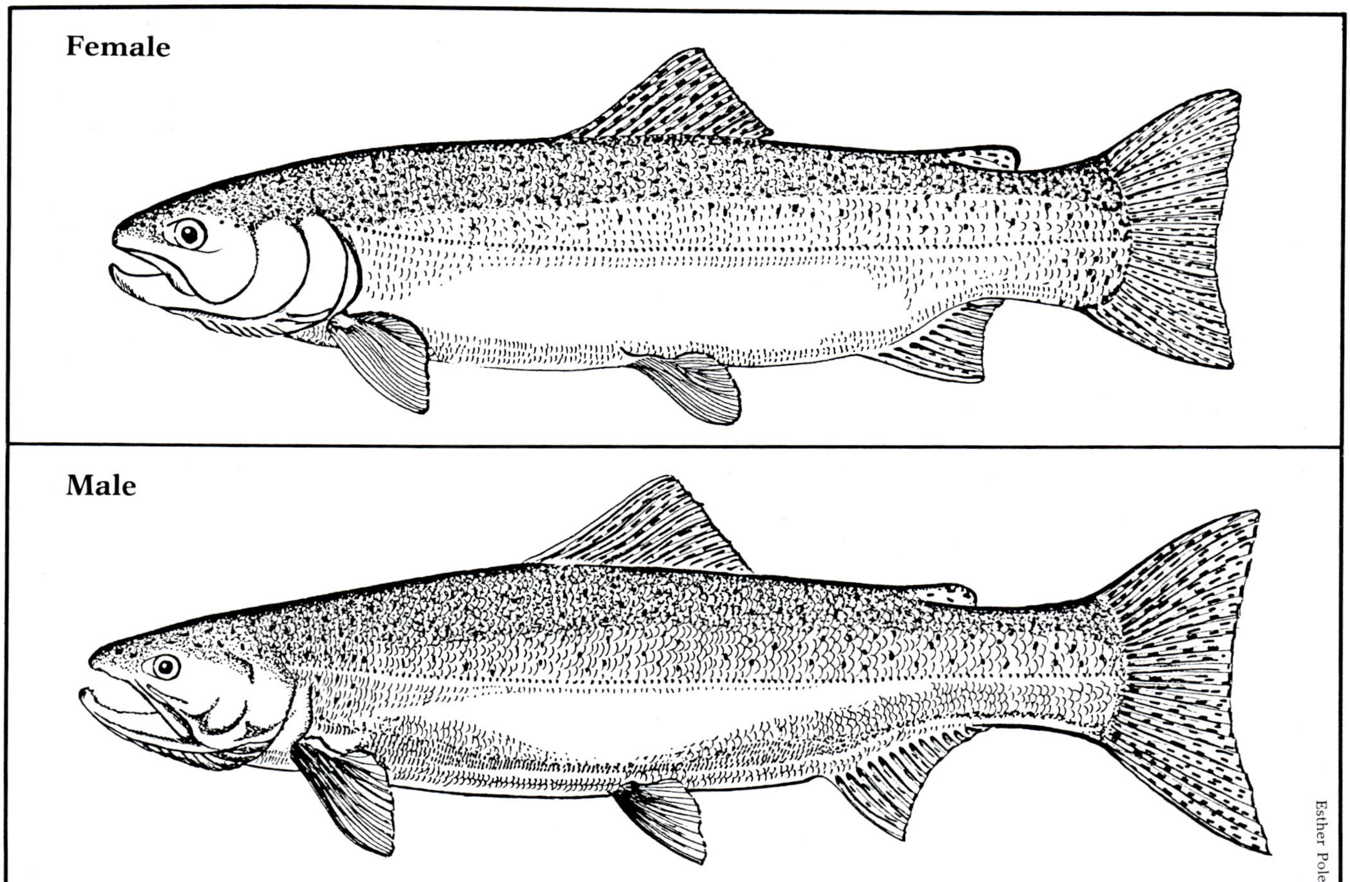

looks in the family...streamlined like a fat torpedo, with smaller, well-shaped head. The males develop surly, underslung jaws that have a definite kype or upthrust point by the time of spawning.

A 47 1/2-pound steelhead, caught from the Babine River in an Indian net, tops the recorded size range of this species. Rod and reel steelhead catches are headed by the Alaska fish young David Robert White outfought from a rubber raft in Bell Island's Bailey Bay in 1970 (June 22). That tremendous 42-pound, 2-ounce fish was first assumed to be a Chinook salmon, but designated for mounting to commemorate the 8-year-old's big catch. Through a fortuitous chain of events, that humungous catch was properly identified by the taxidermist, then acclaimed a *bona fide* steelhead by a University of Washington fish biologist, and finally given its just due.

Tremendous steelhead continue to appear among catches every year. For instance, during a few weeks' time in one season, five steelhead well over 30 pounds were caught from Washington State streams. And, whether the tale that follows is true or not, there almost certainly are larger steelhead that are not taken...as evidenced by a rumor of two huge buck steelhead that showed up in Washington's Cowlitz River salmon hatchery at Salkum on the same day. One weighed 42 pounds and the other 40 1/2 pounds! They were transported back to below the I-5 highway crossing and recycled into the river, but never reappeared. The kicker? Well, when salmon hatchery personnel first viewed the whoppers, the 40 1/2-pounder was grinning around a hook, leader and clown pattern Okie Drifter. Can't you just imagine the skepticism that met the unfortunate fisherman who lost that hummer?..."Oh, right, Harry, it was at least 30 pounds! You sure you weren't hung on bottom? You've told us that story 25 times and every time the steelhead gets bigger!"

Kinship with salmon and char and descent from the same common ancestor does not consign steelhead to a fate of one return, one death. Like its nearest salmonid kin, the Atlantic salmon, a steelhead can spawn and live to return from two or more additional replenishing trips to the ocean, while all six Pacific salmon species die after reproduction (this number includes the *masu,* or Japanese cherry salmon, a rarity seldom seen except by northern British Columbia and Alaskan ocean trollers). The estimated 12 to 16 percent of steelhead that spawn more than once, however, do not attain the tremendous size of fish that stay more than two or three years at sea, fattening themselves and avoiding the travel travail, chemical and body adjustments, food deprivation and rigors of reproductive rites. A three-time spawner would do well to spin a scale's needle around to the 20-pound mark.

Both winter and summer steelhead unerringly return to rivers in which they were spawned or released, as though guided to them by internal road maps. By the time of their return, numbers have thinned drastically. Most west coast fishery biologists agree that only 3 to 5 percent of steelhead from either hatcheries or wild births make it back. A return of 6 or 7 percent may be the maximum anticipated and such prolific numbers would provide tremendous fishing. Spawning pairs of steelhead will lay their eggs and sperm in almost exactly the same areas from which they once eased their tiny bodies out of the gravel. Summer and winter steelhead may dig their nests side by side, but pair by subspecies and their progeny carry imprinted in their genes the instincts that tell them in which season to start their river return.

Salmonids are able to detect by scent – both by nose and through the sensors along their lateral lines – the waterborne, individual chemical trace odors of the rocks and soil comprising the make-up of their home streams, down to one or two parts in a million. Experiments have shown, also, that they are deterred from upstream passage by the smell of a canine's paw dipped into the water, a bear's scent, or odor from a human washing his hands. The key element appears to be the chemical *L-serine* present in human's and the dog family's perspirations. Detection of this smell has been demonstrated to cause a school of steelhead or salmon to retreat as much as a quarter-mile downstream for 15 to 20 minutes at a time.

Winter steelhead begin to slide upstream in late October and continue to increase in number until late March. Often, early fish will be feisty, 4- and 5-pound males, but some rivers sport November appearances of hulking 20-pounders that can overpower an unsuspecting angler before he gets his act together and eases off his drag or rod pressure. Next to appear in the first half of December are mixed schools of hatchery fish...bucks and does in nearly equal numbers. By Christmas and New Year's Day, hordes of mint steelhead are slipping over river bars and into range of their spawning beds. Gun metal blue/green backs are sharply separated from dime-bright silver sides and alabaster bellies, with the steelhead fat, firm and full of vim and vigor. The division between back and sides is etched as keenly as though cut with a surgeon's scalpel. Profusely scattered black spots are strewn from head to tail on the steelhead's back, dorsal, anal and caudal (tail) fins. Distinguishing characteristics that identify steelhead and which salmon do not have are: spots on the lower half of the tail, 12 or less rays in the anal fin, and cream/white mouths...roof, bottom jaw and gums.

Early January is prime fishing time in many rivers for the hatchery-reared, salt-spangled ocean travellers. In February and March, wild natives join the fishing fray as deep-bellied, long-finned behemoths from the brine. Many steelheaders consider these late-winter wild steelhead the epitome of fishdom. They are wary, often difficult to hook, and the largest bucks are possessed of a power awesome to behold. My fishing partner once laid the steel to a huge February steelhead that inhaled his bait in a deep and long run in front of him and he sorrowfully related to me the action as follows:

"When I came back on the fish, it never stopped...it just swam steadily upstream, jumped once 100 feet from me and in front of another fisherman, and kept

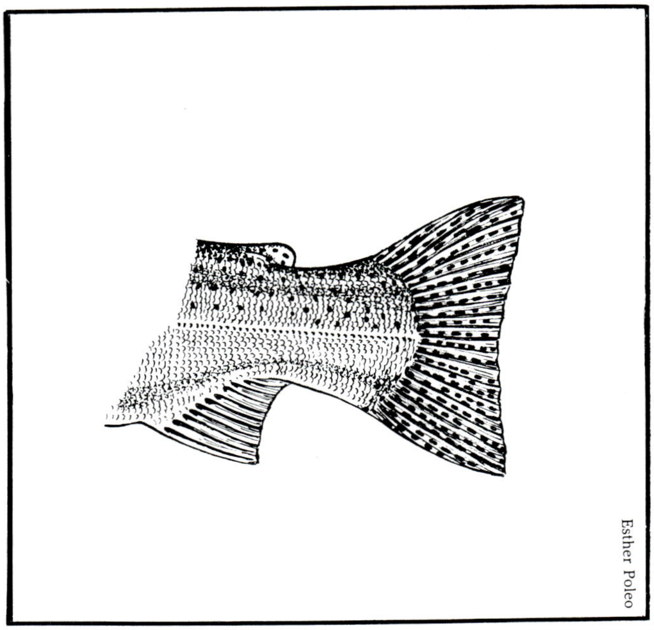

Spotted tail markings are characteristics of the steelhead.

going. When I saw two or three wraps of line left on my reel spool, I pointed the rod at the fish and he broke my leader as if it was thread! The angler above me said it would weigh at least 25 pounds and maybe go a lot bigger than that."

I could very easily sympathize with him. Late in February of the previous season a similar overachiever had left me talking to myself. I'd coaxed a strike from a heavyweight steelhead lurking in a position extremely difficult to fish. It took a short, low, upstream cast under a hanging tree branch and gentle reeling to allow my bobber/yarn combination to fall into a spot only 15 or 16 feet in front of me where a tiny underwater gully contained a lick of current that would move it on downstream. I edged my gear into the "slot," felt a thump that was not a rock, and set back heartily on the 9-foot rod only to watch in dismay as my rod tip whipped down into the water and began sawing back and forth as though it was caught on a railroad engine's piston rod. Upset by my tether, the submarine slugger I'd hooked surged steadily out of the lie in a long, slanting, mid-river run while my spinning reel whined in complaint. One stop at a boulder bed encouraged me for a bare breath of time, but that unseen sockdolagar scarcely paused there, setting a course back to the Pacific...which it probably made, because I had no choice other than to pop it off at about 60 yards downstream and over the next riffle! (I suppose that's why the sport is called steelhead *fishing,* rather than *catching.*)

All that strength comes mainly from bellying up to the ocean training table, since winter steelhead rapidly undergo changes to their bodies, upon entering fresh water, which prepare them for the pending reproduction of their species but sharply curtail their gourmet tendencies. Their digestive tracts shrink, making room for burgeoning egg skeins in the female steelhead, while the bucks' sperm sacs swell to replace their food recycling systems. In just a few days after leaving salt water, winter steelhead are neary unable to ingest or absorb a meal...but that doesn't seem to prevent them from trying. There are too many instances I've personally noted in which ice-month ironheads have done very good imitations of swallowing baits, lures and other substantial objects – all the way down their gullet and into their shrunken digestive tracts – to say that winter steelhead don't and can't feed.

Buck steelhead also color up quite quickly after entering natal streams in the wintertime. Gill cheeks become rosy and a pink/red stripe traces their lateral line from pectoral fin to tail, sometimes becoming a double stripe. Their gleaming sides turn a dull gray first, then a mottled, sooty, rust color, while their backs dull to dirty gray or brown. Hen fish retain their beauty longer...a two-month female resident of spawning water may show a delicate tint of rouge on her cheeks and her oyster-tone abdomen may have shaded to ashen hue, but her now-slender sides generally remain only a slightly tarnished silver. The inside flesh color of new-run winter steelhead is bright pink, which fades slowly to nearly white after the fish is a month or more in the river. After spawning, the spent fish is dark, and its scales are lusterless. In some streams, however, the recovery of spawned steelheads' scale tone and gleam is rapid, and downstreamers will quickly return to bright, glistening silver color.

Summer steelhead show up in natal streams anywhere from early April to late October. (In today's hatchery/wild mixture of fish, there in fact are bright, fresh and bouncy steelhead that will appear in streams almost every month of the summer. Some rivers seem to support a spring-run subspecies of fish, while others produce a fall run of bright fish from August through September.) These sunshine season steelhead bring their appetites with them! They may arrive fat and frisky, jam-packed with ocean energy, but have a long wait ahead of them before spawning in February and March just as the winter steelhead do. They'll not only eat, but chase down an intended dinner with zeal and abandon, making them a fisherman's delight to pursue. They can be close-mouthed, and often are, but when you find out how to trigger their feeding instinct the net results can be terrifically gratifying whether using bait, a twinkling spinner or deceptive nymph imitation.

Summer steelhead normally are leery of moving shadows, and they are easily spooked in low water that can be as clear as a greenhouse window. Also, the self-preservation instincts of the steelhead may retain dim memories that the last passage through this same water was rife with snapping jaws and clutching talons, so shirt-sleeved summertime fishermen are attempting to tango with a wary, suspicious partner. In order to supplement their stores of fat laid on in the ocean's rich feeding ground, however, summer-runs sometimes go on binges of ferocious predation on small fish and large insects. In the gray light of early morning, and again at twilight, they will savagely charge upon and chomp their chosen prey.

In general, summer fish tend to be most numerous in long rivers. Winter fish are most prolific in short-run streams. As for size, both seasons can produce real wallhangers. Many Snake and Clearwater River (upper Columbia River) long-range summer steelhead will vie for big fish honors with any other steelhead pound for pound and inch for inch. Some rivers, such as British Columbia's Thompson, Babine, Skeena and Kispiox, have a reputation for giants. On the other hand, short, coastal streams also can deliver huge, powerful winter steelhead to match their swift, tumbling currents.

Winter, spring, summer and fall, steelhead are available to be caught. All that is necessary is the proper tackle, some tips on rigging and technique and enough fishing time to pay your dues and you'll be banking some of those bright battlers.

Angler releasing a hefty summer-run steelhead. Chances are high that this fish will be hooked and released more than once.

Chapter 3

Steelhead Tackle: Rods and Reels

Where you fish for steelhead, how you fish them, and the kind of water you're tackling will influence your selection of the rod/reel outfit needed to enjoy the most comfortable and efficient angling. Many of the steelheaders I know have several tackle combinations that vary in length, action and weight, allowing them to choose from among their rods the one (or two) that will best suit their intended day's angling.

Rods generally range in length from 7 1/2 to 15 feet, with the greatest majority of steelhead sticks taping from 7 feet, 8 inches to 9 feet long. Light tackle anglers and lure fishermen prefer rods having a fast tip action, which will allow them to obtain distance casts. Bait-fishermen prefer a slow (or parabolic) rod action, which is less likely to snap off their baits on the cast. Modern fishing rods now are almost wholly two-piece and self-ferruled, although some few veteran anglers still elect to buy one-piece rods, considering them to have the finest action.

By self-ferruled I mean that the ferrule – the connection between rod halves – is of the same material from which the rest of the rod is built. A few years ago, nearly all rods had metal ferrules, which eventually created some problems. One or the other ferrule half worked loose from the rod, or the top portion of the rod became stuck in the ferrule. In addition, the ferrules' lips, no matter how designed or finished, created wear and break points at which the rods could snap while casting, playing a fish, or, in most instances, by the fisherman striking while his hook or sinker was hung on bottom or a snag.

Action describes where and how much rods will flex, and is the key to their sensitivity, hook-setting and fish-playing capabilities. Action is determined by the wall thickness of the rod blank and its taper from tip to butt. A relatively uniform taper from tip to butt will provide a soft action rod ideal for playing a fish, but which only lobs a bait or lure. A rod that progressively and swiftly tapers to a fine tip in the top 20 to 25 percent of its length will zing a spoon or spinner across a medium size stream with little effort, but might also frequently snap off soft baits as you cast. Most steelheaders will select a rod best suited for either fishing with bait or with lures, but capable of doing both...which generally turns out to be a medium fast rod with most of its taper in the upper 25 to 30 percent of the rod. This gives them good casting ability, tip sensitivity, and progressively tougher fish-playing capability as the rod bends into the middle and, with a real hummer on, into the stiff butt.

Weight and strength are design factors that are carefully balanced in the manufacturing process to produce a rod that is as strong and resilient as possible, yet as light to handle as the materials used will permit. Rod materials most used today are fiberglass, graphite and boron. (The fiberglass is far advanced from solid glass, and most rods are made of a fiberglass composite that also has some graphite or other reinforcing material in it.)

The three standard types of steelheading outfits you will normally see on a walk down a popular steelhead river's bank are bait-casting, spinning and fly-fishing rigs. Each successfully catches steelhead. Each fulfills its basic purpose...getting your bait/lure/fly down to a steelhead's eyeball level, where you must have it to draw a strike. However, beyond this similarity, the selection of which steelhead tackle you choose to use depends on your preference for a particular angling method, the width, speed, depth and clarity of the river to be fished and the amount of bank brush or trees that might limit your casting and thus effect your choice of gear.

There are combination rods that can quickly convert from fly-fishing use to spinning/bait-casting function by reversing their handles and attaching the appropriate reels. These rods generally come in several pieces, are commonly referred to as pack rods and are good alternate choices for anglers who hike or backpack to remote, upstream steelheading locations. For day in and day out steelheading, however, the short length, light weight and number of pieces that make them so useful back of beyond become drawbacks to serious steelheaders.

For the most consistent, easy to learn, rewarding steelhead fishing, I strongly recommend a beginning angler choose one style of angling – spinning, bait-casting, or fly-fishing – and get some expert assistance in putting together his first outfit. Buy the best quality rod, reel, line and terminal gear you can afford, as it is much easier to cast and fish with equipment that will do its job smoothly and efficiently while you are gaining in skill.

Let's look at the three styles of fishing outfits, the uses for which they were designed, and the features that make them different:

This hatchery origin steelhead was marked on the back near the head for scientific purposes.

SPINNING TACKLE:

Pinch your monofilament line between forefinger and rod handle, open your spinning reel bail, flip your spinning rod forward and, when it's pointing toward where you want to fish, let go of the line. *SPLASH!* Turn your reel handle to close the bail and raise the rod...you are steelheading. The simplicity of learning to fish with spinning tackle is one of the strongest reasons for a budding steelheader to choose this method. Another, in my opinion, is that hardware such as spinners and spoons can best be cast and fished with the tackle designed specifically to use these lures. Spoons and spinners have flat surfaces that often catch a bit of wind or plane in air by virtue of their design, slowing the line, which has little effect on a spinning reel but is disastrous when using a level wind reel because it causes birds' nests. Also, in fishing them, spinners and spoons are better worked by the long-handled spinning reel, which gives an angler more sensitive control of their swimming action.

A steelhead spinning rod is generally 7 1/2 to 9 1/2 feet long, has a straight, fat cork or *Hypalon™* handle that will reach from your elbow to first finger knuckles, a fixed reel seat on its underside, and as many guides as it is feet long. The guides, too, are on the underside of the rod, opposite the back, or spine of the rod. Spinning rods are designed to be fished with the reel down and the reel handle is cranked away from the angler in a rotary fashion. (Screw rings for the reel seats ought to be above the reel, allowing the rear of the reel foot to be set under the cork or foam handle. Since most of the angler's hand grasps the rod behind the reel foot, covering as much as possible of this metal will reduce its winter chill factor.)

Most anglers will agree that the first requisite of a steelheading rod is tip sensitivity that will betray a fish gently mouthing their bait or lure. From that point on, the increasing stiffness (or *action*) of the rod down to the butt is subject to anglers' preferences, meat for many long debates, and exact ratios of flex per foot of rod are closely-guarded manufacturers' secrets. I select rods that have most of their action in the top fourth of their length, while other anglers with whom I fish like to have almost a full third of the rod take an easy, deep bend. My favorite rods progress from this light tip into medium action, which I feel is more forgiving of errors I might make in playing a fish and also keeps more soft, relentless pressure on my catch.

Rod actions depend on the kind of fishing you plan to do and whether you're going to need tackle with which you can snub down a rampaging heavyweight to keep it out of snags or brush or, if the water is ice-clear and unobstructed, with which you can play out the fish with a light drag and soft touch. There are some fishermen, generally plunkers and plug anglers, who like stout steelhead sticks I refer to as pool cues but, on the other hand, I'm sometimes guilty of teasing and taking steelhead with a slender, flexible rod that a few friends have called a buggy whip substitute. Light line enthusiasts will go skinnier yet, fishing 4-pound test lines and 2-pound test leader on special-use noodle rods to 15 feet long that will bend from tip to butt in a wide teardrop shape.

Line guides on a spinning rod are largest near the butt of the rod and taper to small diameter at the tip-top. This is so the first guides can gather and channel the coils of line peeling off the open front of the reel and form them into more or less a straight line as they go through the diminishing ring sizes of the upper guides. Good quality guides now are made of space-age ceramics, silicon carbide, or aluminum oxide, instead of the stainless steel and carbaloy guides of yesteryear.

Today's steelhead spinning rod materials are strong and light fiberglass, graphite or boron and most of them are superbly designed and crafted. Prices ratchet upward from inexpensive to top-of-line fiberglass, less costly graphite sticks start below the upper limits of the glass rods and go upwards again, while boron rod costs lead from the higher graphite rod bracket to another plateau.

I have suggested to friends who are just getting started in steelheading that they would do well to consider making their first rod a spinning model, inasmuch as it may be the least expensive to purchase, surely will be the simplest to learn to handle, and also may be used to try out a bait-casting reel. (A bait-casting rod with uniformly small guides, on the other hand, cannot perform adequately with a spinning reel attached.) A spinning outfit can be cast sideways, overhand, or upside down with only a short, snappy wrist movement. This will allow you to fish where there is little casting room. For instance, against a tight, steep bank, under trees, or in brushy spots where you would not care to try other tackle. This means you can fish in more different parts of the river...perhaps even spots that most anglers don't try.

Selecting steelheading spinning tackle is much like learning to throw a curve in baseball. There is a certain grip that feels right. Try out a few friends' outfits for this feel, for balance, the ease with which they can be cast, and whether they seem heavy or light. Balance can be checked when the rod is fully equipped with line and lure or bait rig, by holding your forefinger under the rod at the front of the butt grip (or fore grip, if it has a two-piece handle). There is a point within an inch or less one way or other from the end of the cork where the rod will balance horizontally on your one finger. This rough test will reveal whether the rod, as you would normally equip it, would be a butt-heavy or tip-heavy armbreaker to cast and fish all day.

Every fisherman has name brand preferences as to which rod works best for him. I suggest you do several things to determine which of the many excellent rods available today will suit you. Talk to a number of steelheaders that own different makes of rods, and ask what it is about their particular choice of rods that they like. Visit your local tackle dealer and see what he recommends (and remember, he wants your repeat business, so he won't tout you into this week's special if he hopes to see you again).

Finally, for an excellent way to check on a rod company's reliability and longitude, go to your library and look up several magazines and/or newspapers that cover steelheading. Read the advertising, not the stories. Were the steelhead rods you've been inspecting and considering made by companies that were around 15 or more years ago, two to five years ago, or even last year? If so, that's a very good indicator they are producing satisfactory rods.

However, don't overlook the possibility that a newly-formed rod company might be able to furnish you with a prime quality lifetime spinning rod too. There are very few bad rods on the market today. With meticulous anglers pressing for better and better tools with which to fish, adverse word-of-mouth publicity shortly chops off their production lines. Have a close look at the quality of the guides, reel seat, the wrapping detail, and the finish. Top workmanship in construction of the rod is likely to mean top quality for fishing, too.

Spinning Reel

The spinning reel is truly the angler's friend because it is practically impossible to make it backlash...that dreaded bait-casting reel's involuntary overrun that robs you of precious fishing time when a hot bite is on, or may cause you to cut half your line off to get past the snarl. Instead, the spinning reel just chunks your gear out, time after time. And, if you want to change your line to better match the fishing conditions, you can simply and quickly pop off the reel spool in use, snap on a different one, and resume fishing.

Open-face spinning reels, not the closed-face models, are the standard for steelheaders. (Closed-face spinning reels have neither the line capacity nor precision drag control needed in this type of fishing.) These open-face spinning reels have a long foot by which they are mounted underneath your rod. A half-round bail or a pick-up finger steers line from rod to reel spool, which is mounted on a spindle within the reel's cup-like front. The spindle shaft extends through to the rear of the reel and the anti-reverse mechanism and beveled drive gears are mounted there within a narrow housing. On one side is the crank handle (often interchangeable from left to right on newer reels) and the free spool lever. Line drag adjustment mechanisms may be mounted either at the front of the reel spool or at the rear of the reel.

When a cast is made, with the bail flipped aside, the line peels off the front of the non-revolving spool. Small weights can be cast very easily with spinning reels. Turning the reel handle drops the bail back into position and line is retrieved at anywhere from 3.5:1 to 5.6:1 ratios, which means that each full turn of the reel handle will cause the reel spool to revolve 3.5 to 5.6 times.

When playing a steelhead on spinning tackle, anglers should pump their rod upward to gain line and then reel as they lower the rod. Continuous reeling against a running or stubborn fish will fatigue their monofilament and cause it to break, much as you can break a coat hanger wire by rapid twisting. Lightweight, modern materials such as graphite, titanium, stainless steel, Teflon, zinc and nylon may be incorporated into a reel that is as precision machined and built as a fine Swiss watch. Ball bearings are almost standard, line guides now are of wear-resistant aluminum oxide, silicon carbide, or at least of stainless steel. Snug-fitting reel spools may be further guarded by protective skirts that prevent line from creeping behind the spools.

Excellent quality spinning reels can be purchased at very reasonable prices. You can, of course, buy models that have all the bells and whistles of a tiny computer. There were spinning reels sold last year that would tell you how much line you had cast, would remember the cast length so you could repeat it, show how many feet of monofilament per second you were retrieving, give you the time of day so you could clock how long you fought with a particular fish, and even ring a preset alarm that might be used to advise you of the peak period of moon phase, tide and best bite.

I suggest a "plain Jane" spinning reel for beginners. Your major concerns should be getting the gear you're fishing in front of a steelhead's nose and then sensing when it is taken. This is aided by laying your fingertip along the line just ahead of the reel, eyeballing your mono for a sudden stop or twitch, and watching the tattletale movements of your rod tip.

Spinning outfits can be used for any type of steelhead fishing, from pulling plugs behind a boat to casting extremely light or sinker-free bait or lure drift rigs and may also, with split shot added on the line or leader, drop flies to a wary ironhead's lie. They have many advantages.Two things spinning rods cannot do well, however, are to feed line from the spool while fishing (although they can be back-reeled), as a bait-casting reel does, and make long casts of a relatively weightless lure, as does a fly rod.

BAIT-CASTING TACKLE:

Many oldtimer steelheaders seldom fish with anything other than a bait-casting rod and level wind reel. Most of their rods will measure from 7 feet 8 inches long to nine feet, with perhaps the most popular stick an 8 1/2-footer. If you select for quality of materials and workmanship, a carefully matched and finely tuned bait-casting outfit can be a joy with which to fish.

Bait-casting steelhead rods are made with the spine or back of the rod to be fished on the underside of the rod and the guides and reel seat are installed on top of the rod. The lower guides are smaller than lower spinning guides, since line will come off the revolving spool reel on a horizontal plane only a few inches wide and does not need to be funnelled through the first guides.

Fiberglass composites, graphite, boron and Kevlar are used in bait-casting rod blanks. A good number of steelheaders favor these rods for angling with cluster eggs, shrimp, or other baits and want their rods to be as ultra-sensitive as possible. For this reason you'll see a few more one-piece rods used, and most preferred models will have very light action tips. Fixed reel seats are built into fore-arm length cork or closed-cell foam handles. Again, I look for rods having the reel seat screw rings above the reel, which provides a warmer, more comfortable winter grip.

Price ranges extend from about $30 on up past $100 for good, to top quality, bait-casting rods. Little touches, such as a hook keeper loop added near the butt, underwrapped and snug-fitted guides, added color and pattern in guide and butt wraps and the best guide ring material, all add to the cost and durability, as well as to your pleasure in using a superbly crafted rod.

Bait-casting reels have "come a long way, baby" from their forebears of 25 and 30 years ago. One of the biggest bait-casting breakthroughs was the addition of free-spool gearing that allows a reel spool to turn, while the reel handles no longer revolve to rap and skin your knuckles. High-speed level winds now retrieve smoothly and evenly. Precise control casting drags – manual and magnetic – make backlashes uncommon, and star drag mechanisms help you meter the fish force required to peel monofilament from your reel.

Many parts of today's new, lightweight, small bait-casting reels are made of graphite, which is stronger and lighter than metal. Engineering and design innovations have produced wonders of rugged, efficient, long-lasting, precision mills that will give fishermen a lifetime of enjoyable use. Some new reels are convertible from righthand to lefthand operation. Today's reels snuggle comfortably into your hand, and no longer have any rough edges and nuts or studs where your hand makes contact.

Learning to use a bait-casting rod and reel will take a little practice. You cast this outfit by placing a thumb on the reel spool to hold the line. Push in the free-spool release. Next, bring the rod back sharply and then forward as if you were driving a nail into a wall. You must lift your thumb slightly, allowing the cast line to flow smoothly through your rod guides, when the rod reaches a forward point past the vertical, and either feather the mono with a whisper-light touch of your thumb or trust to the casting drag mechanism. Magnetic casting drags, set properly, generally will give you trouble-free casting with little or no thumbing of the reel. Manual casting drags still must be aided by thumbing the departing line.

Casting Reel

Fine-tuning a bait-casting reel for efficient casting is done by tieing on the fishing rig you will use, then adjusting the drag tension while the reel is in free-spool mode. Hold the rod out horizontally, release your thumb pressure from the spool, and watch for the bait or lure to begin creeping down toward the ground as you back off on the drag tension screw. This is the optimum casting drag tension setting.

When fishing, once you have cast, do not turn the handle, which would drop the reel out of free-spool. Instead, keep light thumb pressure on the top of the reel spool and allow monofilament to sift from under it as the current takes your terminal gear downriver. This does two things for the steelheader...allows the bait or lure to tail downstream (permitting you to cover more river with your gear), and it keeps you in sensitive touch with your line. A slight tug or tap of a fish on the line should be felt under the ball of the thumb.

Expert steelheaders have an uncanny sense of touch with bait-casting outfits. One angler I know will freeze like a pointer scenting birds and say, "A steelhead came up and looked at it, but wouldn't take my bait." Sure enough, in a few more casts, he would sink his hook to the inquisitive fish!

FLY-FISHING TACKLE:

Watching an expert fly-fisherman can be a truly

awesome experience and shattering to an angler's ego. To see Maggie Merrimen, women's world fly-casting whiz, work five fly rods and lines in the air at one time, or World Fly-casting Champion Steve Rajeff shoot a fly line from about the 20-yard mark past the opposite football goal and into the stands of a domed arena can make a non-adept fly-flinger take up verb conjugation like "slink, slank, slunk" in a hurry. But then, when Jim Teeny, a renowned west coast fly-fisherman and fly manufacturer, strolls into an open spot between bait-fishermen on a heavily-fished stream, and hoists two lovely, bright steelhead in less than 25 minutes, you say to yourself "He made that look so easy that even I might be able to catch ONE steelhead on a fly."

Sure you can. And, once hooked, a steelhead can be tired on fly tackle more readily than on any other gear, because of the steady, relentless classic action of the fly rod. It takes a soft, deep bow that constantly works against the fish, sapping its energy. And, most steelhead will take a fly in the lip, roof of the mouth, or corner of the jaw and can be safely released by a sportsman respecting wild fish release regulations or who wishes someone else to enjoy the battle of the same steelhead.

Esthetically speaking, fly-fishing is a thing of beauty and a joy to behold or achieve. Practically speaking, fly-fishing is one of several successful methods of catching steelhead. The sport once called elitist is now acclaimed a challenge by a dedicated and growing core of long-rod users. They point out that, to bring steelhead to hand or net, fly-fishermen have to study their quarry harder, learn to read the water better to find steelhead in their holding spots, and develop techniques and tactics to get their fur/feather offerings through depth and current to writhe seductively in front of the fish.

Fly-fishing rods used for steelheading generally range from 8 to more than 9 feet long. You may still see some beautifully crafted and treasured split bamboo fly rods in use on steelhead streams, but they are becoming rarities. Most modern blanks now are made of graphite, fiberglass composites, or boron materials, in about that diminishing order of use. Precisely constructed, wrapped and finished, these rods generally are two- or three-piece sections that travel to and from the river in a solid protective case.

Stainless steel snake guides or aluminum oxide guides should number as many as the foot-length of quality fly rods and there should be a hook-keeping loop or ring wrapped into the butt windings. Handles of fine species cork are considered the best, but some excellent fly rods feature closed-cell foam handles. Graphite or other lightweight reel seats are standard, to reduce the overall weight of the rod.

Fly rods are not balanced against their reels. Instead, rods and fly lines must be matched, because it is the line that is cast, not your fly, and the line carries the fly to its touchdown spot. Many fly-fishermen remember the early days of ABC letter codes designating fly lines...and that every third line maker used his own different weight. My D might have been your E or C or...just about any weight. Next came a

Fly Reel

number system which is largely still in use. A No. 9 line goes with a No. 9 rod, and so on. Some fly-rod shops today market systems in which rod and line are prefigured to match and a System II anything will work with another System II component.

Because of the relatively low numbers of fly rods sold, and the expensive production procedures in making these rods, they are among the most costly fishing equipment you might buy, and they are at the same time the easiest to damage or destroy. (You only toss a flat tire into your trunk on top of a $180 fly rod once.)

Steelhead fly reels are not the simple storage places many trout reels are labelled. While many are 1:1 ratio, elementary arbors from which to feed, and in which you collect, line, fly reels for steelhead, salmon and other large, strong fish should have 2:1 or 3:1 retrieve ratios, a better drag mechanism than a crescendo series of clicks, and exposed rims that may be palmed to slow a sizzling fish.

Top quality fly reels are made from light, strong materials, many using quite a bit of graphite or silicon/aluminum alloy in their manufacture. Frames having the least number of assembling screws, or unitized bodies machined from one piece of metal, are your top choices. Perforated spools, interchangeable from left to right side operation, wobble-free brass or bronze bushings or steel roller bearings, and counterbalanced handles are other desirable fly reel features that add to their overall efficiency. As you add all these extras into your fly reel selective process, however, be aware that your wants are pushing its price tag higher.

Learning to use fly-fishing tackle does take longer than to acquire skill with spinning or bait-casting gear. There are many good books on the subject, and fly-fishing schools appear every spring, summer and fall to help you get a proper start. If you can spring for lessons from a competent instructor I advocate you do so. Your other recourse is your public library and backyard practice. My one piece of advice on this learning process is that you wear a broadbrimmed hat and safety glasses when you do so.

Chapter 4

Lines and Leaders

After you set your hook into something that feels and acts like a Trident submarine bound for points west of our continental shelf is a poor time to wish you hadn't saved a few dollars on the line and leader linking the two of you.

On the other side of the coin, if you're using top-notch quality line and leader and know your knots are strong, well-tied ones, it can increase your confidence in playing and successfully landing even the biggest of steelhead. An angler should be able to land a 16-pound steelhead on 4-pound test line. Some fishermen have formed "4 To 1" and "10 To 1" clubs, meaning they angle for and take fish weighing 4 to 10 times the breaking strength of their lines. The gear will do it...it's up to you to avoid snags, boulders, the eagerness pitfall of trying to bring a green fish in too quickly, landing mishaps and all the other mental errors.

If you could always have the best quality line on your reel at half its cost, would you do it? Of course! Well, you can, and here's how...use only half as much of the expensive line by filling the inner diameter of your reel spool with durable linen or braided monofilament line backing and then spooling the rest of the reel with the best monofilament you can buy. You generally need only 15 to 30 yards of line for casting, and another 20 to perhaps 40 yards of line with which to play a strong fish. If a steelhead gets farther away from you than the far goalposts of a football field (which river distance generally includes two or more bends, half a dozen logs and snags and 40 huge rocks) you're in a heap of trouble! Casting length, playing length, and another 15 yards for extra security and line-shortening knot changes generally will average from 65 to 80 yards...which is all you should require. Most one shot line spools contain twice this length, so you can have two reel refills, atop the backing, for the price of one.

Keeping your reel filled to maximum recommended capacity with A-one quality line serves two helpful functions. Your reel casts best when loaded to the manufacturer's guideline (often marked on the reel spool by a guide line) and, by halving your costs, you are encouraged to change line more often, ensuring you have fresh and unimpaired line with which to better hook, play and land a steelhead.

Monofilament lines today offer a steelheader a wide variety of choices, among which you should be able to select one or more to suit every type of angling for these silvery splinters from the salt water. Tremendous improvements in manufacturing and quality control have created lines having many options of stretch, color, flexibility, knot strength and resistance to abrasion, and reduced "memory" (that used to cause coils to spring from the reel), which are major characteristics an angler considers for his specific method of fishing. It seems as if every line color in the rainbow can be obtained, from glowing gold or fluorescent blue to water-matching teak or green. Monofilament line with small, uniform diameter and highly rated breaking strength is commonly available through tackle shops and other suppliers. In fact, you are not limited to monofilament any longer, as now there are available new lines of *copolymer* and *tripolymer* manufacture, which combine the most desired qualities of uniform strength, size, sensitivity, flexibility, low "memory" and high knot or abrasion resistance into one line.

Light lines used with noodle rods and such slender sticks as my buggy whip normally start at 2 pounds breaking strength and progress by even-numbered increments upward to about 6-pound test. (Few odd-numbered line strengths are manufactured between 2- and 20-pound test, except for 15- and 17-pound test, and most manufacturers' lines shift to 5-pound breaking differences at 20 pounds and above.) The tiny diameter, wee, wispy filaments almost always are used with spinning reels, which demand a flexible line that will accept without damage the abusive 90-degree retrieve angle from bail to spool, and they have a calculated amount of stretch to complement the slightly softer action of spinning rods, which are very tolerant of angler error. Standard breaking strength line choices for commonly used steelhead spinning tackle may vary from labelled strength of 6 or 8 pounds in summer to 12 or 14 pounds parting point in winter.

Modern level wind reels now are built with tight reel spool tolerances, which allow small diameter lines to be used without fear of them jumping behind a reel's side plate, a common fault of many early casting reels. Summer anglers often load 8-pound test monofilament on tiny level wind reels, with wintertime line test husking from 10 pounds up to 20 and 30 pounds on heavy-duty reels used mainly for plunking or plug fishing. On the average, most steelheaders will use lines that break at around 12 to 15 pounds on their bait-casting tackle.

Level wind reel users prefer line that is slightly stiffer and more sensitive than that favored for spinning reels, to give them increased ability to interpret the underwater action of their terminal gear and to identify the gentle touch of a biting fish. Uniform diameter, consistent breaking point, smooth wraps on the spool, and good abrasion resistance and knot strength (to offset frequent contact of at least some of the line with bottom) are needed.

A good rule of thumb for choosing line color is to match the normal hue of the stream or streams you habitually fish. Some lowland and pasture-fed streams seem to stay a rich green all year around save for their swollen brown flood stages. Other rivers are glacier-fed and their most common color is milky green or blue. Still more streams often are tinted like rich tea or coffee from old timber slash or trees littering their bottoms. If you stick with line that most closely approximates the river color of the streams you regularly fish, you should have better success than when using a line having a contrasting color that might alert steelhead something strange has entered their area.

On that same subject, in my own experience, I can testify a fluorescent line may be useful to winter steelheaders and catch success in dim light and roiled waters might be improved by its better visibility and subsequent angler control, but this highly visible line is more likely to put steelhead off the bite in summer. When fishing water that was virtually transparent from top to bottom of a stream, I've observed steelhead seemed to spook from a fluorescent line as though it carried a quarantine label!

KNOTS, AND HOW TO TIE THEM:

Between your line and leader there normally is one or more knot connecting you to whatever bait or lure is fished. More fish will succumb to steelheaders who follow a rule of Use the fewest, best knots you can tie. Knots are very critical to steelheaders, as each knot in your rig increases the Russian Roulette ratio of points at which you and a wildly cavorting steelhead might be prematurely separated by a long line release not sought by one (guess which?) of you. However, just like the U.S. Marine Corps request, "We need a few good men," you need only learn to tie well a few good knots to enhance a lifetime of fishing.

Every fisherman, and especially a steelheader, should know the line/leader *HOOK SNELL* connection that allows direct linkage of a hook to your line. When a fishing situation calls for bait or lures to be fished with no weight this tie is your strongest, and is least visible to fish. Follow the directions in our Hook Snell diagram to fashion this knot-free connection...knot-free, because it is wound and wrapped, rather than tied.

HOOK SNELL

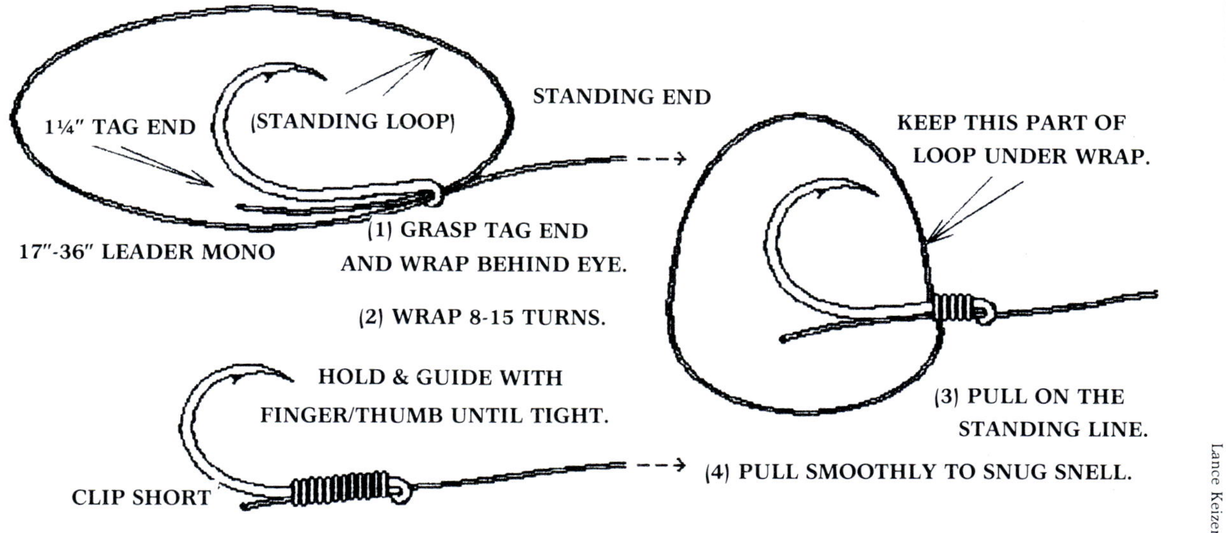

A Hook Snell is the basic rig for steelheading mainliners who attach a hook directly to their main line, using no leader, and slip a small length of surgical tubing on their line to hold pencil lead sinkers against the mono at adjustable distances from the hook to create leader length. This is a very effective and relatively simple and economic way to fish steelhead, as few accessories such as swivels, snaps, or split rings are needed. However, it has some drawbacks...the line and lead in continual abrasive conjunction being one, and the number of times that snags and other hang-ups cause the tubing/pencil lead to slide down to the knot and cause everything to be lost, necessitating frequent rig tieing, is another. This reduces fishing time on the river and shortens your main line by several feet every time you tie on a new hook.

Probably one of the next most useful knots steelheaders may wish to tie is the *BLOOD KNOT.* It makes a smooth, secure tie for line-to-line knots or solidly connects lines to backing. For more years than I care to admit, I've tied this knot in the standard, first-one-end, then-other-end fashion you see in most fishing and knot books. It is awkward to learn and difficult to perform, but forms a superb, strong knot. From now on, however, I will no longer have to fumble back and forth, switching line ends from fingers to opposite hands to tie a standard blood knot, thanks to Jim Ruppert, a well-known Seattle steelheader who is always willing to share with other anglers his innovative and successful light-line steelheading methods. Our diagram of *JIM'S BLOOD KNOT* depicts a one-direction tie infinitely easier for me to manipulate into what I feel is a smooth, near-perfect knot for connecting two lines of equal or relatively equal diameters and for line/backing linkage.

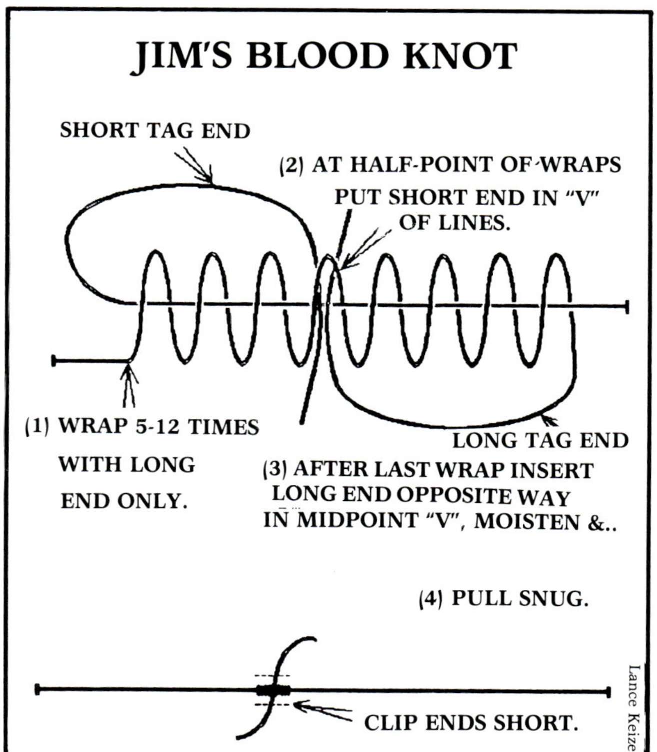

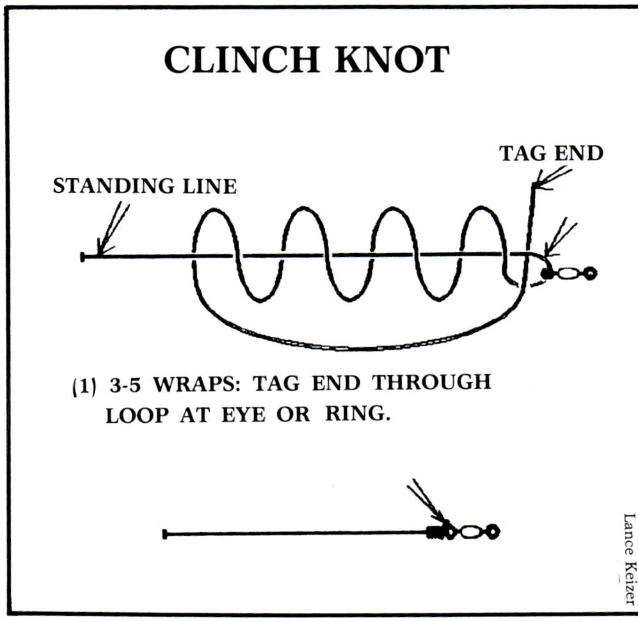

A large majority of steelheaders rig up their terminal gear with either a barrel swivel or snap swivel at the tag end of their line, then add a hook-bearing leader measuring from 14 to 30 inches. This allows them to tie leaders at home, carry them in a leader dispenser or leader wallet and, when a break off occurs, to whip out and tie on a fresh leader at streamside and get back to fishing quickly, while a hot bite is still on. The two knots at the opposite ends of a swivel or snap swivel connection can be tied in a variety of ways, among which choices are the *CLINCH KNOT, TRILENE™ KNOT* and a fisherman's own adaptation of these or other knots. I have for years been very content with a strong, easy tie which has been dubbed

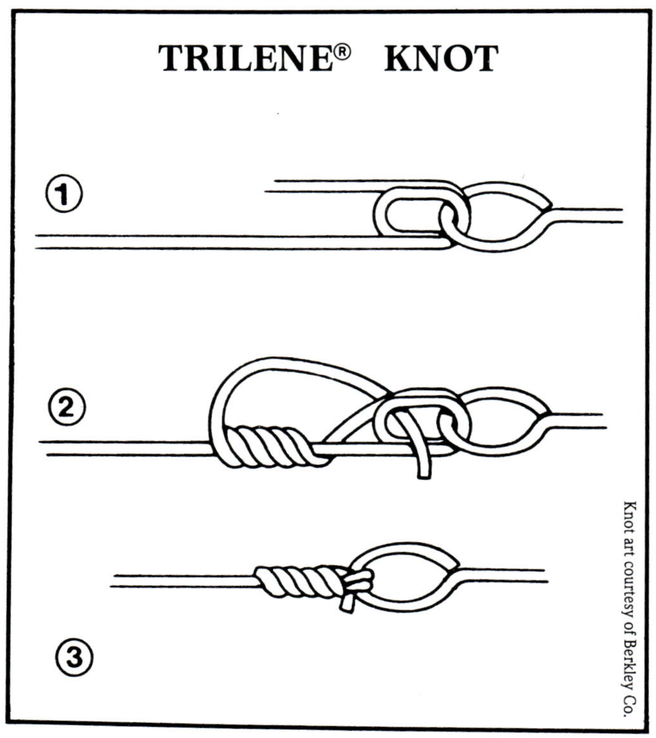

MILT'S MAXI KNOT. Tieing diagrams for your choice of these knots are pictured here.

MILT'S MAXI-KNOT

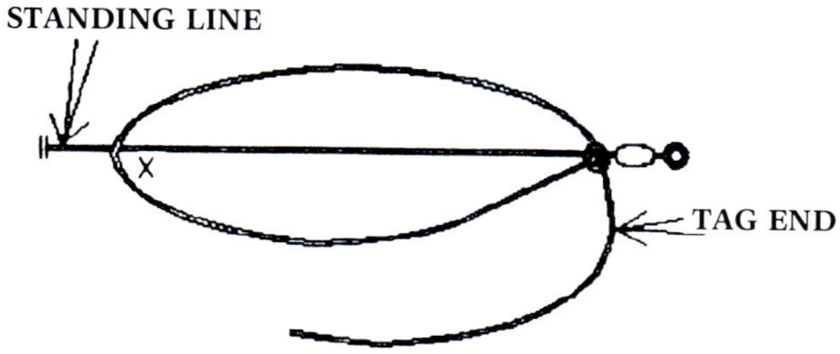

(1) PUT TAG END THROUGH EYE TWICE; HOLD LOOP WITH A FINGERTIP AT "X".

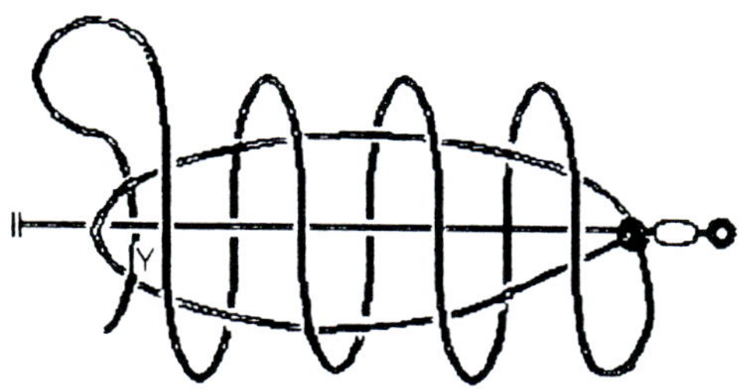

(2) 4-6 WRAPS AROUND ALL LINES; TUCK TAG END THROUGH LAST LOOP AT "Y".

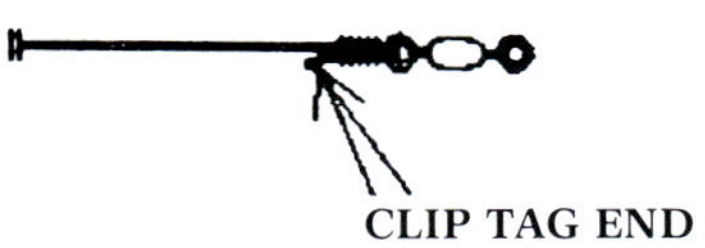

(3) MOISTEN; PULL SNUG.

Lance Keizer

BUMPER TIE/EGG LOOP

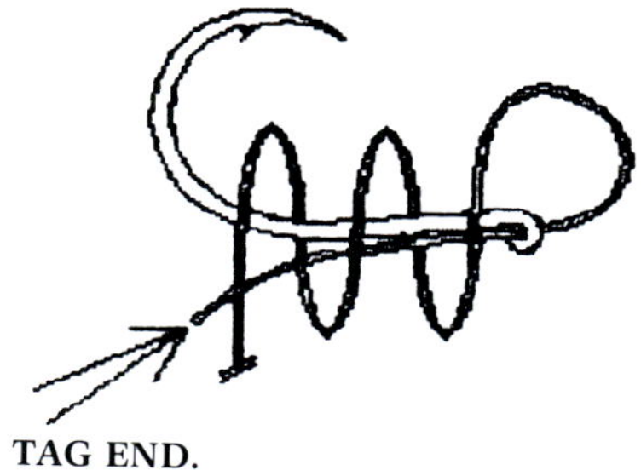

(1) INSERT TAG END 1¼" TOWARD SHANK THROUGH EYE, 4-8 WRAPS, STARTING BEHIND EYE, WITH STANDING END.

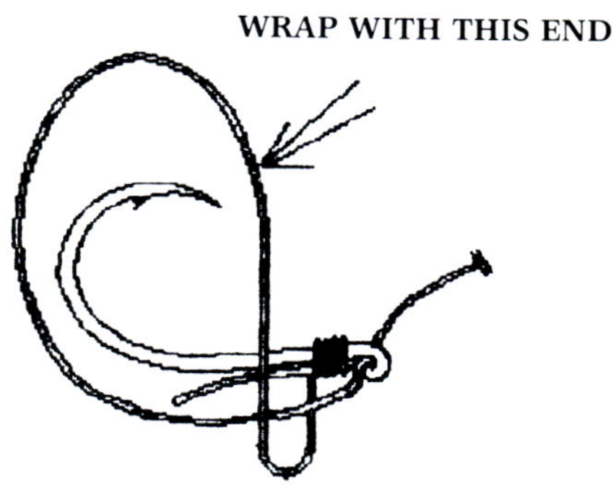

(2) BRING STANDING END AROUND HOOK AND INSERT FORWARD THROUGH EYE; MAKE 4-8 WRAPS OVER TAG END AND LOOP.

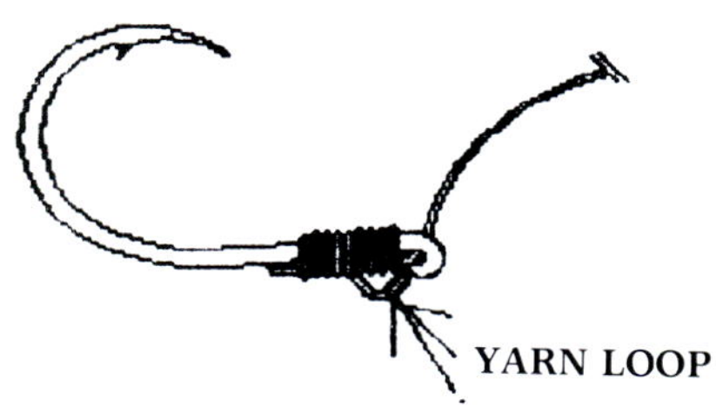

(3) PULL SNUG, CLIP TAG END.

Lance Keizer

Bait fishermen most often use a *BUMPER TIE* or *EGG LOOP* tie, both names referring to the same wrapped tie, which provides a short section of line, emerging from the center of their wraps and leading through the hook eye, into which yarn may be laid or tied, and which can be opened to accept and help hold cluster egg, roe bag, or shrimp/prawn baits. Leaders fashioned by using the Hook Snell also are favored by bait fishermen, with the snell wrapped and cinched tight partway down the hook shank, which permits baits or yarn to be snugly held by a loop pulled into the leader between the top of the snell and the hook eye.

It is important to rig Hook Snell and Bumper/Egg Loop ties on hooks having no baitholder barb (the tiny spike or spikes found on the hook shank about 5/16 of an inch below the hook eye), or to flatten these barbs before you form your tie. The sharp edges of the baitholder barb can carve their way through the tie and cost you a good fish.

Light-line steelheaders, fly-fishermen and anglers who fish flies on long leaders with their drift tackle outfits should know the *TURLE KNOT*, which is minimally visible to steelhead and very simple to

TURLE KNOT

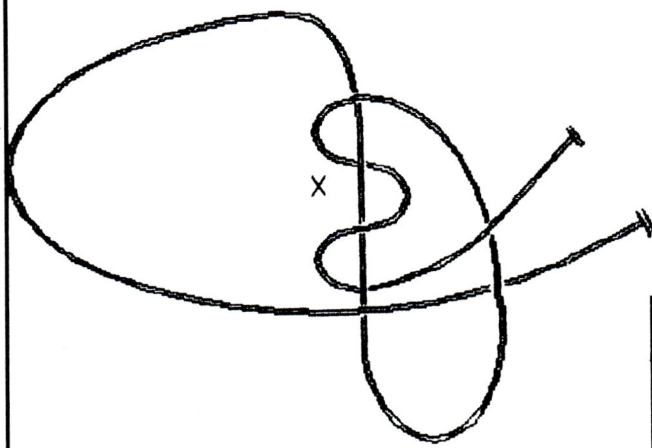

(1) FORM END LOOP; PASS TAG END TWICE AROUND SELF AT "X".

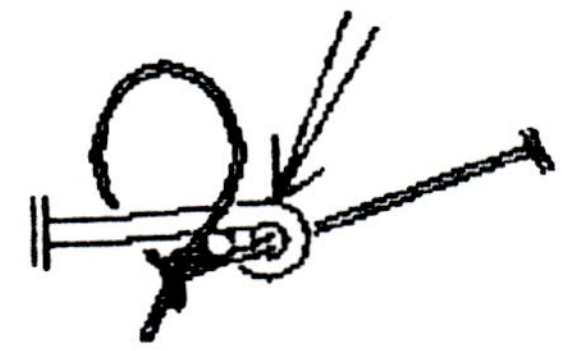

(2) PULL SNUG. USED AT REEL ARBOR, TYING ON FLIES AND FOR TINY HOOKS.

Lance Keizer

form, closely resembling a slip knot. (The Turle Knot also is an easy, long-lasting and effective way to attach your monofilament or backing to your reel spool.)

And, for fishermen who wish to add a light leader to much heavier line, or leader to fly line, the *NAIL KNOT* has reigned supreme for decades. Today's plastic age steelheaders, however, generally dispense with the nail and use in its place a short section of thin tubing, such as a cut-off old ballpoint pen filler, thin drinking straw or hollow mixed drink stirring stick. This allows a Nail Knot to be wrapped over the main line and tube, the leader to be passed through the hollow tube, and the tube withdrawn so the knot wraps can be snugged down tightly on the larger diameter line. See our diagrams for tieing these handy knots.

NAIL KNOT

(1) LOOP MONOFILAMENT AGAINST FLY OR LEAD CORE LINE, HOLD ALL AT "X", AFTER WRAPPING, PASS TAG END THROUGH TUBE, PULL TUBE OUT TO LEFT & SNUG KNOT TIGHT.

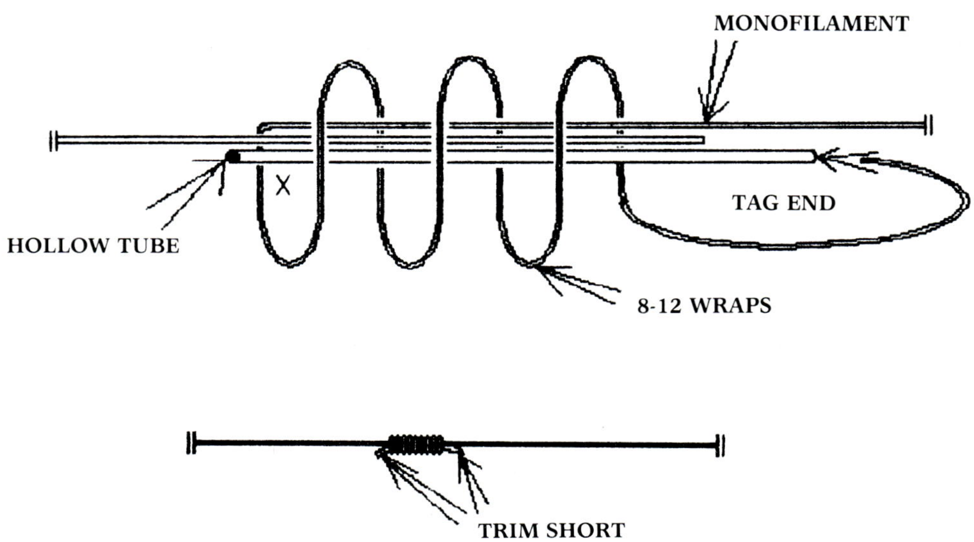

Lance Keizer

LEADERS AND SINKERS:

Steelheaders can find leader spools of all weights and colors for every type of fishing application. Leaders testing 1, 2, 3, 4 and 5 pounds breaking strength will match a light-liner's tackle, and heavier leaders then succeed these by 2- and 5-pound differences from 6 pounds on upwards to 30 pounds or more for use with sturdier outfits. Leader is available in colorless to mahogany hue for clear or dirty water and all shades between the two. Some leaders have the ability to become nearly invisible in whatever water you fish, while others attempt to match blue or green tints of the streams.

An important consideration of steelheaders is the flexibility of the leader chosen for their particular mode of fishing. If an angler does mostly bait-fishing, generally he will select a brand of leader having excellent flexibility but with some stretch, which allows bait to make a drift along bottom much as a bit of natural food would be borne by the current and yet instantly sock the steel to a fish's jaw on the strike.

The opposite extreme – a stiff leader – is chosen by fishermen who prefer to add wing bobbers to their bottom rigs or fish these lures alone, sans bait. They require leaders that will not twist themselves up into a tangled mess if a stray bit of weed or grass lodges on the lure, or when making a fast retrieve. A leader that does this is soon weakened to the replacement point and, if used with "coil springs" in its length, probably won't help attract fish very well and might even warn off steelhead by its unnatural action and appearance.

Knot strength and abrasion resistance are even more important in leaders than line, since a leader is intended to ramble among the rocks and boulders on the river bottom and is exposed to far more abuse than is your line. Leaders should have only a minimum of stretch, basically needed on striking and again in beaching struggling fish. Better ability to sense bites and hook fish is credited to anglers using low-stretch leaders.

All too often, steelheaders will lose good fish at their feet when leaders "pop" as they are landing fish... and many times it's not the fault of the leader. Remember, there's only a very short strand of leader between swivel and hook and it IS designed to break at its designated 8 or 10 pounds. When your line is retrieved to nearly the rod tip and you're levering a steelhead into port on a bar or gravel beach, you can do two things to increase your landing ratio: one is to make sure your drag is set lighter than when playing the fish (use thumb or finger pressure to control line drag) and you're ready to give line if the fish charges back for the river; the other is to lead the steelhead to its final berth upstream from you, so that the current aids you to beach it rather than helps the fish put weight on the leader.

Steelheaders who tie up their leaders at home rather than on the river have an advantage in fishing time over those who tie their rigs at streamside that often means more opportunity to catch a fish. Sure, it only takes a few minutes to fashion a leader... if your fingers aren't so frigid it's hard even to open a snap swivel! But, sometimes steelhead will bite only for a brief period and, if your line is out of the water while you are rigging up a new hook, yarn, bobber, bait, etc. you are not fishing. An hour's television show often is enough time to tie up two dozen or more leaders and store them in a leader wallet, leader dispenser, or in zip-top or sandwich bags. Your carefully fashioned and tightly snugged leaders are not only ready for quick replacement, but guarded from any scrapes and nicks that monofilament on a leader spool might suffer banging around with other items in your vest or parka pocket.

One of the handiest gadgets I've seen for keeping your supply of leaders is the Pip's leader dispenser, patented by Denzil Pipkin and now made by Mack's Lures. It is flat and round (looks like an oversize powderpuff case) and you can barb well over 100 hook/leader ties into its center cork, lay the leaders half a dozen at a time through slots in the bottom half, clap on the top and "crank" the leaders all into the rim space between the two dispenser halves by turning the upper half of the case. When you want a new rig all you do is pluck out a hook and pull smoothly and easily until the entire leader gently slips out. I use two or three color-coded carriers each fishing trip, keeping different pound test leader rigs in separate dispensers.

Leader lengths will depend on river conditions a steelheader anticipates facing. Most fishing regulations booklets require a hook and any sinker weight to be separated by at least 12 inches, to avoid any semblance to snagging gear. Ice-clear water, on the other hand, may be more successfully fished with a 36-inch leader that removes eye-catching sinker, swivel and surgical tubing as far as possible away from the fish.

Each steelheader's standard leader length is a compromise between achieving the greatest visual separation of a bait or lure from the rest of your fishing rig, versus the shortest length leader that will do the job, so that you can more quickly sense the bite of a steelhead and set the hook. For an example of what's happening down on the river's bottom, assume a steelhead lies in one position and you make a perfect cast that will bring your hook right to its mouth. The river current is carrying your bait/lure downstream ahead of the sinker. The fish obligingly opens its mouth and sucks in the hook. You will not feel the bite until the sinker moves a full leader length past the steelhead and the line tightens, having stopped. Meanwhile, the fish has begun trying to eject the hook by opening its mouth and shaking its head to get rid of that sticky-sharp thing pricking its jaw. How soon you sense all this activity largely depends on the length of your leader.

If you are using a 12-inch leader your sinker will travel two feet before it picks off bottom and your tightening line transmits a signal to strike. If your leader is 36 inches long, the same message won't come up your line until your sinker has continued tapping bottom from three feet above the steelhead to three feet below its position, a total distance of six feet!

Somewhere between 12 and 36 inches is the desirable length of leader that will work best for you.

Perhaps my home tied system of postponing the final determination of this length will work for you also. Pull a length of monofilament off your leader spool that comfortably spans the width between your upraised hands as you are sitting with elbows tucked back on each side of your ribs. After you attach the hook (I use the Bumper Tie or Milt's Maxi Knot with yarn added while tieing), the leader still spans about 20 to 26 inches. When I reach the river, my leader length is "fine tuned" by cutting it down to what looks right and fishes best.

Let's put everything together now and make up a basic "drift rig:"

DRIFT RIGS, THE BOTTOM LINE:

The steelheader's "drift rig" generally consists of a barrel or snap swivel, pencil lead sinker, surgical tubing, leader, yarn, bobber/bait and hook. There is an astronomical number of ways to combine these elements into the one that will best suit your preferences. I'll diagram some choices and point out what I feel to be their strong and weak points.

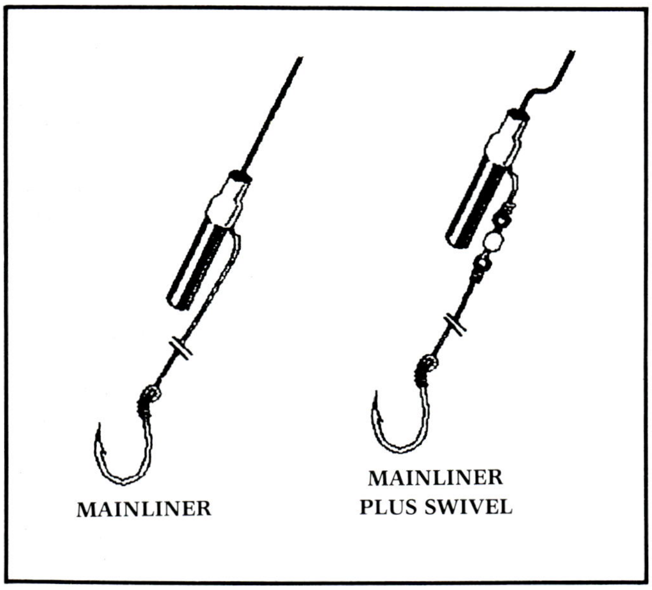

The MAINLINER RIG has only one connection of line to hook that might conceivably be a weak spot and, if you've wrapped a good Hook Snell, that point should be as strong as the rest of your line. A 3/4-inch long piece of surgical tubing is slid over the hook and run up the line 14 to 20 inches, held there, and a chunk of pencil lead sinker is forced into the tubing about 5/16 of an inch. The tubing can be moved to increase or decrease your leader length.

This may be the least expensive rigging system and easiest to pack and use. A supply of hooks and bait, some yarn, perhaps a few drift bobbers, extra tubing and lead and your tools are all that need be taken fishing. Disadvantages are that the sinker lead sliding on and scarfing the line's exterior can weaken it, or a hang-up can cost you a lot of line, since it is all the same strength from hook to reel spool and could snap anywhere, and you will lose some possibly critical fishing time while tieing up each fresh rig from scratch at streamside.

Add just one tiny barrel swivel to your set-up betweeen main line and leader and your system now becomes better organized for speedy rigging. Surgical tubing and sinker go on the main line above the swivel, and you can pack ready-made leaders along to swiftly tie on and get back to fishing when using a *MAINLINER PLUS* drift rig. An added benefit to this arrangement is that you can position the surgical tubing and lead right on top of your barrel swivel, so wear and tear of the abrasion is metal-to-metal, rather than metal to line. Again, the hang-up potential is nearly all on your main line and the odds are that you will lose everything on a break-off.

Perhaps next in simplicity is the *PINCH SINKER RIG*. Tie on a barrel swivel and leave a tag end hanging four or five inches from the leader knot. Pinch on two or three split shot or a piece of hollow pencil lead to get proper bottom-bouncing weight. A variation of this arrangement might be to split one end of solid pencil lead, lay your tag end of line through the split and crimp it tight again on the line end...or punch a hole near the end of the pencil lead and tie the loose main line end through the hole.

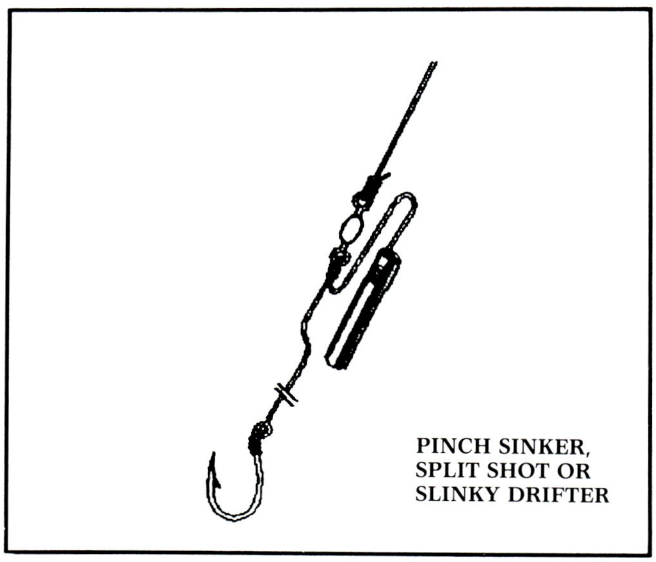

The principle is the same in all of the above rigs whatever you pinch on the sinker drop line...if the sinker is the piece of rigging that becomes hung up, a short jerk or steady pull should cause it to pull or break off, leaving you with the rest of your drift rig intact. Generally, leader breaking strength used with these drift rigs is about two pounds less than the rated line strength. If your leader is snagged, it should pop before the line will, and you ought to have swivel and weight still on the line, to which you tie a new leader and renew your fishing. The largest drawback in this rig is that the added distance a sinker is separated from the swivel increases the likelihood that it will find a crack in a rock or a protruding stick on which to snag and this set-up will cause you to replace a lot of sinkers.

SLIDING SINKER drift rigs are created by adding your pencil lead or a bouncing ball style sinker on the line above the swivel connection. The ball sinker has an eye through which you run your main line. For attaching pencil lead, using a snap, or a snap swivel and a small piece of surgical tubing, steelheaders run their main line through the eye of the snap, open the snap and force it through one wall of the surgical tubing, then close the snap and stuff the pencil lead into the tubing. The weight is free to slide on the line. This is an extremely effective method of rigging to feel a steelhead taking your hook. No weight on the leader also may cause the fish to retain it longer, giving you more reaction and hook-setting opportunity. However, the sliding metal-to-line contact can damage your main line and you should remember to redo the main line knot every few dozen casts (and adding a bead as a bumper between knot and sliding snap also helps). When your sinker gets snagged, since it is above the swivel on the main line, you're going to part with your entire drift rig a good number of times.

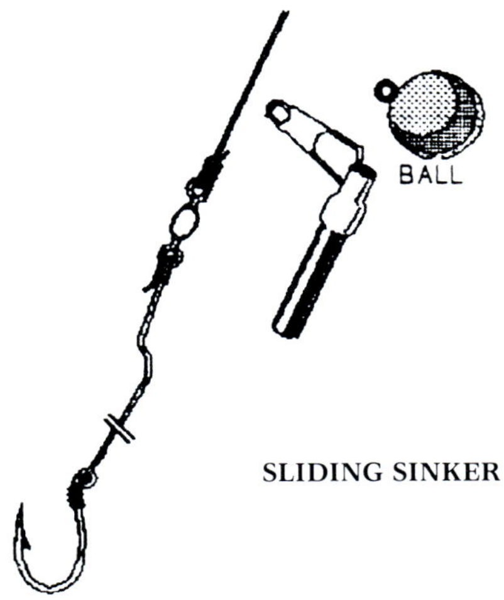

SLIDING SINKER

Many steelheaders prefer to tie their main line to the upper eye of the barrel swivel in a snap swivel, then affix their leader to the opposite eye of the barrel swivel portion of this item and let the snap hang loose to accept their surgical tubing and pencil sinker. It is less sensitive than a sliding sinker rig, but snags less often because the "Y" formed by the snap swivel, sinker and leader is a short, snug one that does a good job of fending off hang-ups. When you do hang bottom with this *SNAP SWIVEL RIG*, what happens most frequently is that you'll pull your pencil lead out of the surgical tubing and, by adding new lead, may be able to almost immediately get your line back in the water.

Pencil sinker lead comes in several sizes and in both hollow and solid choices. There are different surgical tubing sizes and wall thicknesses available from which to select either thin, easy to tear tubing or thick, strong lead receivers. Both lead and tubing can be bought by the foot or, in the case of pencil lead, by the pound on spools. Popular diameters are 1/4, 3/16 and 1/8 inches for lead and tubing. Bouncing ball

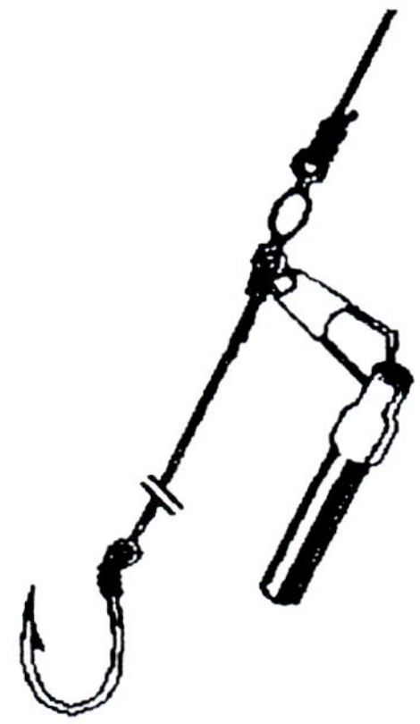
SNAP SWIVEL

sinkers can be obtained in a variety of weights. You will seldom see pyramid, flat, or dipsy sinkers used in drift fishing. (There are other sinker choices...I've seen steelheaders utilize solder wire, pieces of coat hanger, plastic-coated strings of split shot and sections of old speedometer cable as sinkers.)

Tired of hanging bottom and popping off lead or abrading your line and leader? Try a slinky sinker...it's new and works slick as a whistle. The slinky is a nylon sheath in which round lead buckshot is stuffed, with the ends sealed with a flame. It slithers over and through rocks, catching far less frequently than pencil lead because of its smooth, slippery nylon surface. Prong it snugly close to your line with a snap swivel and it will hang you fewer times, allowing you more fishing time.

Solid pencil lead should be wet, then an end is pushed into the surgical tubing only 5/16 of an inch or so. You want the lead to pull out on a hang-up, so that you can free the rest of your gear and get back to fishing quickly by adding new lead to your rig. If you stuff an inch or more of your lead into the tubing you can kiss it goodbye on the first determined rock!

Swivels and snap swivels should be as small as you can work with...the tiniest ones are stronger than your line or leader. I prefer the more costly, die-formed barrel swivels, rather than the twisted wire models, and choose black barrel swivels that are less likely to attract fish or give off warning sparkles when hit by sunlight. (It's frustrating to see steelhead strike a bright nickel swivel rather than at the lure on the same line!) Snap swivels are a different story, however. I use the cheap, Japanned brass snap swivels. Yes, there are some mighty sad tales of huge fish tearing up brass snap swivels, and I've pulled some apart in my hands after attaching them to my lines. But I test every snap swivel by pulling on line and leader before using it, and have lost no steelhead I could blame on this inexpensive snap swivel. Since the snap is used only to hold your surgical tubing and pencil lead, you really couldn't care less if it does disintegrate after a fish strikes!

When you're fishing a drift rig that has strong, well-tied knots, proper color and length leader and a bait or lure that you know steelhead will take it can build confidence that the bottom line you've come up with also is going to come up with fish.

Chapter 5

Steelheading Wear and Gear

It doesn't take long for a beginning steelhead fisherman to accumulate a widely scattered litter of lures, accessories, tools, boots, clothing and other angling-related items. To save several trips to the garage or carport, den, closet, vehicle, workbench, top of the refrigerator and dresser top every time they plan to go fishing, serious steelheaders get organized. All it takes to force you to this decision is 50 to 100 miles of highway between yourself and the lunch, vacuum of coffee, steelhead vest, or fishing license you've left at home.

Somewhere in your residence there must be an area three feet by about seven feet you can adapt for this purpose. It doesn't matter if the rectangular space is horizontal or vertical, as you can readily use either. What works well for me is a corner in which I have mounted a "reject" interior house door across two metal two-drawer filing cabinets. Tackle boxes, pasteboard boxes, duffel bags and shipping cartons stored underneath it still give me kneehole room to sit at the home-built desk. I can tie up fishing rigs, clean a reel, or pour out a whole bunch of lures and sort them, on top of the door. That still leaves me the file drawers for paperwork, fishing catalogs and maps, and plenty of convertible desktop area for a typewriter. A small study lamp will brighten the desk surface for close detail work.

Parts organizer cabinets are just super for storing bobbers, spoons, spinners, hooks, swivels and beads, surgical tubing and precut pencil lead, plus all the small tools and accessories I use. These terrific storage sets come in models having from nine to 48 drawers and I have no difficulty keeping several of the medium and large ones filled. I drop a lot of miscellaneous, non-rusting items in cans ranging from 9-ounce Almond Roca containers to 3-pound coffee tins, some with plastic lids and some open. Large, plastic ex-whipped cream or dip dispensers will hold tangled rigging brought back from the river and the jetsam that collects in your jacket or vest pockets over a few days of fishing. These are sorted later, some of it discarded, and the good stuff is cleaned and returned to the parts organizer drawers.

A simple wall-mounted rod rack is easy to make from a short piece of 2 X 4. Measure the diameter of your fattest rod butt and then bore slightly larger holes two-thirds of the way through the four-inch height. Next, cut the 2 X 4 into a 2 X 2. The half with holes bored completely through is the top of your rod rack and your rod butts go in the pockets left in the bottom rack piece. Mount the two pieces on the wall about 44 to 45 inches apart and you'll find it easy to insert two-piece rods (broken down and the halves rubber-banded side by side) by sliding the tips up through the top rack holes and then tucking the butts into the bottom of the rack.

If there is a heat source below one end of your storage area, such as a wall register or hot air vent, leave space against the wall so heat will rise into the legs of hip boots or chest waders hung above it by their toes at ceiling height with special boot hooks held by a screw eye or bracket. Plastic (no rust) clothes hangers on another hook or bracket will help dry your rain parka or jacket in the same location.

Hey, that was pretty easy and inexpensive, wasn't it? Now you have a place for everything and everything in its place. OK, let's take a look at some of the things a steelheader needs that overflow from streamside to home storage area:

STEELHEADING TOOLS, ACCESSORIES AND GADGETS:

You can start steelheading with little more than

your fishing outfit, serviceable outdoor wear and a pocketful of lures. After that first trip what you should obtain next ought to be determined by what you needed and didn't have with you. (My first steelhead fishing trips required only a bare handful of spoons and a 35mm used film canister containing snap swivels and a few extra Siwash hooks, all tucked into the small pocket inside the top of a pair of borrowed chest waders.)

Steelheading is one angling pursuit for which medium and large tackle boxes are not very convenient streamside items. They are awkward, extra objects to carry, are easy to dump over when open, might get bumped off a bank into the river, thereby floating all your gear away and, because of the nature of the sport, contents carefully arranged at home always seem to have all found new hideyholes by day's end. The best use for tackle boxes is to carry a boater's supply of plugs.

Right on top of your steelheading accessory list should be a good needle-nose pliers. This is a nearly-indispensable tool at home and at the river. The kind that has long, thin jaws and a set of cutters for wire or lead up to 1/4-inch diameter works best for me. Buy a medium size pliers to pack along fishing and another one slightly smaller to work with at home (tuck it into a parts organizer drawer, so it won't wander out to the kids' play area or into your toolbox). Spend a little more to get top quality, smoothly-functioning pliers less likely to rust and be sure that you can readily open and close the jaws with one hand.

The pliers will cut or trim your pencil lead sinkers to size, clip line and leader, open stubborn snap swivels, hold split rings while you're changing hooks, and help you release wild fish steelhead without touching them, simply by grasping the hook shank with the pliers and upending it with a slight shake and twist. (This can also be done with a surgeon's forceps.)

Monofilament can dull cutting edges of your good knives and pliers, so a small fingernail clipper can save you sharpening or replacing these costlier items. For now, tie a 20-inch chunk of 15- to 20-pound monofilament through the hole at one end of the clipper and form a loop on the other end that can be fed through a shirt pocket buttonhole so you can quickly fish it out and drop it back in the pocket. Get at least two clippers, and stick the extras in a parts drawer. After you buy a steelhead vest, there are clip-on, spring-loaded reel buttons that let you whip out the clipper or a file, use it, and then the retrieve mechanism zips the tool out of your way.

Another cutting tool steelheaders put to good use is a pair of sharp scissors. Small, folding, surgical steel scissors snip yarn cleanly to make neat leader rigs either at home or while fishing. These will pack along easily in a pocket or vest. Also, get a large scissors or shears for your home area. These are ideal for cutting egg skeins in your cluster egg and roe bag preparation.

A file, hook hone, or other type of hook sharpener is a vital item in every steelheader's pocket. Touch up your hook point every dozen casts on general principles and every time after you've been temporarily snagged. Having a sharp hook is critical when you're trying to stick it in an "ironhead's" jaw. They earned that knickname honestly, with thousands of hard-mouthed steelhead lost off anglers' hooks annually because the hooks were not struck home securely past their barbs. I carry two files, one in my vest and a spare tucked into my leather license wallet.

Even new hooks taken right out of the maker's box generally are not sharp enough to suit longtime steelheaders. A small ignition/point file will slick them up so that the hook point will drag when gently moved across your thumbnail. There are special fishermen's files also, ranging from pencil type to a file that has two surfaces per side and a floating handle. Hones and stones are sold by your tackle dealer and he might also extol the virtues of a little battery operated hook sharpener that puts a keen point on your hooks with just a touch or two on each side of the tiny, whirring wheel...which I like for home sharpening.

A split ring pliers is handy if you work with or make up your own spoons, spinners, plugs, three-way plunking spreaders or wire-mounted wing bobber rigs. With this special tool and a stout Boy Scout or Swiss knife, even the balkiest heavy split ring can be attitudinally adjusted without having it spring away and roll under the couch. I also have several large, roundheaded straight pins handy at home, for clearing the drilled holes in bobber lures and picking paint out of hook eyes. I pack one of these pins along to the river in my bobber box and also carry a tiny, plastic crochet hook for picking tangles out of bait-casting reels.

A fly-tieing vise will help whip up the latest killer steelhead fly pattern, yarn tie, or come in handy for snelling hooks and creating egg loop leaders for use with drift rigs. The fly vise is especially handy for beginning steelheaders learning to tie their own leaders because it gives them a third hand to hold the hook while they loop and wrap the leader with their two.

Don't ever discard any small, sturdy plastic box you can lay your hands on. Sooner or later you'll find a piece of essential tackle that will fit into it for safer transportation or storage, or a pocket in which it fits while loaded with something critical to your success on the river. Line spool boxes, the plastic containers filled with small nails or screw assortments that you get from the hardware, hard plastic staple refill boxes and some Tupperware *(Oops! She heard that!)* pieces meet this category and often fit your shirt or steelhead vest pockets better than other containers.

If you requisition a few zipper top or fold-over large sandwich bags from the kitchen and slip them into a 3-pound coffee can to store odds and ends too big or oddly shaped for your organizer drawers, your area will be a lot less cluttered.

Add a tube of liquid rubber to be used for repair of waders or raingear, and that just about covers the general types of tools, accessories and gadgets many steelheaders gather in their home fishing centers, but in no way approaches a complete list.

WADERS, CLOTHING AND RAINGEAR:

I do not want to lose any of my fishing friends...either the ones I know well now or those whom I have yet to meet. Therefore, the FIRST item outside the normal on-the-river fishing tackle I'm going to recommend you consider buying is a flotation coat, jacket or vest. These are buoyant devices worth every penny they cost if you only need them once! Even if you plan to fish only from river banks, you might conceivably slip or fall in. Or, if a friend comes along in his boat and invites you to go with him for the day you need a flotation device...and you're wearing it.

Boat fishermen, especially, should wear flotation vests at all times when on the water. Safety cushions stuffed under the boat's front deck or a seat may satisfy the legal requirements in many areas, but in all likelihood will not be anywhere near if you unexpectedly wind up in the water. My flotation coat keeps me safe and warm and, beside that, it's a classy looking outfit for other fall/winter/spring activities. You can find flotation coats or vests in sporting good stores and tackle shops, or they can be ordered through mail and discount catalogs. There are jackets and vests, also, that are rapidly blown up into a buoyant lifesaver by a carbon dioxide cartridge triggered either by yourself or water pressure. Choose one of the above, buy it and wear it.

Steelheaders face more ways than one to get wet, however, so your next consideration might be a good rain parka or rain suit. Rain and spray, mist or dew on trailside bushes, and wet boat seats all are good reasons to don this protective gear. Staying dry and comfortable will make you a better fisherman. If you're soaked and shivering, it's hard to tell if there's a steelhead biting on your hook or you're creating all that tip action by yourself.

The best quality, and thus more expensive, rain suits and parkas probably are your best buys. They last longer, and are designed to let air in and keep water out, preventing condensation from sopping you down on the inside. I buy rain pants large enough to go on over my hip boots or pacs and benefit from a dry seat when fishing from a wet boat. I steer clear of full-length rain coats, because I do quite a bit of hip boot-depth wading. The longer coats trail in the water and you could be knocked off your feet by river current filling your coattails at the wrong time. A parka length is just fine, or a fingertip-long jacket. Just ensure the raingear reaches past the tops of your hip boots far enough so the run-off won't drain down your legs.

The color of your rainwear is important. Bright red, orange and yellow should be avoided by bank anglers, while green, khaki, and camouflage hues better match your streamside background. You can spook every steelhead in a given stretch of river by walking along the water in a bright jacket or parka. Years ago I startled a huge steelhead from at least 50 feet away when approaching him in a stoplight red parka. He left a wake like a PT boat and didn't stop until finding a deepwater slot half a football field downstream! (That parka now is reserved for hunting.)

Calf-high "pacs" having lug or cleat soles are excellent bank and boat fishing footwear. Get them in large enough size so that in winter fishing you can wear a couple pair of sox. Tight boots or shoes cause cold feet and make it very uncomfortable to stand for long periods of time in your favorite bank-fishing spot. The same advice applies to hip boot and wader foot size too.

Hip boots and chest waders are the normal garb of most dedicated steelheaders and, unless you believe ice-cold trickles of water running down your shins are unimportant, you should buy quality, well-fitting equipment and take good care of these thin shells between you and wintry rivers. Hang them to dry after each use and, if you must store them away between seasons, roll or fold them loosely once and sprinkle them down with talcum powder.

Your choice of steelheading clothes is optional, depending upon the season and weather. Wool is excellent in winter, because it retains body heat even when wet. Flannel and denims also make good winter wear if layered, trapping air between. Many anglers wear net style, synthetic, down or wool longhandles next to their skin in winter for added warmth. Keeping your feet warm, dry and comfortable will require thin socks on the inside layer and thicker ones on the outside. Topping off everything with a brimmed hat or cap to shield you from sun and rain is a wise move. Rain hats can be carried in a pocket or the back of your steelhead vest. Pocket-size handwarmers are nice added extras to warm your fingers on a bitterly cold winter day.

Bait-fishermen generally clip their bait canteens on an extra belt that goes outside jackets or rain wear. When fishing in chest waders, this bait belt is cinched snugly at the upper ribs and will help keep water from spilling into your waders in case of a sudden dunking. A small towel or hand rag is tucked under the belt to use in wiping off borax and egg goo.

Landing nets are very useful to bank steelheaders at spots where there is no way to get into the water to beach or hand-land fish. Boaters consider landing nets mandatory. Some wading anglers will carry folding nets on the end of a cord slung over their shoulders, but they are few in number.

A many-pocketed, canvas or heavy cloth steelhead vest is the steelheader's home away from home in that spare equipment, line, prepared leaders, lures, file, water thermometer, pencil leads and other sinkers, his lunch, coffee, and even his raingear may be carried turtle-fashion along with him from vehicle to fishing spot to next fishing spot.

Most good steelhead vests have a minimum of 9 capacious pockets, while some have as many as 12, and it is startling to discover just how much one of these garments stores. Mine has a folding gaff, cleaning knife, pair of fingerless wool gloves, a small flashlight, miniscule but deadly priest to administer last rites to keeper fish, a bundle of small plastic bags for eggs and large ones for fish, a couple lengths of cord with which to carry steelhead on a cut branch, a packaged but rigged Side-Planer and plug combination, plastic bottle of fish scent, spare reel in thick, soft bag, extra plastic box of spoons and spinners, maps, extra line in a pouch, polarized fish-spotting glasses, sun glasses, extra spinning reel spools and a spare pack of cigarettes.

That's just the back pocket! In the others I carry my fishing gear at my fingertips in the front outside pockets where I can get at items readily even when the vest is covered by a rain parka. On the inside of the vest there are two wide pockets I find useful for pencil lead and surgical tubing in one, and folding scissors, pliers, discarded rigs, and my and other people's fishing litter in the other. When I buy a new vest, the first thing I do to it is add Velcro™ strips to the tops of these inside pockets to prevent spillage while wading.

Most steelheaders never zip the vest front, so that they can shed it quickly if they want to free themselves of its weight to fish or if they take a sudden dip in the river. Even worn under a rain parka, which I buy extra large for the purpose of covering me and my traveling warehouse, I figure I can dump all that anchor weight in a hurry if necessary. When I pack a camera along, plus snacks and a jug of coffee, and maybe tuck my raingear in the back pocket, the vest starts to resemble a mountaineer's backpack!...OK, we're all equipped, rod in hand, boots or waders and rain gear on, vest crammed with fishing gear and accessories and we're ready to head for the river...will someone give us a slight push to get us started?

A moment of great happiness. Ron Lane, Baseball Co-Commissioner of the 1984 Olympics, poses with a Dean River, British Columbia fly-caught steelhead his son just landed.

Chapter 6

Steelhead Baits, Sources and Care

West coast fishermen use a wide variety of baits to coax steelhead to their hooks. Perhaps 60 to 65 percent of steelhead caught from coastal rivers of mid-California to upper British Columbia are tricked by tidbits that appeal to their appetite.

There's an adage that always seems good for stirring up a little debate on whether and how much steelhead feed in fresh water. It goes something like this, "Winter steelhead don't eat, but summer-runs like meat." This saying is based on the rapid organic changes a winter steelhead undergoes upon leaving salt water in fall or winter (most Pacific coast winter-runs come "home" from early November to as late as April) to make a relatively short-time trip to spawning gravel in its home stream. Digestive tracts shrink, and egg skeins in the female steelhead and milt sacs in the male swiftly swell to fill their belly cavities, preventing winter steelhead from swallowing and digesting food.

Summer fish, however, coming into rivers any time from May to October, are fat, firm and frisky on arrival, but must continue to feed somewhat in order to preserve themselves for their December-February spawning ritual.

Effectively, shortly after swimming into fresh water, winter steelhead cannot make full use of what they try to ingest. But it is possible they may be able to utilize some small morsels of food for several days to a week or two after pointing upriver. After that time, they continue to try to eat. I've seen concrete proof that they'll grab whatever they can that remotely resembles an entree, salad, or main course and attempt to pork it down.

In one instance, a January angler stopped by my fishing partner's front door to show him a thoroughly bedraggled, chewed-upon ouzel, a small bird that hops among streamside rocks and ducks underwater to poke about for food as comfortably as it does on land. This bird is familiar to steelhead anglers as a western dipper. Asked why he had brought such an obvious goner over, the smiling fisherman swung his other hand from behind him and replied, "Because this 4-pound winter hen steelhead was doing her best to swallow it... its head was halfway down the fish's throat!"

Can't you picture the underwater scenario when Ollie Ouzel discovered he was on the menu? "Hey! Whoa, lady," (with his outspread wings backpedalling) "not me! Let's talk this overrrrrr!" Tell him winter steelhead don't eat!

Almost every steelheader I know has a similar story to relate concerning what they saw a steelhead take, or what they found in its stomach when cleaning one they had caught. Winter and summer steelhead alike will pick up and mouth – sometimes swallow – small and bright wood chips, rocks, leaves, berries, glass, feathers, pop-top tabs, insects, larvae, crustaceans, minnows, bits of plastic, rags...and steelheaders' flies, lures and baits.

Most steelhead will immediately reject the majority of these objects, since they are not palatable. A steelhead's intake and expulsion of trial food can be equally swift. Objects are sucked in by flaring the gills, with wide-open mouth, creating a siphon flow that carries things into the mouth. Ejecting them is controlled by the fish opening its mouth, along with a sudden closing of the gills, propelling unwanted things back into the river current. Acceptable items, or those that need further taste testing, are retained in the fish's mouth and its jaws thoughtfully chomp them several times.

This period of time a steelhead will mouth small objects is critical to steelheaders. Anglers often scrub lures free of all human scent, add various attractive scent juices, use strands of soft yarn to tangle in the steelhead's tiny teeth, or attach chewy plastic bodies or enticing tails to their lure or bait. All these painstaking preparations are intended to increase the retention time an ironhead will keep their bait or lure in its mouth and thereby allow the fisherman time to feel a sensitive strike.

Baits are effective any time your favorite steelhead river is reasonably fishable. They sometimes are the only things that work well when the water is high and muddy or just the opposite, low and clear as a Vodka Martini. Baits fished alone, with yarn, with bobbers, or with yarn and bobbers, are excellent choices for coaxing bites from steelhead. Before electing to fish baits, however, every angler should carefully *READ THE REGULATIONS HANDBOOK* for his state or province, to determine whether, when and which baits are legal.

Beginning steelheaders often are told that it is very difficult to sense the subtle nibble of a steelhead sampling their bait. The problem is not necessarily feeling the soft take of a biting fish, as it is in recognizing what is happening. Veteran anglers will eyeball a newcomer's rod and ask, "Why didn't you set the hook on that fish?" and the neophyte steelheader will reply, "I didn't think it WAS a fish." With properly chosen, sensitive tackle and matching line/leader rigs, a bait-fishing beginner soon learns that, if there's any difference between his first several drifts and the next one, it's likely a steelhead may have his bait in its mouth.

After catching a few "suicide" steelhead – those that give emphatic tugs on your gear and solidly hook themselves – it's much easier to determine what is and isn't a bite.

A good bait fisherman can be recognized by the quality of his baits. Lively, racehorse night crawlers or worms, active shrimp, grasshoppers, meal worms, grubs, periwinkles or prawns, carefully prepared cluster or single eggs, or fresh crayfish tail sections produce far more steelhead catches than stale, lifeless offerings.

Here are some good baits that steelhead will take:

THE NIGHT CRAWLER/WORM CONNECTION

Easiest and most inexpensive to obtain, fat, wriggling worms or night crawlers (also called dew worms) are prime steelhead baits. Since steelhead spend their first year or more in streams, these enticers are readily accepted as familiar food objects. Night crawlers and worms are universal baits that have freshwater appeal to all species of fish, including steelhead. If Will Rogers had been born a steelhead, his oft-repeated statement might have been, I never met a worm I didn't like.

Night crawlers are readily available at bait and tackle shops. They also are caught fairly simply and their pursuit can be a good father/son activity in which quick young fingers often outdo age and experience. Night crawlers may be found in most grassy back yards, parks, golf courses, cemeteries and some school yards...or anywhere grass is kept well-mown and watered. Permission to collect them should be obtained when seeking them on property other than your own.

You'll need a large, clean bait can, such as a three-pound coffee container or small plastic bucket, and a flashlight with red plastic over the lens. 'Crawlers are sensitive to white light, and will quickly disappear down their holes if touched with an unshielded light. They generally have their tails still in their hole, so your best tactic is to locate a night crawler, move the red flashlight glow slightly off the quarry, then pounce with a flat hand on the 'crawler, pinning it to the ground. Next, grip it as close to the tail as you can and exert a steady pressure on the night crawler to overcome its tail grip in the hole.

Never keep a broken night crawler (or worm) in your bucket. One dying bait can cause the entire batch to spoil.

For one day's fishing, a bait canteen full of wrigglers will do, or a two-pound coffee can is an ideal carrier. Cut both ends off and use two plastic lids, with a pair of strong rubber bands holding everything together. Since the worms or 'crawlers all try to hide at the bottom of the can, the best way to get one out is to turn the can over, open the lid that formerly was the bottom, and select a choice, fat one to barb on your hook.

A dozen or two dew worms that are going to be used soon may be kept alive and healthy in sphagnum moss, worm bedding, a clump of thick grass, or in a wad of crushed, slightly damp, shredded newspaper at the bottom of your container. Your unused 'crawlers may be seeded in your lawn...they are good for the soil and may ensure a future supply of bait, thereby saving you the $1 to $3 a dozen cost of purchasing them from a bait supplier.

Also, for best travelling, carry the baits on a layer of ice in a small cooler. Foam plastic cups, oleomargarine, cottage cheese or other dairy products containers also make good bait holders after you punch a dozen or more airholes in their lids. (If you've an understanding and forbearing wife, these ready-to-go bait preservers might be stored overnight in the family refrigerator.)

There are many ways to hook a night crawler and individual fishermen may do it differently from my preferred methods. With a No. 2 hook or larger, I slip the hook through once about an inch above the tail, then spike the hook downward through the collar near the head. If using a No. 4 or smaller hook, I'll insert the point downward through the tip of the head, pull my hook and leader through, then insert the point downward through the collar that holds the reproductive organs and rotate the hook, leaving most of the shank buried and just the barb exposed.

Large earthworms can be hooked much the same, but smaller worms should be strung, two to four at a time, through the head and out the collar, then another worm, until the hook is covered.

Worms can best be dug from moist, dark soil, with good spots being garden edges, drain fields, or near mulch piles. They also can be purchased from bait shops or the traditional barefoot boy in bib overalls.

Worms and night crawlers may be kept for long

periods of time in commercial bedding maintained in clean, slightly damp and cool condition. An old refrigerator in the basement or carport works fine for this purpose. These baits also may be raised in sturdy wood boxes 8 to 10 inches high by a couple feet square. Fill the box two-thirds full of commercial worm bedding, shredded newspaper, or a mixture of peat, dirt, and old rabbit or cow manure (fresh manure is too acidic). Your crop of 'crawlers will fare better if you line the box with black plastic, leaving one end or side long enough to cover the top. Use an old spray bottle to lightly mist the surface of the bedding once or twice a week, taking care not to get too much water in the bedding, which would drown the wrigglers. Feed your potential baits vegetable tops once or twice a week. You can improve the fish-getting action of night crawlers and worms if you condition them before taking them along on your next fishing trip. Get them in racehorse shape by selecting a dozen or more of the most active wrigglers and placing them in a separate bait container that already is about a quarter filled with a mixture of fine gravel and dirt. After 10 to 24 hours in this Spartan weight-reducing spa, your prospective baits will have excreted inner wastes and scrubbed their outsides clean. They become lean, mean, catching machines with a lot of lively appeal to steelhead.

If steelhead won't take these sassy mouthfuls, they're being very picky. That might be the case, so there are other baits to try...

Dave Kaffke hooked this eastern Washington summer-run steelhead with a spinner.

FISHING WITH EGGS

Single eggs, egg clusters, roe bags and artificial eggs have been successfully used to catch hundreds of thousands of steelhead in this century. Oldtimers rate them the No. 1 bait and many veteran fishermen use very little else to take season limits of ironheads year after year.

Fishing steelhead (or salmon) eggs presents a problem much like solving the question, Which came first...the chicken or the egg? Baits are processed from the egg skeins of a freshly caught female steelhead or salmon. If you've a good fishing friend, he'll probably volunteer some eggs to get you started. Or, there are commercially prepared single eggs, egg clusters and artificial imitations of these that may be purchased.

After you take your first hen steelhead or salmon, your buddy very likely will show you how to cure your own eggs and put them up in ready-to-use containers. Or, if you fish a lot of artificial lures and hardware, as I do, which seem to appeal more to female fish, while my angling partner catches mostly bucks on his egg and shrimp baits, you might strike a bargain such as we have. My partner cleans my hens AND any deer I might take during the hunting season. In return, he gets our total egg supply, from which I can borrow on the rare occasions I want to use these tempting, productive baits. (Before you make this trade-off, check your regulations to see if and how you can legally transfer any parts of a game fish to another person...in our state, a note stating the gift, your fishing license and steelhead punch card numbers, plus the day's date, are required.)

Curing your own egg baits is relatively easy and you soon will develop your own personal formula for giving them just the right color, consistency and smell calculated to make steelhead swim a half-mile past other baits and lures to happily close their jaws on your offering.

Loose eggs may be put up as singles by boiling them in a large container half-filled with water. Throw in some salt and bring the water to a rolling boil for several minutes. Ladle out an egg after a minute or two of boiling and test it between your forefinger and thumb to see if it crushes easily or whether it is becoming a trifle spongy. You're looking for the eggs to slightly harden, giving them enough body to stay on the hook, but not stiffen to the point they become like hard rubber. Some of each egg should still be juice, so that a hooked egg will milk into the water you're fishing, enticing steelhead to the smell. Attractive scents, such as salmon egg oil, herring, anise, shrimp, general-purpose fish scent, sugar or molasses, may be added to the boiling water to enhance the odor your eggs will emit when used.

When you take a female of the salmonid species that has tight, not-quite-mature egg skeins, you've got the prime requisites for cluster eggs or roe bags. Handle the fish's two egg skeins carefully. Some anglers pack along several plastic sandwich or zipper top bags in which skeins can be kept safe and clean, preferably on ice in a cooler, until getting them home.

Putting up cluster eggs and roe bags takes a little

time, space and effort. The end result, though, when properly done, is several containers loaded with succulent, colorful, juicy baits no steelhead in the right frame of mind should refuse. A 6-pound female steelhead generally will yield about two to three cottage cheese cartons full of clusters, while the most we have obtained was over eight cartons of cluster egg baits from a heavily-laden 22-pound hen that now hangs on my living room wall.

There are good commercial cures available that produce very fine baits having excellent color and texture. Many anglers prefer to use their own curing formula, however, and come up with equally effective baits.

Standard procedure for almost all steelheaders is to rid fresh egg skeins of excess moisture by wrapping them in paper towels and then newspapers and storing them one to two nights in their family refrigerator (they're almost odorless at this stage). Check them periodically, to make sure they don't dry too much. Then, clear a large space on which to work...kitchen table, workbench, or half a sheet of plywood on sawhorses in a cool spot.

First, you will need to cover your work area with lots of old newspaper or a cleanable oilcloth. Obtain your own large size scissors, as I guarantee you won't be allowed to borrow your wife's sewing scissors twice for this job! Next, you have to decide which kind of curing process you are going to follow and how large or small you will cut the clusters.

Baits nearly the size of golf balls appeal to salmon and the largest steehead, but most fishermen prefer clusters or roe bags to range from about quarter size to approximately the size of a nickel. Your two main choices of curing process are to use powdered borax (do not confuse with Boraxo soap powder) or sodium sulfite (not sulf*ide* or sulf*ate*), either of which curing agents provide excellent clusters or bags.

Borax Cure

Borax curing is done by spreading a thin crust of powdered borax over a serving tray-sized work area, cutting skeins in half lengthwise, then into the size of baits desired, laying each on the borax. Make sure to leave a small piece of the egg sac, or skein, on each bait, as this helps hold the bait together and on your hook. As each bait is snipped from the skein, roll it several times in the powdered borax, and wait to box

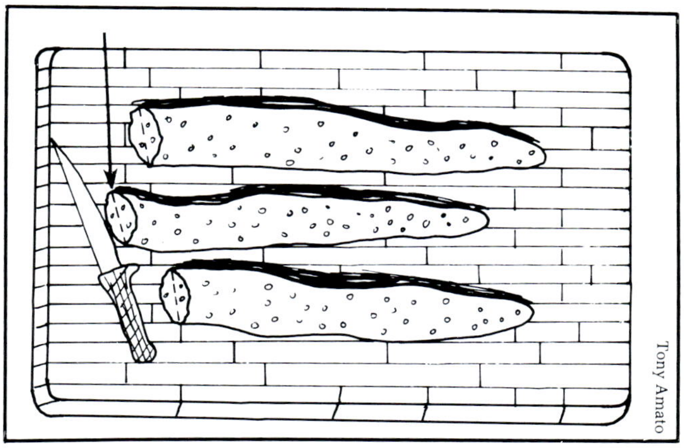

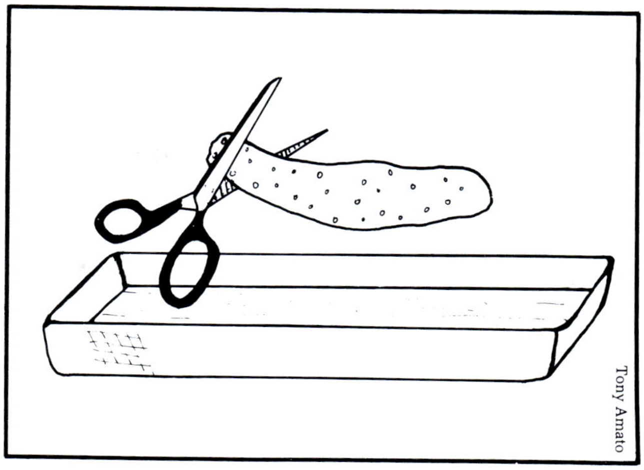

them until you have finished cutting all the clusters, allowing all baits to further drain off unwanted juice.

Ideal bait boxes are dairy products containers about three inches high and five inches across at their tapered top. Glass jars – such as jelly comes in – or the larger baby food jars make the best receptacles for storage, but are too easily broken in transporting them to the river or while fishing.

Put in the container a layer of clean powdered borax, then a tier of baits, fill and cover that layer with more borax, add another tier of clusters, then more borax. Depending on the size of your baits, you will get two or three layers of prepared fish-tempters.

For roe bags, purchase a supply of maline cloth...a fine-meshed net material that will hold the bait in a rounded shape and through which your hook barb will penetrate to help keep the bait on your hook. (Old nylon hose also will make good roe bags.) Cut squares of the material to a size that will fully wrap the clusters, place the baits in the center of the mesh square and bring up the ends. Turn the folds to the inside, and snugly tie a bit of thread or light cord around the maline just above the bait, then cut the cloth off squarely a half-inch or less above your tie. Store the roe bags in the same manner as cluster eggs.

For the best longevity, it's a good idea to keep your finished boraxed baits for about two or three more nights in the refrigerator so the borax can have a longer opportunity to cure the eggs. Mark the date of processing on the top of each bait container before you store them away in a freezer. Use your oldest baits first.

Sodium Sulfite Cure

A good cure that delivers bright, juicy, milking egg clusters can be achieved with sodium sulfite, available from many larger drug stores or from sporting goods/bait dealers.

After draining one or two nights in their paper towel and newspaper wrappings, the skeins are cut to size as above, but without using powdered borax. This can be a juicy undertaking, so be sure to have several layers of newspapers on your working area. Spread the baits out in one layer only in a flat glass or Pyrex™ dish so they can be salted down like a layer of codfish.

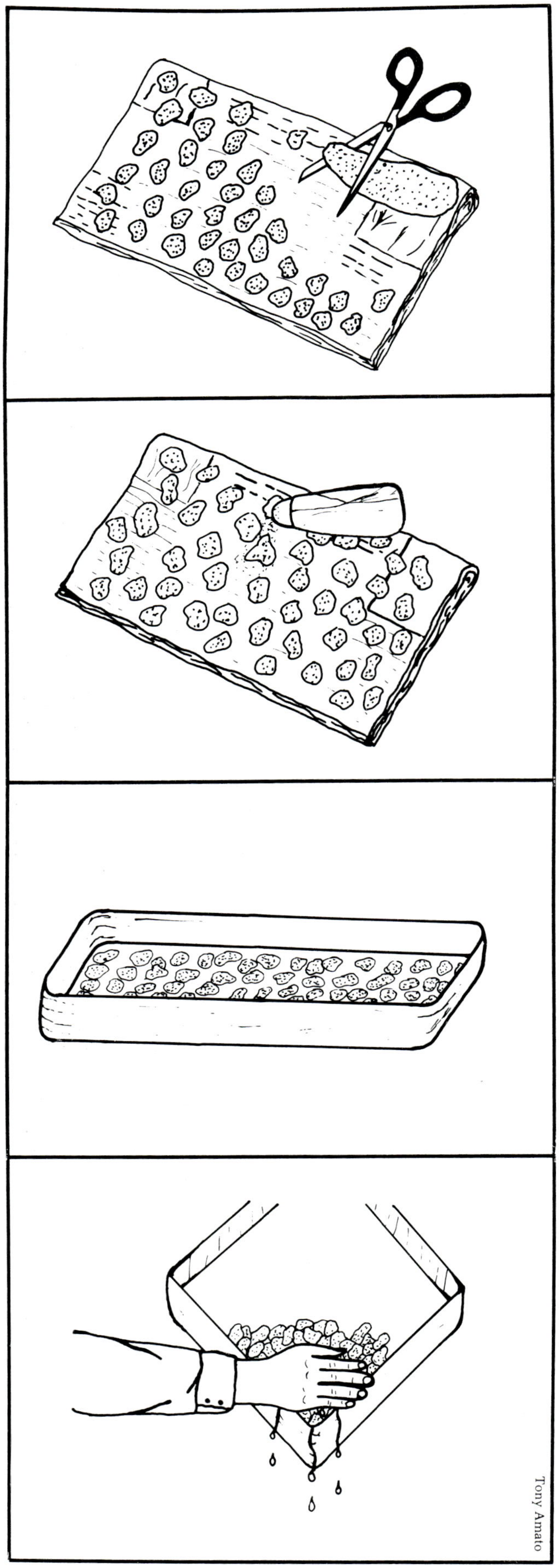

You will need an old, large salt or pepper cellar, table salt, sugar, and the sodium sulphite. Mix a batch sufficient to fill the shaker one time and consisting of one scoop table salt, one scoop sugar, and 1½ to 1¾-scoop sodium sulfite. Stir and shake until this is thoroughly blended, then use it in the cellar to dust all the baits well, but not heavily. Turn the clusters over and hit them with a light sprinkling on the other side.

This curing procedure will generate lots of excess juice, so it's best to put the dish in your refrigerator for about 10 to 12 hours. Check it every three or four hours, and pour off the extra liquid. When the baits stop "bleeding," they are ready to put in containers (no borax) and then into your freezer.

Baits put up by either the borax or sodium sulfite curing method can be used "as is" or wrapped in maline roe bags. (In addition, loose eggs also can be bagged for baits after being boiled or treated with either borax or the sodium sulfite cure.)

For many fishermen, it's often more pleasurable to catch a steelhead on bait you have cured yourself, adding a more personal bent to the contest of skills between man and fish. If, however, you wish to skip this step, you generally can find single eggs, cluster eggs and roe bags or scented, plastic imitations of all of these for sale at a nearby large bait shop.

Properly fished, egg baits will deceive steelhead in almost all types of water, from skinny glass-clear trickles to murky, near-flood conditions. They are topnotch treats for finicky fish, but not the only baits that are effective...

SHRIMP

Tasty, tender and fresh sand shrimp (also called ghost shrimp) or fullcourse meal size ocean prawns are terrific temptations for steelhead. Having fed upon these in the past, steelhead coming into freshwater streams often will accept shrimp or prawn baits more readily than they take anything else.

If you wish to fish sand/ghost shrimp live, there's a way to keep them fresh and frisky even though you plan to use them far inland and several days from their capture time. Taken from sand-gravel-rock beach beds, these small shrimp are fragile, and will easily succumb to rough handling, heat, or lack of salt water.

You can retain bait shrimp alive for days if you dig and handle them with care, keep their container on ice, and pack along some of their water. This can be done quite easily by cleaning out several half-gallon cardboard milk cartons before you go shrimping or clam digging (the shrimp inhabit much the same areas as most Pacific clam species), and fill the cartons with sea water and some gravel taken from near your digging site. Freeze the cartons and use them to periodically change the water in which your shrimp are kept by pouring off two-thirds of it and adding a block of native ice. As this melts, the shrimp's habitat is freshened and cooled at the same time.

As long as the shrimp or prawns are fresh, their hearty odor wafts a come-hither appeal downstream

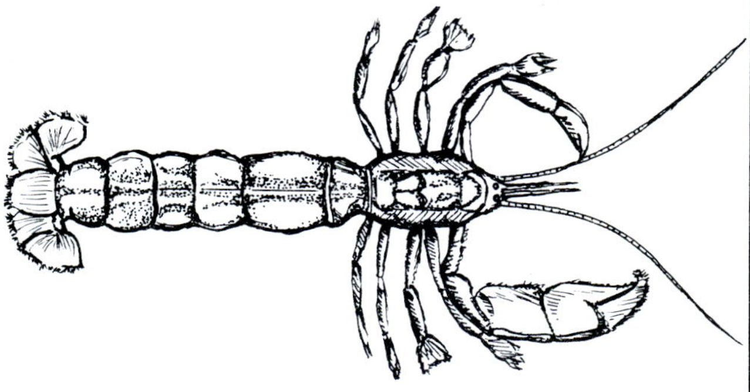

Sand (ghost) Shrimp

to steelhead. Many anglers feel they don't need the baits to be alive, provided they are fresh, and most steelheaders are convinced they can better hook steelies if the shell of their prawn is removed. A pinch and twist will pluck off the head and the tail shell then will peel off quite readily.

It's very easy to lose these shelled, soft baits off your hook when casting, so your best bet is to snug part of their body under the bait loop of your leader tie, use a rubber-band bumper loop, employ a two-hook leader or fasten the shrimp to the hook with a few turns of thread. Some anglers fish shrimp alone, while others choose to include strands of yarn in their rigging so as to tangle in the teeth of steelhead. This causes the headshaking that betrays a fish trying to rid itself of a clinging object in its mouth. Shrimp or prawns also may be successfully fished with a round drift bobber or winged bobber added above the hook.

Fishermen can freeze day packs of shrimp or prawn baits if they want to have fresh baits at hand without trekking to the ocean beaches every couple weeks. Store five to eight baits in a zipper top or fold-over sandwich plastic bag and tuck away a few dozen bags in your freezer. To use them, pull out two or three bags a good two hours before you'll need them to fish with, and tuck bags and all into your bait box. They'll thaw by the time you are ready to rig the first one on your hook. These baits do not refreeze very well, so be careful to draw from your frozen stock only the amount you're sure to use.

Bait shrimp and prawns can be purchased from most well-stocked bait dealers, and prawns often can be located at food stores that deal in ocean fare. In a real pinch, you might make do with cocktail shrimp as baits, but these tiny, delicate shrimp are so soft they come off the hook too easily to be used in their canned condition. Cure this problem by heating a pan of water to a scalding boil and dumping in the shrimp for one to two minutes. This will make them tougher and a little more chewy, although their small size often causes them to split when being barbed. They are, however, a last resort if you have located some steelhead that seem to want only shrimp baits.

Are you sure you've tried all other baits? Here is another good possibility...

ANOTHER SHELL GAME; CRAYFISH:

The rich, oily, white meat of the freshwater crawdad holds strong appeal for steelhead and has an additional side benefit that makes it effective as, or better than many other baits...it is very hard for minnows and other bait-stealers to rob it from your hook. Whether a small, whole tail is used, or segments of the shelled tail, the grainy, tough meat can be savagely attacked by small fish such as sculpin, chubs and trout, and still will be on your hook when a steelhead fins over to check on the menu.

I have found crawdad tail segments to be productive in fishing situations where there is very little current and you have to give your terminal rig a little movement by gently reeling line. Generally, a special rigging is called for, in which you add a medium to large size Lil' Corky or tiny red/white bobber to your leader halfway from hook to barrel swivel. This holds the bait just above bottom and a steelhead swimming past it creates a current that rocks the bait enticingly. Normally, the strike under these conditions is a vicious, jarring one!

Crayfish can be obtained by fishing for them with worms or meat baits. There's one peculiar habit crayfish have that you should know in order to transfer them from their habitat to your bait box. They will grab and hold on to your bait all the way from the bottom of a stream or pond only to about six inches from the surface...then let go and scuttle for cover. So, the trick to taking them is to net them with a small dip net before bringing them all the way to the surface.

Another easy way to take a quick supply of crawdads is to net them (check your regulations first) from a pond or stream with a flat, mesh net having lift cords that will close the net on crayfish attracted to a center-pinned bait. Check the net every half-hour to hour, and move it near weedbeds and undercut banks or ledges until you find the best area.

A barrel trap, made of either wire or wood slats, is an oldtime, but efficient, method of taking a supply of craws sufficient to last many weeks (again, see your regs). Sunk in a productive crayfish area, the baited trap allows crawdads to enter a hinged or cone-shaped entry, but not to escape. Overnight sets often yield a dozen or more claw-waving baits. (If you score a real bonanza haul, fresh crawdad tails are scrumptious people bait too!)

Tiny crawdads of 1½ to two inches may be declawed and fished live, in the shell. However, most steelheaders will use only their tails, shelled to expose the meat and better allow the tantalizing odor of the crawdad to sift downstream. Larger crayfish are shelled and only one or two segments of the tail are barbed at a time. Fished with a couple strands of red or orange yarn, these delicacies can be deadly.

Crawdad tails can be frozen, two or three to a plastic bag, for long periods of time. However, once thawed, it's wisest to use them up or pass them on to another angler, as they take on a very strong odor. Take a bag or two out of your freezer a couple hours before intending to fish them...it's hard to put a hook through an ice cube! (If you can run faster than your fishing partner, one quick way to thaw them out is to drop them in his coffee cup to soak.)

Let's hop along to the next baits...

CRICKETS AND GRASSHOPPERS

Wherever grasshoppers and crickets abound, you have a ready supply of steelhead baits...if you can catch them. Steelhead are accustomed to seeing these terrestrials in and on the water and many an errant 'hopper's leap terminates in a splashing gulp.

Large, black or brown field crickets are tempting to Ol' Ironhead also, barbed singly or in twos on a small hook. They are perhaps the easier of the two species to collect. Take off your cap or hat and use it to snare the crickets in grassy spots or, if your landing net has small mesh, it will pin the crickets just long enough for you to capture them.

Moricetown Falls on the Bulkley River in British Columbia.

Steelhead strikes drawn by cricket or grasshopper baits often come quickly and violently. I watched a summer angler one hot, sleepy day on Washington's Klickitat River (southwest region) bait up a grasshopper and, clad in swim trunks and shirt, settle into a lawn chair seat-deep in cooling water, tipping his straw hat down to shade his eyes...for about 20 seconds. His rod thrashed like a firehose getting its first shot of water and a bright, and very angry, steelhead literally tore up the river surface in front of the chair.

That fish threw water over the angler in several splashing leaps, sawed around for a minute or two near his feet, leaped again, and then streaked for the far downstream shore. Believe me, the angler was by now wide awake! (And he landed the feisty 7-pounder.)

Again, a landing net can be used in flail fashion to collect grasshoppers during the day. A heavy shirt or a jacket also can be pressed into similar service. Perhaps a better way to trap half a dozen or so 'hoppers is to catch them by hand early in the morning, when they still are stiff from the previous night's cool temperatures and reluctant to move.

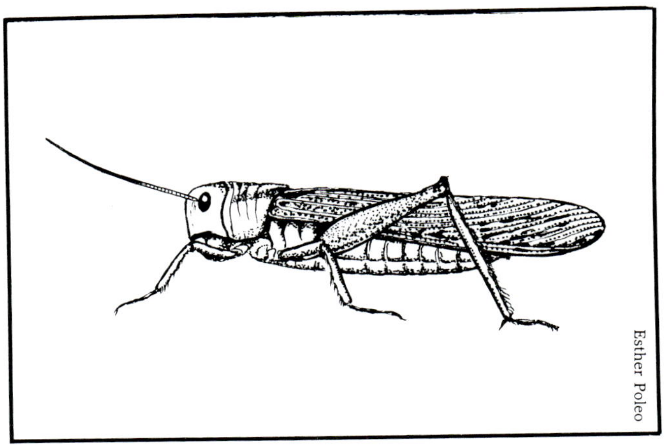

Grasshopper

Grasshoppers or crickets should be kept in a tall can (large fruit juice tins are good choices) with a handful of damp grass loosely bunched in the bottom and an old nylon stocking held across the top with a rubber band. They will not keep well, so you'll probably do best by releasing unused baits at the end of the day and garnering a fresh supply for your next fishing period.

Still looking for a never-fail bait or additional bait choice? Here are more...

LARVA, GRUBS AND OTHER GOODIES:

Almost anything that creeps and crawls on Planet Earth may at one time appeal to the eyeball or appetite of foraging steelhead. A large periwinkle or two on your hook can turn a fishless day into fast action. This larva of the western caddisfly is found clinging to rocks and boulders in most Pacific coast streams and, shucked from its stick-like shell, will beckon trout, steelhead and other river fish to your terminal gear.

You can pluck these from the rocks of the stream you are fishing, or hold a small screen or cloth downstream while your partner turns over and churns up a rockbed. The periwinkles will be dislodged and swept into your net.

Goldenrod grubs make fine baits. Found in the galls or knots in the stem of the goldenrod plant, these grubs have good bite appeal for steelhead and a variety of other western fish.

Meal worms (maggots), cutworms, and garden grubs also can be used, with some degree of reward, fishing for steelhead. Don't knock the mealies if you haven't tried them, because these ugly little squirmers do produce. Ask any whitefish angler about the number of steelhead that chomp his fly/maggot or bare maggot baits and then proceed to just tear up both his peace of mind and his light tackle!

Grub

The "grub group" and meal worms can be kept very easily and for lengthy periods in ex-dip containers half filled with sawdust and a few light pinches of corn meal or oatmeal.

Other baits than those described above often are used in local angling where they are hot for brief periods, or serve as secret, last resort offerings. I've heard of tuna balls served up to California steelhead in maline bags, salted herring, dried minnows or anchovies, bits of octopus, doughbaits, pork rind and just about anything else you can name being tried as steelhead bait. And, sure as there's a steelheader somewhere who will try a strange and unusual bait, there is a steelhead that just might latch on to it and give the angler a morning ride.

BAIT FISHING TACTICS & TIPS:

Baits are used in several methods of steelhead angling. They are excellent choices for drift fishing, plunking, bobber fishing, and variations of each of these angling methods. Just as the tempting aroma of bacon and eggs draws you into the kitchen to ask, "What's cooking?" the underwater bouquet of enticing food odors can be counted upon to bring curious, perhaps bite-ready, steelhead to your hook. Baits are reliable in high muddy water, normal flow, and low, clear water. They can be fished alone, with yarn, with a bobber, or with a bobber/yarn combination to help float them off bottom and provide added attraction.

DRIFT FISHING

Drift fishing is the most common method used to present bait to steelhead. Bait-casting outfits with level wind reels are the top choices of many veteran steelhead baiters, although spinning outfits also work well. Monofilament line having rated breaking strength of 8 to 18 pounds generally is used, with bait-fishermen normally opting for 12- to 14-pound test in winter and slightly lighter in summer. Many bank anglers and boat anglers alike are dedicated followers and drift fisherman's "feed 'em" philosophy (as opposed to hardware and artificial lure user's "fool 'em" approach).

Two things govern the success of a drift-fisherman...keeping hooks absolutely sticky-sharp, and developing the ability to sense and recognize a steelhead's take, or subtle bite. Beyond those requirements, some skill in reading the water to determine where steelhead will lie or hold in the river and the ability to cast your fishing rig into that area is needed. Just as in any other sport, the rest of the learning process is practice, practice, practice.

Persistence in pursuing steelhead is rewarded sooner or later. There are tales of anglers who have fished half a dozen to a dozen times annually for several years in an attempt to catch a steelhead. But, these are balanced by reports of newcomers heading out to the nearest river, plucking two fish in an hour or so from the run currently in that stretch and asking, "What's the big deal on steelhead being hard to catch?" They are...and they aren't. Any fishermen who pays his dues in time spent fishing and efforts to learn how to tie up and properly fish his steelhead gear should be reasonably successful. Many steelheaders feel that what and how you fish is not as important as repeatedly getting your lure or bait in front of sufficient steelhead jaws that one pair of them eventually will open wide and inhale the offering.

Both bank anglers and boat fishermen cast identical baits and bait rigs, but boaters often use lighter sinkers, since they can get closer to the possible steelhead lies and, in some instances, as they are drifting (boondogging), to reduce hang-ups.

A bait-using bank drift-fisherman's typical approach to a section of river is at the head of a run or pool, where he will fish the nearest water first, extend his casts to the middle and far side of the river, and then work his way in the same manner down the length of the fishable water to the tailout. Floating fishermen have the option of pulling their boat up on the shore of a likely stretch to do the same bait-fishing, drifting through a likely stretch of river while trailing baits alongside and behind them, or of anchoring in midriver positions to reach the best fish-holding water. Starting at the head of the hole, the boaters may lift anchor several times to move 15 to 25 feet, fishing all of the potential steelhead lies as they work downriver.

Drift boat fishermen, relying on oars and the downstream current for their propulsion, may switch to being bank anglers when they chance upon a whole wad of willing steelhead in a river section not normally reached by fishermen afoot. Once they are launched, they have a take-out spot downstream as their one-way destination, so must stop to spend some time on the better fishing areas or they will likely only experience a long boat ride. Jet Sleds, on the other hand, may sample a few miles of water and, deciding the first drift they fished held the best opportunities for catching steelhead, return to it to drift through several times or to anchor in the hot spot and probe with their bait rigs every foot of the potential holding water.

Bait-fishing rigs normally will have leaders from 14 to 36 inches long, with the average leader length approximately 17-20 inches. (See the section on lines, leaders and rigs for the ways of tieing up this type of terminal gear.) A pencil lead sinker intended to slide on the line above the barrel or snap swivel at your line end, or affixed to the swivel, is standard fare, although a round, bouncing ball sinker may be used, or in soft sand, a light, cone-shaped or flat bottom sinker might be tried.

The ideal bait-caster's drift will allow his baited cluster eggs, shrimp, or night crawler to be carried downstream by the current at the river flow speed or slightly slower, with his sinker tapping bottom at regular intervals. Nine out of 10 winter and summer steelhead will be hugging bottom, or using the shelter and shade of boulders, logs or ledges providing the cover these fish favor. Successful anglers will alter their sinker weights by switching the lead used to longer or shorter lengths, or snipping pieces from the original, to get drifts that are just right, in their estimation, to pass in front of or beside these waiting fish.

As successive casts reach further, and the drifts get longer, the angler will raise his rod tip to keep as much line as possible out of the water, reducing the belly in it caused by current, and keeping in more sensitive touch with the bait. Here is where the convenience of a level wind reel comes into play. With the reel in free-spool after the cast, it is possible to tail the rig you're fishing a considerable distance downstream, increasing the amount of river bottom over which your bait will trundle. To do this, simply let line slowly slip from under your thumb as the current pulls it, yet maintain a light pressure on the reel spool to feel any sudden tugs or cessation of movement.

You are prepared to clamp down with your thumb, holding the reel spool firmly as you come back on the rod to strike and set your hook into the jaw of a steelhead. Any change in your drift is cause for action. This may be an upstream movement of your line, tiny tugs as though your bait was caught on a soft rubber band, a hard stop that might be a rock, log, grass OR a steelhead, or the flash of a fish's side rolling and twisting in the river near where your gear is thought to be.

Drift Fishing For Steelhead From Shore or Boat

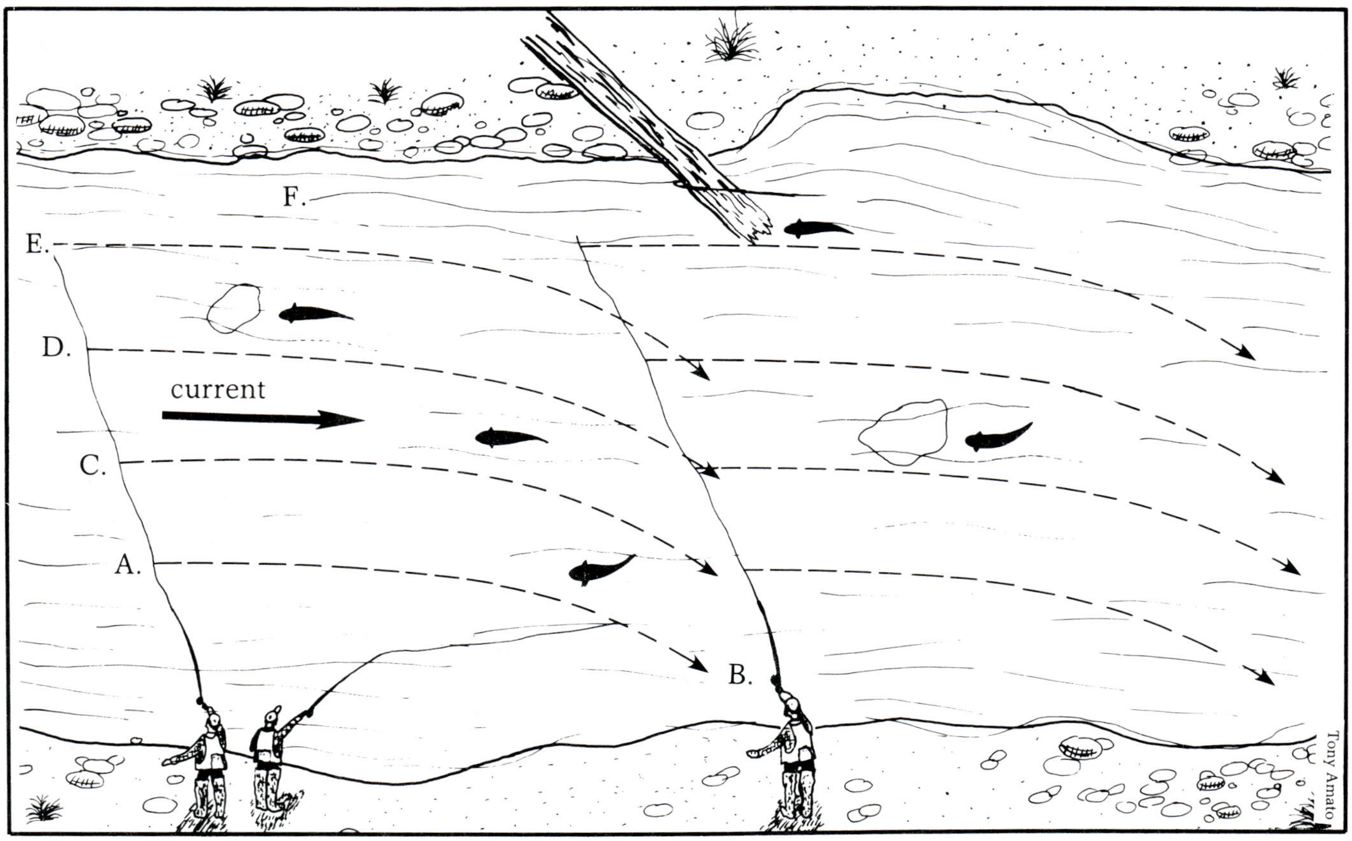

Starting at or near the top of the run or tailout the angler makes his first cast to point A and follows his line with his rod down to point B. At an imaginary line between the angler and point F the lead should first come in light contact with the bottom and occasionally touch bottom until the end of the drift is realized. Covering the water methodically, the next cast is several feet farther, and so on until the water is covered. At that point the angler moves down anywhere from 10 to 40 feet to repeat a thorough series of casts. If a bite is detected or the angler is sure there are fish present, much time is spent on the run. If not, it is best to move on after about half an hour to a new run, tailout or hole.

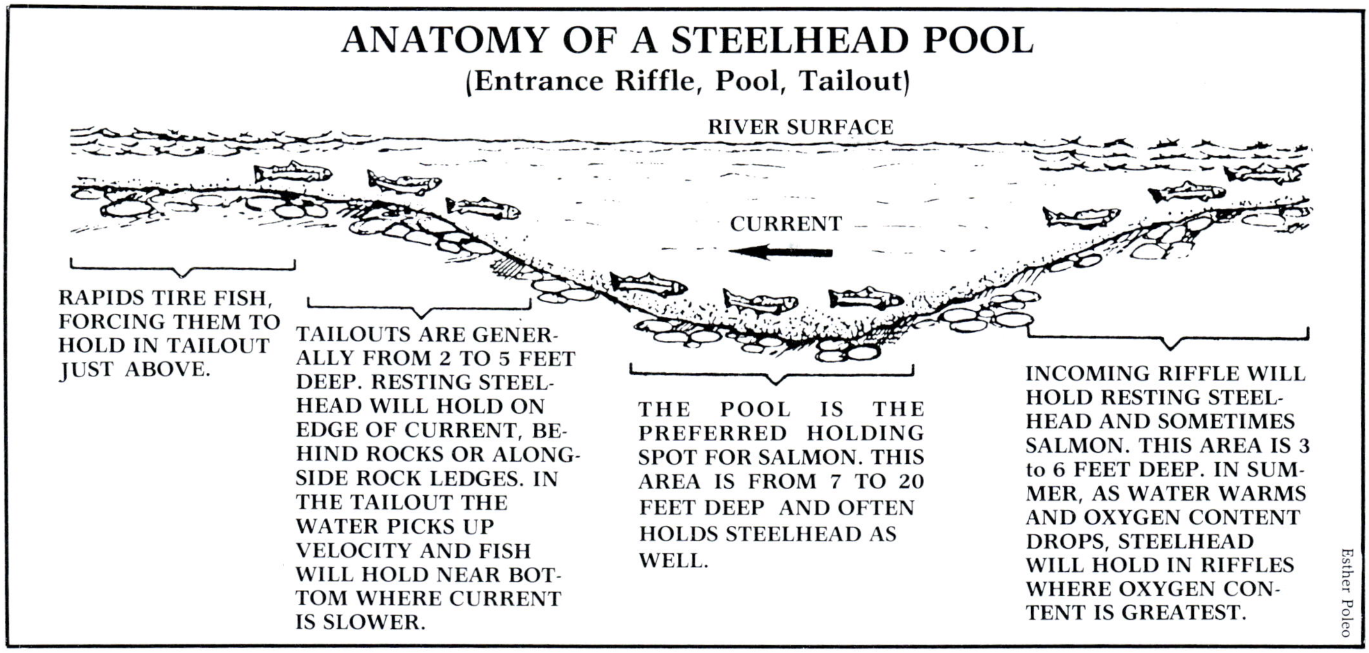

HIT IT! Come back hard and fast on your rod and don't worry about popping your line, as it's practically impossible to do with your thumb as the stopper on the free-turning reel spool. Even in direct drive, the hardest strike you could generate is lessened by the resilience of your rod, line brake mechanism, stretch in your monofilament, and the belly or slack in your line. Go ahead, cross their eyes and get their attention!

My personal preference in striking and setting a hook in a steelhead's hard mouth is to strike twice. First, as forcibly as the bite permits, then, after the fish stops its initial bouncing or running and faces back in the same direction as when it was hooked, to give a second, very short, firm forward and upward stab of the rod butt to drive the hook barb securely home.

An alternative to fishing steelhead baits on bottom or near it is to try for suspended fish with bait angled under bobbers or cast on light, weight-free line. Summer steelhead, especially, often are found suspended only a few feet below the surface of the water in long deep pools. A drift rig on bottom won't attract much attention from these fish. Using a bobber to float a bait to them at their level might trick them into striking. And, when the occasion and circumstances fit,

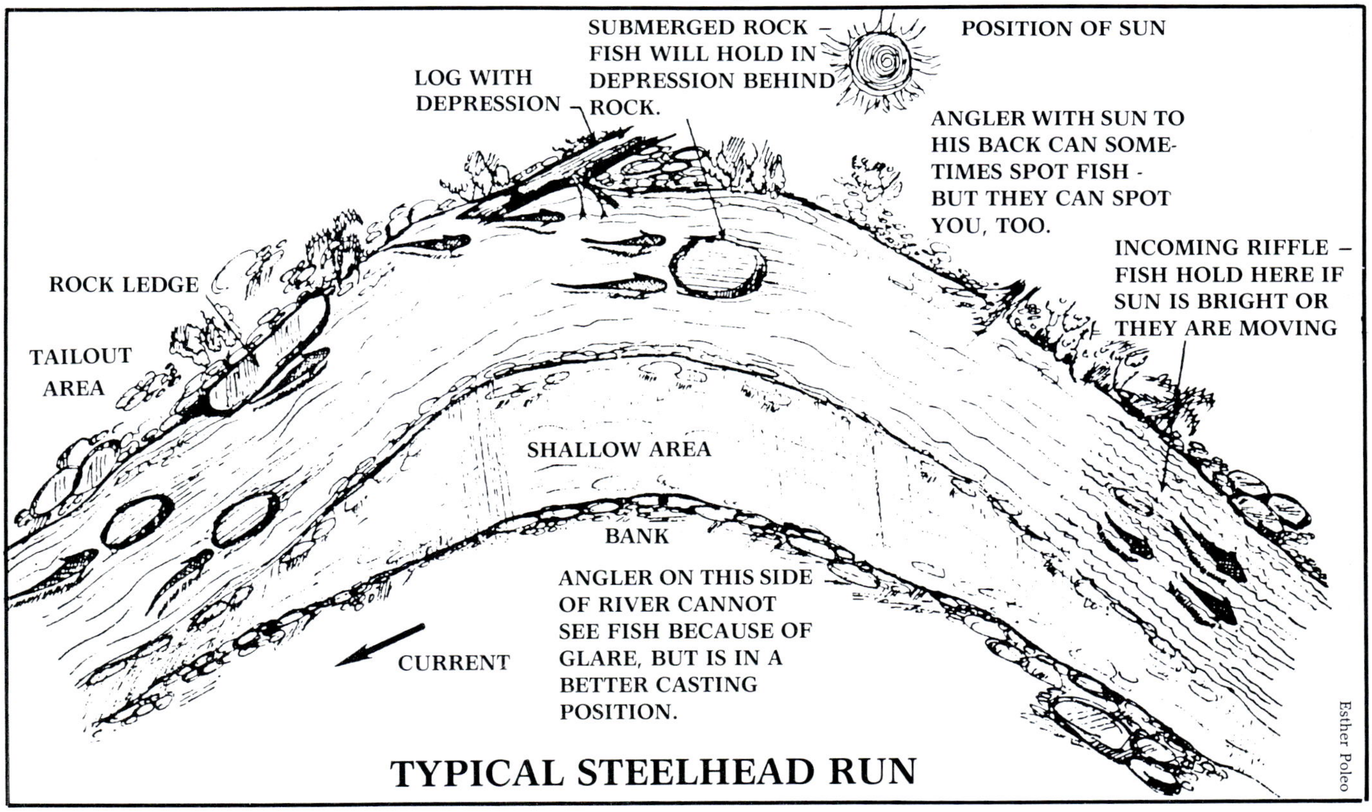

winter steelhead also can be bamboozled by baits floated to them under a bobber.

Large, plain, cork bobbers work best for this fishing, with many fishermen preferring the type of bobber having a center hole through which the line freely runs. A stop of thread, light monofilament, or thin rubber band is tied on the line above the bobber to limit the depth of line fished under it. Tiny split shot may be used on your leader to provide sufficient weight to pull the bait or lure down below the bobber to the line stop. The stop passes through the rod tip quite readily, and when the floater rig is lobbed into the head of a hole and fished on a slightly slack line, the baited hook descends until the line stops feeding through the bobber and your offering is carried along by the current past the steelhead's noses. Shrimp or night crawlers make good bobber baits, and bass/panfish jigs also can be fished under bobbers with v-e-r-y interesting results! Steelhead seem to relish smacking these suspended baits or lures with exceptionally vigorous strikes.

Light-line anglers often fish baits with no attached weight to reach and interest suspended summer fish in ice-clear pools or winter ironheads in slow, medium depth water. This is where you will see noodle rods and other willowy steelhead sticks casting 4-pound or even 2-pound test wispy lines laden with only shrimp, 'crawler or single salmon egg. It is delicate fishing that takes a light hand in playing hooked fish, but might be the only way to trick line-wary or heavily-fished steelhead into taking baits. A leader may be attached to light monofilament with a blood knot, thus creating only one break point, since no barrel swivel or snap is then needed, either of which requires two knots (for a super-simple, slick way of tieing this knot, see "Jim's Blood Tie" in the sections on lines, leaders and rigging).

In all instances, the bait-fisherman's initial approach to the stream should follow the same pattern. Look for the nearest piece of water in which a steelhead may be finning (polarized or Polaroid™ glasses are helpful). This should be fished first, as, if you ignore a fish lieing just a few feet in front of you and begin casting over it, the motion of your arm and rod, and of the line moving in the air or water over the fish, may frighten that particular steelhead into the center of the hole, spooking other fish there, and causing them all to get sudden cases of lockjaw. The clearer the water you're fishing, the more you should take care to use your background to cover movements, and restrict those motions to as slow, few and careful as possible to keep from spooking any steelhead that might be able to see you.

PLUNKING

Plunking is another bait-fishing method that often pays big and bright dividends. It is most rewarding in the lower stretches of rivers, and especially effective on winter steelhead. Plunking is relatively simple, yet requires careful planning as to where to position your line and bait/lure in the river and calls for close attention to your rigging (see lines, leaders and rigs chapter) in order to be sure it is not tangled on the cast, doesn't pick up grass or weeds from the current,

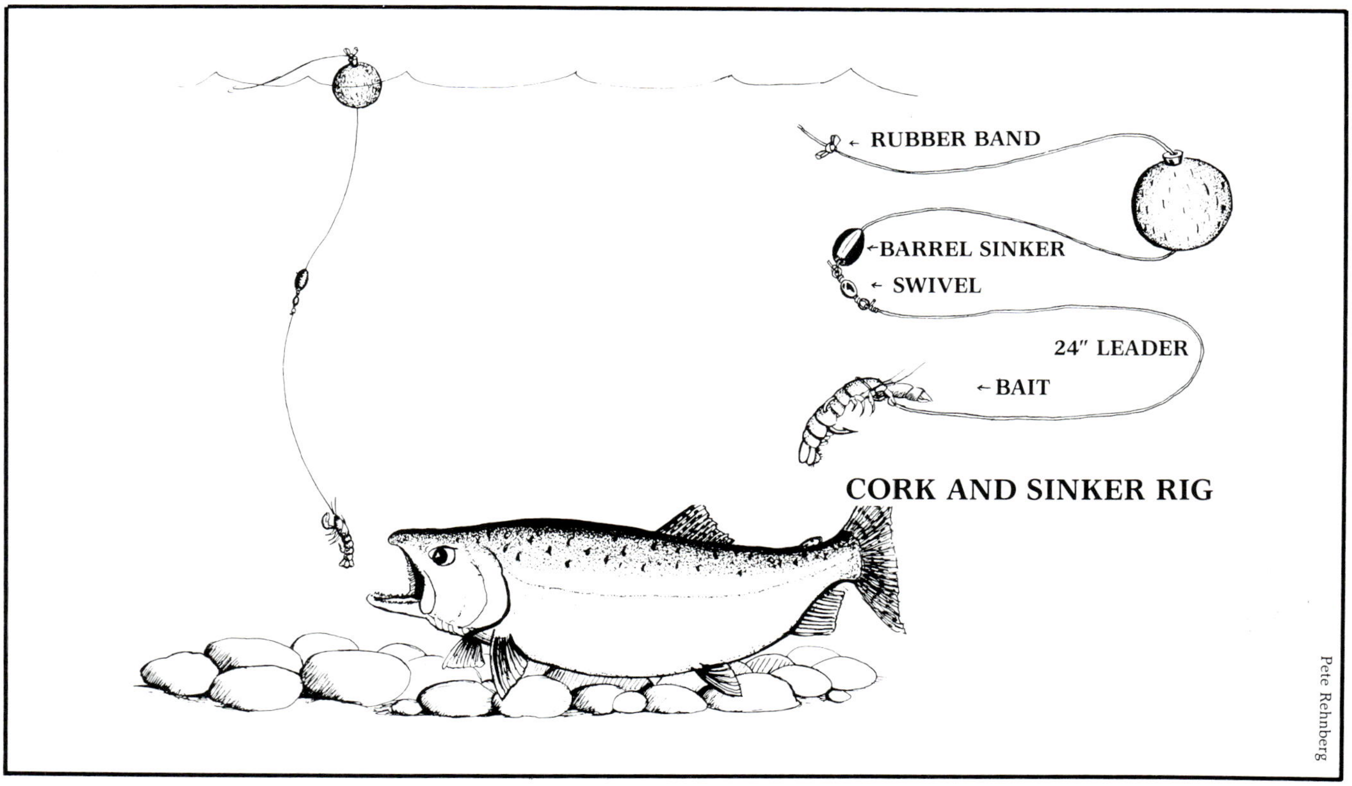

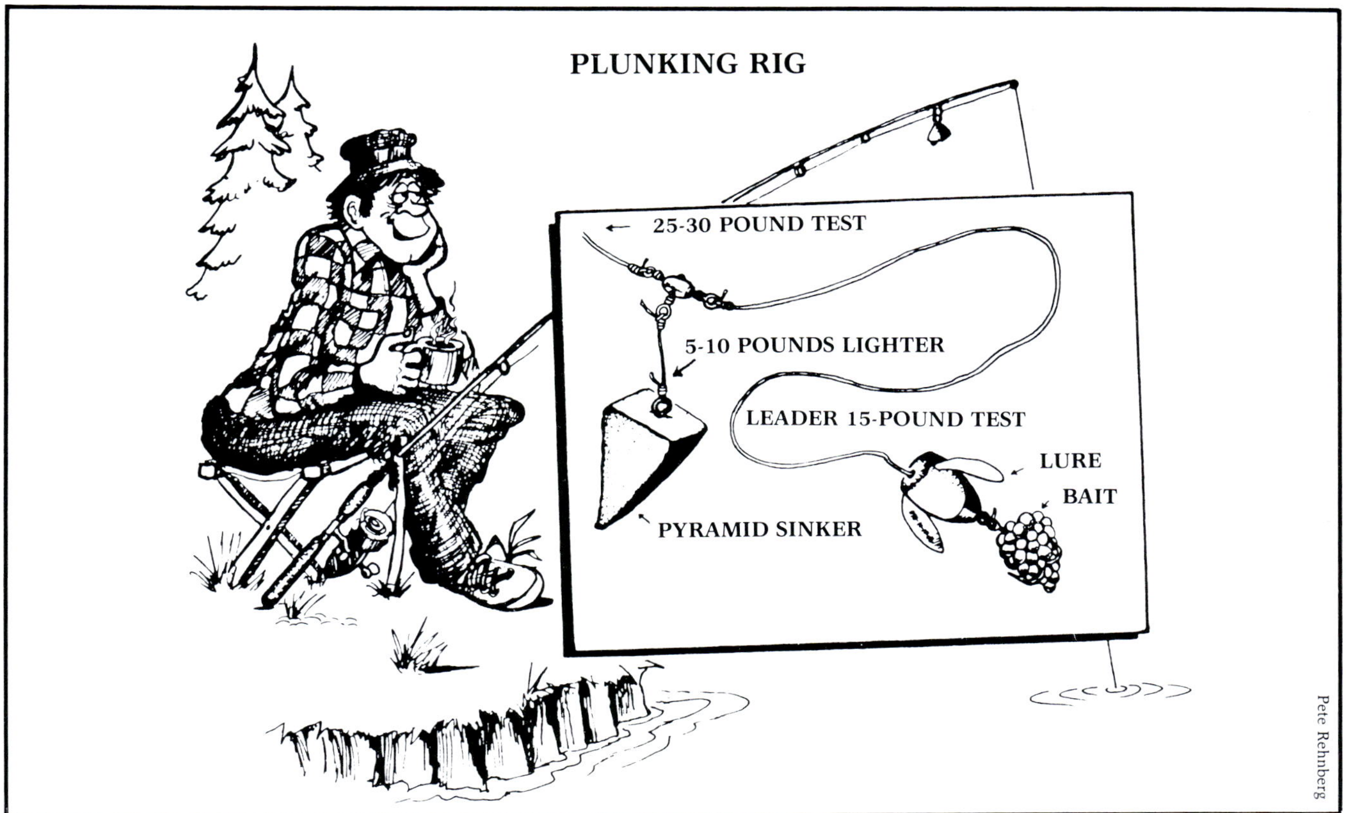

and is doing an effective job of attracting fish.

Medium to heavy bait-casting (and spinning) rods are the best choices for plunking. Lines used generally check out at 12 to 20 pounds snapping point. Pyramid sinkers from half an ounce to several ounces in weight normally are rigged on break-away drop lines to leave an angler and hooked steelhead unencumbered by the added weight. A plunking "spike" or rodholder is sunk into the bank to receive the rod butt after a cast, and a tiny brass bell, bright rag or strip of tape is attached to the upper rod to alert the fishermen when his rod starts bouncing or bucking to a steelhead's bite. (Many plunkers still prefer to use a forked stick for their rodholder, and prop a large rock behind the rod butt to hold it from going into the water.) A folding stool or chair, large landing net, and a vacuum jug of coffee complete the standard plunker's outfit.

After casting, a plunker will watch to see that the sinker holds bottom in the spot chosen, then place his rod in the holder or on the forked stick. Next, slack line is taken up by reeling until his rod tip takes an arc. The reel drag is carefully set so that a fish can take line, yet can do so only against enough resistance the hook may embed itself in the fish's mouth.

By watching the nodding action of his rod, an experienced plunker is able to judge whether his bait is "working" properly, if there is a weed or grass adversely affecting it, or if a subtle bite may be taking place. Sharp strikes are signalled by the bell or flag.

The key to rewarding plunking is to get your rigging into the travelling lanes of incoming steelhead and play a waiting game for steelhead to pass by it. There, next to the main current but not quite in it, baits anchored by the heavy sinkers wave seductively in the current and waft their enticing odors downstream. Anglers often add an artificial lure to their bait, such as a Spin-N-Glo, Glo-Go, Birdie Drifter, Lil' Corky or Okie Drifter, to better float it up off bottom and give the bait greater eye appeal and action.

By adding a second leader a few feet up the line, two bait rigs or combination rigs can be fished, where regulations permit, at one time. Or, with use of a stop two or three feet above the main leader, a Flatfish, Hot shot, Wee Wart, Tadpolly, Hawg Boss, Fireplug, Kwikfish or similar banana-shaped plug can be run down the line on its own leader to be fished above the bait rig.

Again, all hooks must be kept super sharp, as steelhead often will hook themselves when they strike on plunking gear, and this is easier done when your hook point is needle keen.

Even in periods of high, muddy water, plunking produces some steelhead catches, while in normal flow, it continues to hold appeal for both fish and fishermen. Plunking gear is quick and easy to set up or carry rigged in the back of a pick-up truck. It may look like a sedentary way of fishing – even a lazy angling method – but, when it is done properly, "uses your brain to beat brushwhacking" in a manner that catches steelhead as well as, and better than some, other styles of angling. Its advantages are that it keeps your fishing gear constantly in the water in front of steelhead, doesn't require any waders or wading, is relatively easy to learn and do by steelheaders from beginners to oldtimers, and is an enjoyable, congenial way for several anglers to share the same chunk of water.

Chapter 7

Bobbers and Bottom Bouncing

Brightly painted balls of balsa, colorful cork, and perky plastic bodies jiggling and struggling along river bottoms on tethering leaders can draw rapt attention and hard raps from steelhead. Fished with pencil lead or bouncing ball sinkers on drift rigs, these egg imitations – some of which only suggest drifting, loose steelhead eggs – often hold a deadly fascination for winter and summer steelhead.

Bobber is the name given these lures because of their buoyancy, but only a few of these steelhead seducers resemble the red-and-white trout/panfish bobber with which most fishermen are familiar. Those round, half 'n half color pattern bobbers, however, will produce lots of steelhead strikes, as will other bottom-bouncing balls having spotted patterns or a rainbow blend of colors. A more common, solid color bobber also may be just the ticket to entice steelhead to whack your hook.

Bobbers come in enough shapes, colors and sizes to allow choosing one to match nearly all water levels and clarity. There are tiny bobbers scarcely larger than a stickpin's head (like the No. 14 Lil' Corky that fishes shallow, clear summer streams well with a gold No. 4 Eagle Claw hook) and for high and muddy rivers there are huge bobbers such as the No. 00 Spin-N-Glo, which to me looks big as half an apple core, with wings. Some are as knobby as clumps of eggs; a few are elongated ovals; others are round; there are new plastic bobber bodies resembling various underwater creatures; bobbers may be cylindrical; there are winged bobbers, combinations of two small bobbers in one lure and bobbers with seductive sickle tails, spinner blades or propellers attached.

Matching proper hook size to the diameter of the bobber you are planning to use is easily done. Lay a hook flat on your palm and put the bobber in the bend of the hook. If the bobber will freely pass through between the barb and shank or very nearly so, it is the correct size and, when placed on the line above the hook, only half the diameter of the bobber blocks the point of your hook from a steelhead's jaw.

You can fish with bobbers having hollow centers for adding scent-soaked sponges or those with oversize holes for chemical light tubes. Some odd, obviously homemade foam plastic bobbers I've plucked out of rivers while I was fishing were rectangular, with horizontal holes through which several legs of yarn were inserted. The lures looked much like large, fuzzy, wet spiders.

Most steelheaders will fish bobbers with a strand or two of soft yarn in their leader's bumper loop or egg loop, tied into the eye of their hook, or knotted on the main line and draped over the lure. The yarn adds color and wavy motion to the lure and its soft strands catch in a steelhead's teeth, prolonging the time it will retain the hook in its mouth and giving you more time to hook it.

Open the egg/bumper loop on your hook snell and lay yarn strands in it, then snug the leader tight for the easiest way to add yarn. To keep it even and securely held, some steelheaders tie an overhand knot of yarn around the leader's egg loop. My favorite tie is to bind two strands of yarn right in the knot at the top of the hook eye (I don't often use bait, so need no bumper tie or egg loop).

Yarn improves the success rate of many bobbers, but can hamper the action of winged bobbers, which are intended to spin on the line. (The soft yarn tangles between the lure body and hook eye or bead on top of the hook, stunting the rotation needed to attract strikes.) Yarn users should snip off the dangling strands flush with the bend of their hook or slightly above it, to best draw a steelhead's bite above the point. I once watched an angler fishing a bobber/yarn rig with yarn hanging three inches past his barb do everything but turn somersaults on his strikes, trying to hook fish that were grabbing just the yarn. He would bring in the lure, tug a stretched end of yarn back up an inch or so, and cast that same set-up back into the drift only to be further frustrated by the next hit.

Commercial bobber ties, such as the Fenton Fly and Sammy Special, are sold with leaders attached. Lil' Corkies, Okie Drifters and other bobbers also can be purchased ready to fish, most coming with a two-hook leader, one hook below and the other above the lure. You can tie these quite readily yourself, by referring to the chapter on lines and leaders and particularly the Hook Snell.

There are so many choices of excellent, steelhead-catching bobbers available at your tackle store that it's tough to decide between Lil' Corky, Okie Drifter, Wobble Glo, Fenton Fly, Spin-N-Glo, Steelie Stopper, Glo Getter Ball, Roe-Glo, LumaEgg, Birdie Drifter, Glo Go, Float'N Lil Whizky, Crazy Egg, Gooey Bob, Bubblehead, Mack's, Glo-Pup, Skein, Yarn Puff, Sammy Special, Spoon Glo, Cheater, Glo Corker and Mou-Jo bobbers, to name just a few. They all deceive steelhead – perhaps equally well – but you can generate some heated arguments over which bobber is the best one. Every steelheader has his own views on what works best for him...and that's your first key to successful bobber bouncing. Use what works best for you.

My fishing partner is an excellent bait angler and he feels cluster egg and shrimp baits can't be beaten when steelhead are in a biting mood. However, he's the first to also admit there are days when a bobber rig will take steelhead that refuse baits. We proved this to our own satisfaction after about two futile hours of fishing one late morning on our home stream when a fish lightly nudged his cluster eggs but for another 10 minutes would not pick them up again. He then urged me to cast my favorite bobber/yarn rig in the same spot and see if the fish would hit. It did! More bait run through the same area failed to generate any more strikes. Then just a few casts with the same bobber rig garnered my second bright and spunky steelhead. After sitting on the bank, sipping coffee for several minutes and watching my partner, I asked to check his rigging and he swung it over to me. I swiftly snipped off his gear and tied on the hot bobber set-up, which a third steelhead promptly clobbered! No way did they want bait, but the hula dance of my skirted bobber proved just too irresistible for them and turned an otherwise-fishless day into a thoroughly enjoyable and educational one.

Another fishing companion and former neighbor believed the best lure for a particular spot was a two-tone Spin-N-Glo in chartreuse and orange. One day he walked to this hole ahead of me, whipped out his first cast and said, "All right, steelhead, I know you're in there...c'mon out!" His winged bobber hit the water, a steelhead climbed all over it, jumped the log sticking out from the boulder behind which it had lain, and immediately snapped the leader! That's

BOBBERS

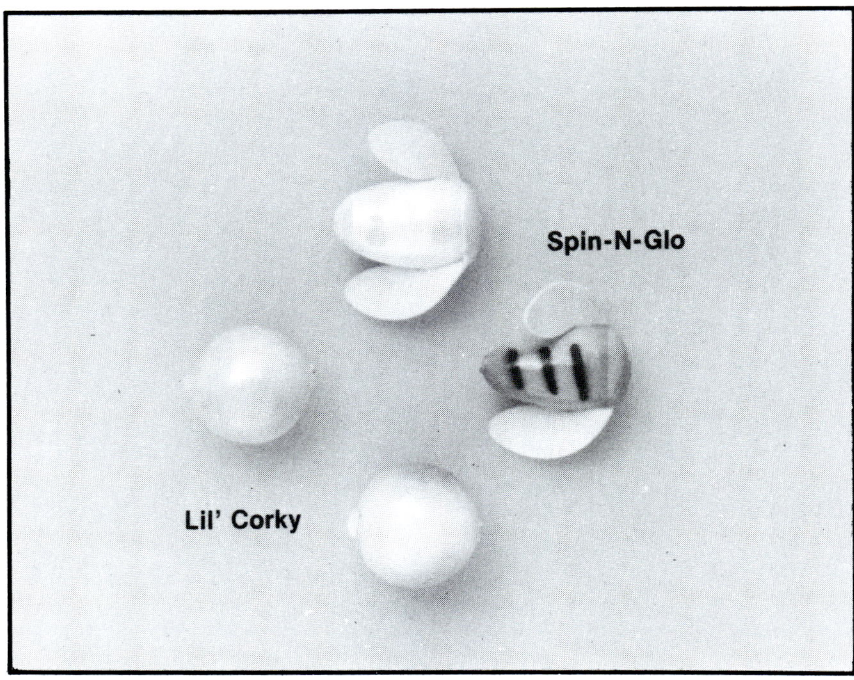

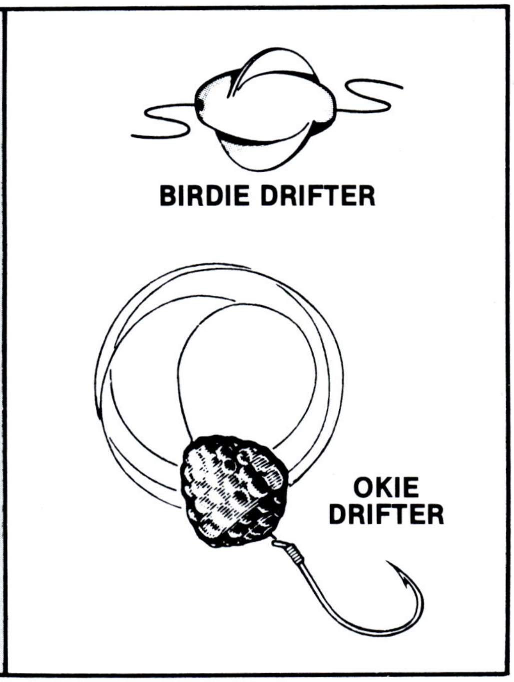

confidence...and tough luck, too.

I would guess 60 percent of my bobber-caught steelhead have fallen for just one of my bobber/yarn combinations...but I have so much confidence in that particular rig that I fish it at least 60 percent of the time I'm using bobbers. There's no secret to it, I just like pearl pink Lil' Corky lures fished with two strands of yarn, one hot pink and the other fluorescent white, because I've taken a lot of steelhead on this lure and yarn mixture. A red or orange plastic bead of 3 or 4mm diameter between the hook eye and bobber is standard in my rigging. It provides a bearing for any winged, rotating bobber, cinches down on top or around the knot I use, and acts as a buffer between knot and rocks when I get stuck in an underwater cleft. This combo is the one that works for me, but there are different combinations that do as well or better for other anglers. I know a fisherman who swears by a cream, red-spotted Mou-Jo bobber (no yarn) and who takes far more metalheads than I do. He's got great faith in that lure, and he uses it about 75 or 80 percent of the time.

That's the second trick to bobber bouncing...sticking with a proven fish-catcher long enough to know how its passage along the bottom feels in almost every underwater situation. The specific tension on your line, the rate at which your bottom rig trundles through the run or hole, the sensation coming up the line and rod when the lure bumps or brushes something...all of these become totally familiar, so that when an alien interruption occurs in the course of a normal drift, you know it is time to set your hook in hopes of crossing a steelhead's eyes.

Leaders used to fish bobbers should be from 14 to 30 inches long, depending on the clarity of the water and your reaction time. (Remember, longer leaders delay the bite indications coming up your mono and rod.) Mainliners normally run a bobber up their line below their surgical tubing and pencil lead, snell on a hook, and then add yarn for extra color. Other anglers who pack pre-tied leaders simply drop a bobber on the leader and tie the upper end of the leader to their swivel or snap swivel and they are ready to fish.

You can get different underwater action from some bobbers according to the way you put them on your leader. Okie Drifters and winged bobbers with integrally molded wings are not perfectly symmetrical. Look at them closely and you'll note that there is a fat end and a narrow end. By installing your bobber with its narrow end next to your hook, the current will work harder against the fat end, causing the lure to do a more intriguing dance in slow water. By sliding the lure on with wide end down and narrow end up, you can slow the frantic struggling of the lure in swift, heavy flow when overly rapid movements of the lure could deter a fish from striking.

Bobbers should not, in my estimation, be pegged on the leader or line by jamming a small bit of toothpick or twig into the hole along with the line. There is no need to do this, and the peg will prevent rotation that might otherwise enhance the allure of the bobber. A bobber moves downstream ahead of your sinker, and the force of the current will keep it next to the hook in all but the slowest water or worst-swirling eddies. (One instance where pegs pay dividends, though, is in fishing heavy, strong-flowing rivers such as on Washington's Olympic Peninsula, where a killer rig on one of those streams a few years back was two Lil' Corkies pegged on opposite ends of a toothpick and sent rocking crazily downriver like an animated dumbbell.)

It may take a few casts and some lead length adjustment to get a good bobber drift, although I have seen veteran fishermen accurately read the flow and depth of water and select a pencil lead exactly right for a good drift on their first cast. What you should try to achieve in bobber fishing is a rate of drift that is slightly faster than you would use with bait.

Bobbers are visual attractors, although scent juices or spray may be used to enhance their appeal, and my experience has been that steelhead will take them better if the lure is not moving so slowly the fish can read the label and identify it by maker, size and catalog number. I like to touch bottom every four to six feet, admittedly a fast pace but one which I think generates more instinctive strikes. The fish see the lure, have only a little time to make up their minds to grab it, jump on the bobber hard, send a good, jarring hit to my senses, and often hook themselves.

Normal bobber rig casts may be from 30 degrees upstream through a fan pattern ranging to 60 degrees downstream. When you begin fishing, start with short casts of only 10 to 15 feet out, even though it appears no clear-thinking steelhead would be holding there. It takes little to conceal a big fish...a rock or two, a slight depression in the bottom, or perhaps only a slight boil of current. If you ignore the nearby water, you could miss a chance at that fish, as well as spooking it into the main hole with your casting motion, where its sudden flight can alarm and put down any other steelhead in the main part of the hole or drift.

Gradually extend the length of your casts until you are reaching close to the distant bank or as far as your tackle will permit. This pattern of casting, carefully done, will search through almost every foot of water for interested biters. Next, move downstream six to eight feet and repeat the process. If you have the drift or hole to yourself, take as much time as you like to work your way down to the tailout, the point where the water shallows before pouring into the riffle or run below. You might be irritating steelhead with your repeated casting, causing them to retreat slowly until they are congregated in the tailout. At this point, one may become agitated enough to savagely maul the next bobber that comes into its range. I've seen, in clear water, up to four steelhead reluctantly fin backward to a tiny pocket just above the tailout of one of my often-fished holes, and kept my lure constantly coming at them until one would explode on the bobber in fury, clamping down hard on the pesky thing!

Bobbers can be fished by casts made almost directly upstream, with their return aided by a slow retrieve until they pass your casting position. This is an effective way to fish a deep slot above you and next to your bank that cannot be reached because of brush or steep banks. It is a tackle-grabber method, however, as your bobber/lead rigs can easily be kicked by current into rocky crevices or hung on debris draped around boulders. Generally, the bobber I use in such an instance is a winged, highly buoyant and slightly larger lure than I'd use if I were able to fish the same spot from a position farther upstream. The steelhead that lie in such places normally are undisturbed except by a few boat anglers, and they often come unglued from bottom when a whirling, colorful bobber dances past their eyeballs.

A long, lonely drift is ideal for "tailing" a bobber rig down its middle. After your cast, let line slowly peel from under your thumb on a level-wind reel, or back slowly on a spinning reel handle, to get as much travel out of your drift as you can. Long range fishing doesn't give you the sharp strikes felt with short lines. A steelhead might pick up your bobber and swim downstream with it, or grab it and head back upstream to its lie, with your line's action the only strike indicator. You must stay alert to spot surges in the rate of drift or a belly suddenly appearing in your line. Crank as much slack from your line as you can when this happens, point your rod tip low, toward the tightening line, and then sweep back as hard as you're able. There's lots of slack mono and line stretch to overcome on a long-line strike, but sometimes shy fish can only be caught by these "south forty" tactics.

There are a few instances where specially adapted bobber rigs repay handsome steelhead dividends. One in particular uses a sliding egg or oval sinker, barrel swivel, and bobber pegged on the leader about 10 or 12 inches above a shrimp, cluster eggs or a crawdad tail section bait. In very slow current, this set-up is cast, then inched back to the rod tip with grudging turns of your reel handle. The bait hangs suspended above bottom and, when a steelhead swims past it, the fish's passage causes both bobber and bait to rock and sway. Keep a tight grip on your rod handle, as the strikes you'll get from this style of fishing can be swift and savage!

Bobber drift rigs readily lend themselves to bottom bouncing with all types of other terminal gear. Flies can be fished much like bobbers, by using light sinker weights. Small plugs also are fine choices for attachig to your leader. Either slowly retrieving plugs or just plain drift-fishing them will dredge up strikes. You can fish any thin-bladed spoons (such as Dick Nites or Triple Teazers) on bottom-bouncing rigs also, and may be pleasantly surprised how many supertrout leap upon the lures normally used for their smaller cousins!

There's another type of bobber fishing that has tricked a lot of fish in British Columbia, Oregon and California, and now is catching on in Washington and Idaho. A large, center-drilled float bobber is used, with main line running directly through the bobber to baited hook, a jig or a large, gaudy fly. Above the hook there's a stop to limit how much line will be allowed to slip through the bobber to function as your leader. Split shot may be added below the bobber to pull leaders holding light baits or lures down to the bobber stop. Some steelheaders use stops both above and below the bobber to prevent their lure zipping out of a willing fish's mouth at the tail end of the bobber's drift when the line comes tight.

Float bobber fishing pays premiums to steelheaders dangling night crawlers, shrimp, cluster eggs, single eggs, leadhead jigs with marabou feather dressing, plastic egg, night crawler and insect imitations, tiny, lightweight spoons or spinners and even miniature plugs over suspended, finning steelhead. The bobbers float your bait or lure at the current's speed, taking it safely over snags in grabby bottom areas, into boils and eddies behind the rocks, and probing along high rock and clay walls or ledges where steelhead lurk in their cover. Little or no action is imparted to the lure/bait by the quiet float, but steelhead nevertheless will sometimes yield to sudden urges to zoom across yards of river to seize your hook. Or, an aggressive steelhead may stalk the offering for 20 to 30 feet, slowly closing in on it to nip sharply at the strange invader.

Float bobber angling works especially well in deep, clear rivers where summer fish often suspend three to five feet below the surface. A long rod, small hook (No. 2 or 4) and light line (4-pound test works well) combination can put these wary biters on the bank.

Bobbers, bottom-bouncing lures, or big float bobbers and the enticers used with them are light and easy to carry. A dispenser full of tied leaders, vest pocket size box of lures, choice of bait, a few extra hooks, pencil lead and surgical tubing supply and some snap swivels are all the gear you need to pack for a day's fishing.

When your bobber lure is struggling along just above bottom, nine times out of 10 you are fishing the right steelhead level. If the fish aren't clinging to the riverbed, give the float bobber system a shot. One bobber or the other could deliver strikes.

Nick Amato displays a Lewis River summer steelhead.

Chapter 8

Hardware for Heavyweights

There's something about a glittering metal blade chugging and twinkling through a steelhead's selected resting spot that sets a fish's fins on edge. I've watched them begin to quiver as a metal lure came into sight, gather their bodies like a tiger would, and launch themselves upon the intruding hunk of hardware with open-mouthed ferocity! Steelhead sometimes will streak over 20 feet to slam a spinner or spoon...and other times they will fin backwards and downstream to hidden lies under brush or behind rocks or boulders, where they come down with severe lockjaw fever.

Hardware is a term commonly applied to either spoons or spinners fished for steelhead. Each of these steelhead size and weight lures has a blade of heavy metal (generally coated brass) that, when the lure is properly fished, creates an action attractive to steelhead. The spoon blade is designed to emulate a minnow or swimming baitfish, while the spinner blade chews an erratic, rotary path through the water and might look like a large, emergent insect or present an alien and space-intruding challenge to steelhead. Spoons are one-piece, needing only a hook, split ring and snap swivel to attach them to your line. Spinners are multi-piece, strung on a stiff wire in an order determined by the maker...beads, weights, clevis, blade and hook. Hardware has many facets of appeal to steelhead...among which are movement, sonic attraction, bright finishes and tantalizing colors.

Which of these qualities best and most frequently spurs the steelhead into striking is a good topic for discussion during a morning's fishing. Some anglers feel metalheads smack hardware out of irritation caused by the lure's intrusion into the fish's chosen territory. Other fishermen believe it's possible the lively, lifelike swimming action of hardware triggers aggressive instincts of larger fish versus smaller fish. Steelheaders also point to the solid bodies of spoons and spinners and suggest they could resemble, at least to the fish, minnows or insects on which they might normally feed and which they grab to eat.

There is no debate, however, that when steelhead climb on a spinner or spoon – no matter what critter they think it is – they are serious about taking it out of the gene pool. That's why many anglers enjoy fishing with hardware...the strikes on metal lures are solid, vicious and often spectacular. Unlike angling with bait or bobber/yarn combinations, in which you have to sense a subtle nudge of your drift rig to realize a fish is sampling your wares, fishing with hardware eliminates indecision as to whether you've been bit by a fish.

I like to label the three major kinds of steelhead strikes I have most frequently experienced on hardware as being divided into categories of "Stop," "Go" and "Look at that!" When steelhead climb on hardware many times your lure will come to a complete stop just as though it had banged into a rock, log or clump of sod on bottom. Strike! You'll leave plenty of spoons and spinners imbedded on riverbed obstructions, but you'll also teach a lot of surprised steelhead how to pole vault. Lightweight steelhead will be stung into running, riverbed acrobatics or some air-walking, while truly huge heavyweights generally react more slowly. When you sock it to a humungous fish, nothing will happen for a long second or two, and then your rod tip will begin to nod slowly and ponderously like a Wyoming oil rig as the big fish shakes its head from side to side. Some of these submarines never show themselves on the surface. They build power like one of the Princess line of excursion ships and either continue upstream to spawn or decide to return to more friendly salt water. You can choose how far you want to tag along in either direction before pointing your rod tip at them, clamping down on your reel spool and waving *Bon voyage* to the travellers.

When a steelhead whacks hardware in the Go style, it can be streaking in any direction almost as it strikes...upriver, down, away or (worst of all) at you. A fast grab, then awaaaay we go! If you've managed to get the point of your hook into the fish on the initial strike it's probably best to just hang on while the fish streaks off on the first run. I've found my catch ratio of these frisky zippers increases, however, if after their first run, I can get in a sharp, forward stab of the rod butt to be sure of setting the hook past the barb. Without this added insurance, many steelhead can exercise your rod arm for a few minutes, then open their mouths and spit out the hardware.

One of the most exciting hardware strikes is the Look at that! variety. Your lure is working properly halfway through the hole or run, and a bright, shining steelhead erupts from the water in one or more shaking, surface-shattering leaps in the instant you feel something twitch your line. If you can set your hook whenever the steelhead spends a little time back in the water you might tame that tiger. But, if you come back on the rod when the steelhead is in the air trying to throw the hook...remember to duck!

Spoons and Spoon Tactics

Spoon-feeding steelhead is one of the easiest ways for a newcomer to steelhead fishing to make connections with his first ironhead. In the late 1960s, I carried only about eight to a dozen spoons and some snap swivels as my entire tackle box but had a hot streak going. I'd put enough steelhead on the bank Ted Wilcox, then my boss and managing editor of *Fishing and Hunting News*, suggested it might increase my work- and lifetime-expectancy if I were to show him where and how I was catching them.

We met early one Saturday morning on Washington's Green River at the Claybar Hole. Ted popped his trunk lid and opened the hangar doors of a tremendous, cantilevered-tray tackle box stuffed to the brim with colorful fishing lures to find the size and color spoon I'd been using with good results. I remember how I envied that goody box, which resembled Santa's Christmas bag in comparison to my plastic bag economy model container for spoons.

Goat-walking down a steep, twisty bank to the fog-shrouded water, we worked those spoons for about 20 minutes through all the likely steelhead lies at the head of the hole, but it looked like we'd picked the wrong morning or place. Ted asked about the lower end of the hole, below the claybar and approximately

Spoons

50 to 60 feet downstream from where we were. When I assured him it often was productive, he scrambled up the bank and and moved down to a spot where I could only dimly spy his western sombrero bobbing to each cast.

Sure enough, only a few casts after he'd begun fishing the tail of the hole, I had a thumping strike and a large steelhead bulldozed its underwater way nearly to the end of the claybar. It fought a tough, non-splashing, determined battle that was not betrayed by my spinning reel's softly-chirring, worn drag. When I beached the bright, totally exhausted 13-pound hen she was too frazzled even to flop. However, the spoon's single hook was solidly imbedded clear down the steelhead's gullet, so I took fish in one hand and rod in the other and clambered up the bank, to walk to a point immediately above my fellow fisherman.

"Hey Ted," I asked, "Have you got a hook disgorger in that big tackle box of yours?" When he turned to answer, I had the fish behind my hip where it could not be seen.

"Sure, a couple of them...why?" Ted responded.

I swung the steelhead into view. "I can't get the hook out of this fish," I told him.

He groaned, "Ohhhh...Why you sonuva...argh!" (or something sounding like that).

Spoons can be hot fishing lures on many steelheading trips, but may rate down there among "the untouchables" on others. Even though I fish with a wide variety of other lures now, I still carry along an assortment of spoons each trip in case that's what the steelhead want on any given day.

There are three general shapes of spoons most anglers pick to pack along for steelheading and you generally will find these are readily available at tackle dealers in the two most-used steelhead spoon weights. These are 1/2 and 3/8 ounces, although some spoons of 1/4-ounce size or a few 5/8-ounce models also may pay you silvery dividends in specific rivers or circumstances. The spoon shapes are: slim, long and heavy; long oval; fat, short and wide.

Popular spoons up and down the Pacific coast have both plain and hammered backs and you can take your pick of nickel, brass and copper finishes. Add to these basic colors some bright spots or slashes of red, orange or black and you've got my favorite go-getters. More color patterns and combinations are commonly purchased by fishermen who like striped coloration on top of the spoon, the stripe created by leaving a curving third of the basic finish unpainted in the middle of the back, or a half-and-half back pattern with red, orange, chartreuse, neon blue or green on their horizontal halves. Solid color backs, too, work well and these also may have spots or slashes of red, orange, chartreuse or black to make them more appealing to fish and fishermen.

Long, slim, heavy spoons are best fished in strong and deep current where their shape and weight help get your line down near bottom, where steelhead are lurking. Short, wide spoons work best in slow, shallow currents where the greater amount of planing surface their shape supplies aids you to keep them in motion and out of the rocks. Standard, long oval shapes are used in almost every other type of water ranging between the slow/shallow and fast/deep river sections.

An assortment of weighted spinners and wobblers for steelhead fishing.

Examples of some of the slim and long spoons you can find in my tackle box are Martin Ace Bait Ottogators, a few Little Cleos and some Luhr Jensen Krocodiles. Other heavy spoons that dig deep to deceive steelhead equally well are the Flutter Spoon, Canadian Wonder, Little Jaspar and a bevy of slab-cut or chunky lures such as Kastmaster, Hopkins, Andy Reeker and Weber Mr. Champ.

Standard long oval spoons I carry are Luhr Jensen Hotrod, Martin Ace Bait No. 4 and No. 3, Wonderlure and Pixie. More good spoons of the same appearance are Dardevle, Blanchard, Acme, Little Jewel and Nebco.

The "little fat boys" I send into harm's way are Stee-Lee, Wob-Lure and Fat Max spoons. Other look-alikes are the Mack's Lure Lucky Glo spoon and Wob-L-Rite.

Midwesterners and anglers from the east coast may have some degree of success with other spoon choices, catching a number of steelhead on Red Eye, Doctor, Kamlooper, Johnson Silver Minnow or Sprite and Hofschneider Red Eye spoons before they lose them to snags or bottom. It will be tough to replace them on the west coast, however, as they are not commonly stocked.

(Thin, lightweight spoons are extremely difficult to cast and do not dig very deep. However, they can be fished on drift rigs or with split shot added to the line 18 to 26 inches above the lure, and Candlefish, Gimpy, Dick Nite, McMahon, Miller Spoon, Needlefish, Trout Teaser, Skiny-Miny, Katchmor, Manistee,

Lucky Knight, Kokanee King, Triple Teazer and similar spoons will draw steelhead strikes.)

Many of the spoons already named also can be purchased with fluorescent paint finishes, mostly chartreuse or hot orange. They show up well in murky water and deep holes. If they aren't bright enough for your taste, there's a new spoon on the market – the *LumaLure* – that has a snap-in light cartridge calculated to draw a steelhead's attention no matter how deep it is fished.

Spoons are extremely versatile lures to cast and retrieve. They can, when strong enough current permits, be allowed to drift much like bait rigs. Flip your reel into retrieve and catch the slack line with a few turns of the reel handle immediately after casting, so that you have control and responsive feel of the spoon's underwater progress. With a bit of practice you soon will sense the lure's swimming movements and interpret what it is brushing, bouncing or scraping. If you get a bounce every eight or nine feet, you're in steelhead country. Any shorter gap between bottom contacts and you're probably going to keep your tackle dealer very happy selling you new spoons. To keep spoons moving properly, all you need do is vary your rate of retrieve for longer distances or raise and lower your rod tip for shorter distances...for instance to swim it over a rock or drop it into deeper water.

Fan-casting from nearly directly upstream to 60 or 70 degrees below your position produces the most effective coverage of water on a river section where you're searching out potential fish lies. If you know the hole has some particular characteristics that cause steelhead to hold in one spot, however, it's often best to devote your efforts to putting your spoon into that chunk of water at just the right angle to interest a fish finning there.

I can recall vividly a three-year love affair with one such rewarding and relatively unfished sweetheart of a hole...a sharp point that projected from the opposite bank of one of my favorite rivers and marked by a bobbing, wrist-thick tree root that broke the surface at medium flow. It didn't look very fishable, as it was a long cast and offered only a narrow slot about three feet wide and seven feet long, but deep enough that most anglers who did try it would not reach bottom until their gear was nearly swept out of the hole.

By accident, I overcast a spoon well above the spot and first discovered how to fish that out-of-the-way hole. I hung a long string of big steelhead – always hens – by repeating the same cast too high for the hole. The secret to my success was that the current slowed below the surface and would suck my spoon deep under the telltale root well before passing under that obvious snag. It allowed the spoon to drop on slack line four or five feet before I began my retrieve through the heart of the slot and Bingo! That first steelhead was no accident, because similar casts produced the same results many more times in the next two seasons. The hens would lie there almost below the bouncing root before moving up through the next run and riffle and, when the spoon came into the exact collision path, it was clobbering time!

I had so much confidence in that spot it was indelibly etched in my memory and became a favorite theme for fishing dreams. In fact, I woke up one morning at 3 a.m. because in my mind there was a thin, insistent long-range voice calling me from that spot, and I hurried to dress and go answer that urgent message. By 7 a.m. I had begun to think it really was a dream and had started my standard reluctant retreat from the river with a countdown of 10 more casts and I've got to go to work. On the seventh cast a mint condition 15-pound female steelhead slugged the spoon hard enough to fully wake me up to a delightful battle! That one hole gave me almost two dozen steelhead before floods cut the corner and chewed out my tree root marker. If you are fortunate enough to find any such honey hole it will pay you to fish it as often as you can and to duplicate the casting and retrieving pattern that delivered your first strike there.

Long spinning rods provide the most control over spoons. They allow you to keep more line out of the water and to slow or speed the return of your spoon better than with a shorter rod. This is especially critical when fishing boulder beds, one of the places where spoons are very good choices to pry steelhead out from the rocky cover. There is one thing to avoid, though, when you switch from a shorter rod to a rod longer than 8 1/2 or 9 feet. That's a spot where the overhead area has branches or clumps of brush that only appear high enough out of your reach to permit a full strike. If you hit a fish, or hang up on bottom, only a brief, sharp slap against a small overhanging twig is enough to snap a couple inches off your rod tip. My pet, handmade 9-foot, 4-inch spinning rod now measures about five inches less than that because I misjudged the branch level twice in one such productive spot. (If you're as forgetful of this as I am, it probably would be a smart thing to carry with you, as I now do, a new tiptop guide one size larger than the one now on your rod and some cement to install it on a suddenly slightly shorter rod.)

Remember what was previously mentioned in the rods and reels section about a spoon's tendency to sky on your casts? If a slight wind catches the flat of your spoon during a cast, it can rise like a kite or jink like Phil Niekro's knuckleball pitch! Spinning reels take this in stride, but bait-casting reels frequently do not. A hitch in the git-along of a bait-casting reel's performance can snarl spooled line so badly you may lose fishing time for long minutes during a peak biting binge. Worse yet, you may even be compelled to clip half your line to get past the birdsnest in order to fish at all. And you then will have reduced casting distance as a result of the shortening of line and subsequent smaller spool diameter.

Spinning reels feed line to a sailing lure on demand whatever the variation in their speed. Bait-casting reels require uniform flow of line off the spools for most efficient operation. If there's some unexpected hang time during the cast, level-winds can provide some very intricate and unusual rearrangements of your mono perhaps better suited as new housing developments for hedge sparrows than for fishing.

Eight-pound hen from the Tolt River, Washington, caught with a weighted spinner.

Good spoon fishermen can tell you what type of bottom – weeds, mud, gravel, rocks or sand – their spoon grazes. They sense the difference purely by the momentary touches of their lure. Some steelheaders also have the fine-tuned ability to check their strike when the tap coming up the line tells them a steelhead is bumping the lure with their noses rather than striking. This is something that I've seen several fish do and a situation that generally causes anglers to react violently, missing the strike and spooking the fish, thus killing the fisherman's future chances for a firm strike on the next cast.

Spoons perform best when actively worked through the water and a spoon's passage through the river is interpreted and guided in the minds's eye by the steelheader, not just cast out and retrieved. I liken it to mentally making your own VCR film of the action underwater, picturing the rocks and logs bumped into, the strand of mossy monofilament hung on a snag and down which your spoon is sliding, a drop-off into deeper, slower water, yardlong shape of blue/silver fish rising to intercept it and...you can add your own grand finale.

SPINNERS AND ANGLING TECHNIQUES

Hardware's other half is weighted spinners, which in my estimation are the most efficient, productive and enjoyable-to-fish steelhead lures on the market. Spoiled by repeated success with Danielson's Tor-P-Do, I was was devastated about 15 years ago when production of this terrific ironhead seducer was shut down. The low price (once 59 cents) and my numerous catches scored with the Tor-P-Do prompted a search for similar spinners that could easily be cast, fished deep, and which had heavy blades properly shaped to create pulsations underwater that could be read by my rod tip and hands and held lots of appeal for steelhead.

There are dozens of steelhead spinners from which to select weights and sizes that might work best for you...and all of them catch their share of steelhead. Some of the commonly available bright-bladed ironjaw-icers you might try are: Mepps, Bolo, CM Spinner, Shyster, Vibrax, Bud's, Max-E, Sonic Roostertail, Metric, Panther Martin, Ilba and homemade variations of your own. (You can get instructions on how to make your own spinners from several sources.

Steelhead smash spinners. Something about the way a weighted spinner throbs and scrambles along bottom triggers a strike reaction in their instinct system. I've seen them streak across a clear stream from the far side to unload a whole world of whack on a spinner! They also will stalk a spinner bumbling downstream and, when it reaches the end swing of your line and struggles upward as though trying to reach shore or the surface, pounce on it just like a bobcat picking off a flushed grouse. They'll grab it, too, when it first smacks the water "just because it's there" as though it were a large insect or tiny bird dropping into the river from a low bush or tree branch.

Spinners are built on a rigid wire that acts as an axle shaft around which an oval, teardrop shape, or elongated, barely curved blade spins on a clevis. Beads and weights follow the blade, with a hook pinned to the tail loop of the wire. You tie your main line directly to the barrel loop at the upper end of the spinner, or attach a positive-closure snap swivel to your line and clip the snap through the loop. Normally, no additional weight is needed to fish spinners, although some deep, fast water might call for addition of a No. 4 or 6 split shot 18 to 26 inches up the main line in order to get the lure down to where the fish lie.

Your snap swivel should be of premium quality, to prevent line twist from weakening the monofilament you're using. Spinners fished without top grade swivels have a built-in tendency to work coils into the last couple of feet of your line and make it hard to cast as well as hampering the action of the spinners. Some of the spinners you can find on tackle shelves and cards come with barrel swivels already on the upper loop, others have no swivel.

Once cast, in the same upstream to 60 degrees downstream fan pattern as you'd fish spoons, the progress of a spinner through the river is guided by first stirring the spinner blade into revolution by a sharp lift of the rod tip or couple quick cranks of your reel handle, then playing with the speed of your retrieve and raising or lowering your rod. Cranking faster will make the spinner rise in the water, and slower reel handle speed will allow the spinner to settle deeper. The same effects can be achieved by lifting and dropping your rod tip.

Exceptionally good spots for fishing spinners are pocket water behind and around boulders, short, deep slots near islands, the dark and deep holes under logs and stump roots, shallow drifts studded with large rocks and any slow, swirling eddies.

Perhaps the major key to steelhead success with both spinners and spoons is that you can keep these hardware lures in the water for more time than most other casting rigs. They are quick and easy to cast, require almost no time to pick from the water and return to probe further good steelhead positions, and seldom need more care than to sharpen their hooks often and retie the main line every 20 to 25 casts or half-hour. They spend more time fishing than do baits or bobber rigs and will cover more area than plunking gear, thus giving you more opportunity to put them in front of a steelhead's nose.

If I had to select one type of lure and no other with which I would be forever limited for steelhead fishing, it would be a chunk of hardware and my problem would be to choose between spoons and spinners. In the long run, spinners would be my first option, since I believe them to be more versatile and slightly more productive. My former neighbor, John Thomas, and I kept a log one summer when spinners were strongly favored by steelhead in our local river. We took 27 eager steelhead that hot season, 25 of which jumped on our spinners, and the other two fell for a Lil' Corky and silver Sammy Special, respectively.

Spinners

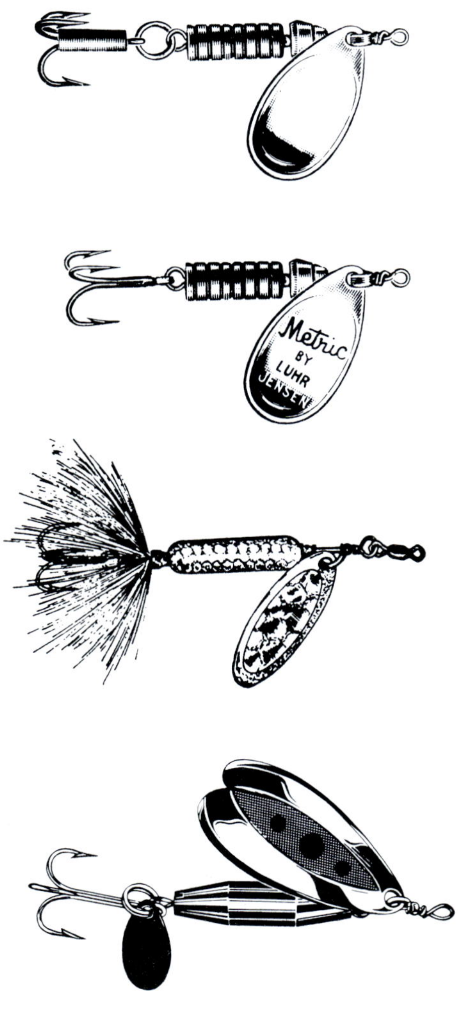

Chapter 9

Plugs, Plunking and Tactics

On one of those bluebird days when livin' was easy and the weather was good lookin', all the steelhead in the river sullenly refused to open their mouths for any drift rigs or hardware we had to offer. So, my partner popped the lid of his boat tackle box and determinedly predicted, "We're going to hook some fish...let's pull plugs."

We needed some suicide steelhead that would throw away all caution and clobber our hooks...and our plugs found 'em! Bait, bobbers, spoons and spinners had been ignored for about six hours, but in just 45 minutes more, we hoisted three steelhead on plugs from one deep run, missed another, and ran out of fishing time or we probably would have netted a fourth fish.

All of our steelhead were caught on deep-diving, big-billed plugs that had orange or green crawdad finishes. The plugs' colors were not the prime factors that spurred the reluctant fish into striking, however. The major reason we woke up those fish was that our plugs were hauled right into their holding territory, in front of the steelheads' noses, wriggling and scrabbling along bottom, where the plugs' actions rasped raw the steelheads' aggressive and territorial defense instincts. Those aggravating, dancing, darting daredevils of the deep kicked up such a gravel-and-sand fuss right in the fishs' faces they just couldn't ignore them.

Steelhead hate plugs. Sometimes they will lock their jaws tightly shut and hunt cover or even flee from the drift when plugs start shucking and jiving down the drift toward them. Often, however, their reaction is to charge into the plug under a full head of steam, crashing their jaws on the offending plastic body and hooks like bear traps snapping... *Crush!... Destroy!... Kill!*

Steelheaders fish a colorful variety of diving plugs in several different, productive ways for excellent catches. Look at their plug box, though, and you'll see there are a couple things all the plugs have in common. Curved like a banana and having long, wide lips or bills at the front, steelheading plugs are designed to dig down into a steelhead's parlor and cause both sonic and visual commotions that will irritate or excite the fish. And, once a steelhead savages the standard double set of treble hooks or two big Siwash single hooks on most plugs, he's generally got a mouthful of stinging steel. Then the fun begins!

Besides attracting lots of strikes, plugs cause infuriated steelhead you hook to battle like wild demons, shredding a river's surface with end-swapping leaps or direction-changing rolls, and making reels sizzle on long, fast runs. Their fight seems twice as fierce as that of steelhead you've tricked to the hook with bait or bobber.

Plugs most often used for steelheading are the Hot Shot, Flatfish, Tadpolly, Hawg Boss, Wee Wart and Wiggle Wart, Shordoo, alphabet plugs such as the Big N and Big O, Hedd Hunter, Wee'R, Reefer, Fire Plug, Deep Lazy Ike, Guppy, Super Scooper, Hot'N Tot, Smilin Minno, Jiffy, Kwikfish, LumaLure, Macadoo, Fishback and similar wobbling divers. These are available at tackle stores in a myriad of color combinations ranging from metallic blue, gold, silver and green to spotted, striped or solid colors such as the fire orange "Big Red" U-20 flatfish. Fluorescent chartreuse or red plugs, or those with blue or green fish scale, perch or crawdad finishes are additional good steelheading choices, as are plugs having subdued body color and bright heads.

Most steelheaders will fish plugs from boats, but bank anglers who carry a few plugs along on drift-fishing trips can switch tactics to cast and retrieve plugs, hang these wobbling lures in the current off points or creek mouths, suspend their plug behind a side-planer, or anchor a plunking line on bottom and slide a plug down their line on a three-foot leader to hassle upstream-bound steelhead while the fishermen crack open their lunches and coffee vacuums.

Even light-line anglers get downright devious every once in a while and attach a huge, gaudy, fire orange U-20 Flatfish or a similar Kwikfish lure to their 4-pound test line to fish slow, deep and clear water. Suspended steelhead that turn up their noses at baits, jigs and flies may go bonkers over Big Red sashaying through their chosen lies. Sure, it will take you a little time with that delicate and cobwebby gear to convince an 18-pound steelhead it should swim over to your gravel bar and take a nap on it, but the constant, strength-sapping bend of the long rod used in light-line angling will do the job.

To avoid spooking steelhead hanging in gin-clear water, cast well above the target fish, then bring your big plug swimming slowly toward the steelhead. Time the speed of your retrieve to direct the plug right at the fish or just to one side of it. If a steelhead materializes behind the U-20 and closes fast on it, do not slack your reeling speed. It works best, instead, to increase the retrieve rate slightly, as though your plug were trying to escape from the punishment that zeroing steelhead is planning to launch upon it.

PULLING PLUGS (HOTSHOTTING)

Working steelhead plugs across and down a productive steelhead drift is far more easily done from a drift boat or sled. The oarsman or motor operator guides the boat from side to side and checks it from sliding downstream with strokes of the long oars or deft touches on the tiller and throttle control. Starting at the top of a drift, run or pool, the boat sweeps the plugs from bank to bank, then is allowed to slip downstream, where the search is resumed, until all the water is covered. The plugs dance, pointed lip downward, as though they were small fish struggling, but being borne downstream by the current. Their long, wide lips scrabble over gravel and sand bottom, kicking up attention-getting cloudy spurts of sediment, and the buoyant bodies bounce against and climb over riverbed rocks and boulders. Occasionally, the plugs will pick up weeds or grass on the hooks, causing them to lose the action needed to attract steelhead. The waterweed decorations on their barbs may affect plugs so much they will turn on their sides and pop to the surface.

Generally, the medium weight and action rods used for pulling steelhead plugs are inserted in rodholders or their butts are propped so that a hard strike won't catapult them from the boat into the river (it happens!) Holding the rods in hand dampens the plugs' action and is wearing on the arms after an hour or so. Anywhere from 20 to 35 feet of line is payed out to get the plugs down eight to 12 feet, good steelhead holding depth.

Fishermen who often pull plugs (the method is called Hotshotting on the west coast after the plug first used in this type of fishing) usually equip their reels with 14- to 17-pound test monofilament. Reel drags are slightly tightened, and anglers need only keep an eyeball on the nodding rods for sudden dips and smashing strikes. When steelhead hit plugs, the bent rod and line resistance might be enough to set the hook but a couple fast, barb-sinking strokes with your rod are good insurance.

Steelhead seize plugs so solidly in their tough mouths they often cannot be hooked until they begin to open and close their jaws to shake out those biting steel barbs. If you don't hit them a few hard shots, you might carefully play a big steelhead to the net, then see it open its chops and allow your plug to float out.

Lagoon and river bay steelheading – such as at many stream mouths in California, British Columbia and along the Columbia River – has promulgated an enjoyable, minimal-tackle mode of angling for ironheads that is extremely effective. Small boats plying protected, calm waters are most effective, since the boats are oared, or operated with electric motors at very slow speeds.

Les Johnson, avid Northwest fisherman with a large Kalama River winter steelhead.

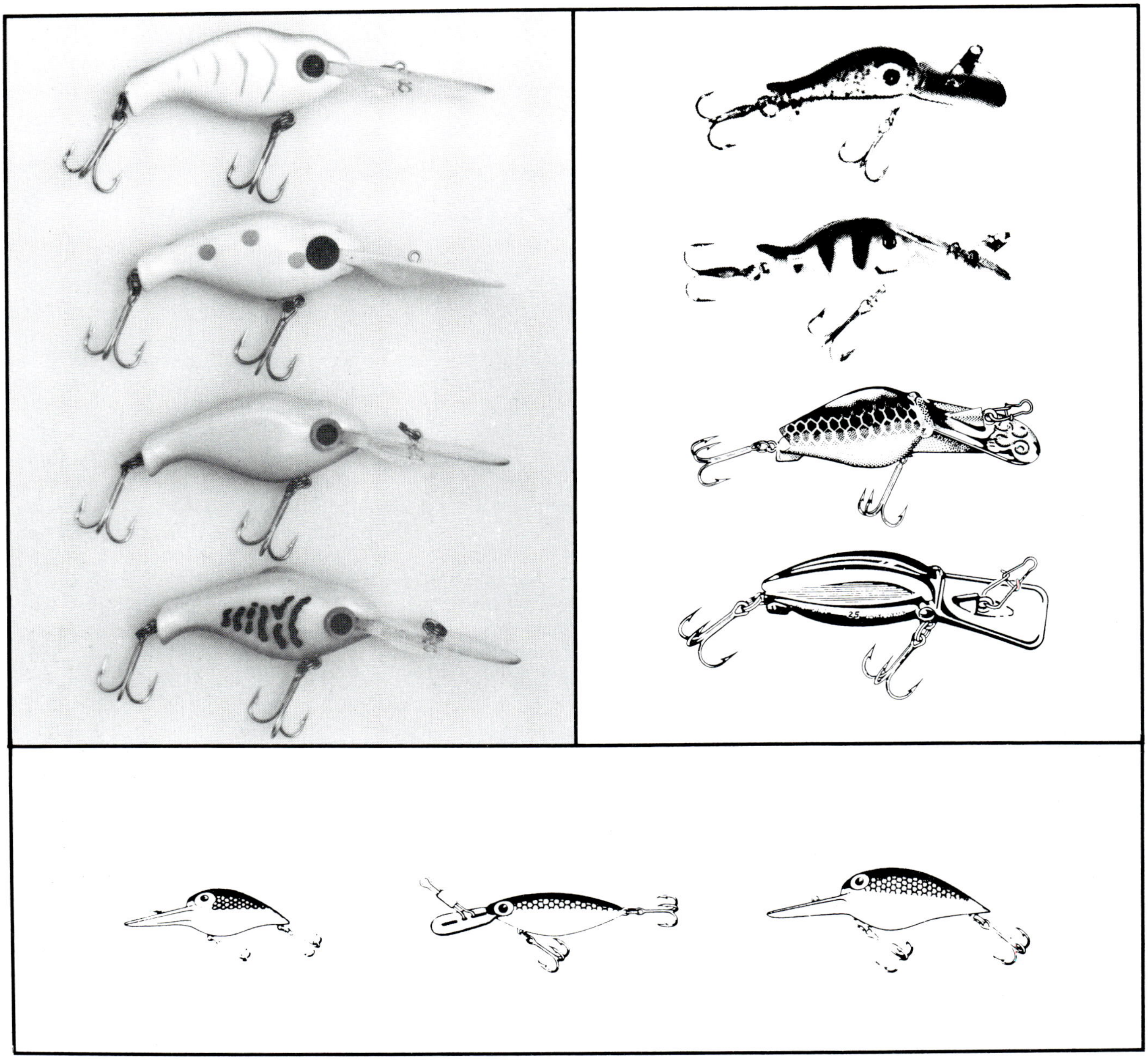

Fishermen using medium weight rods and 12- to 17-pound test line tie on a plug having slow action, such as a Flatfish, Lazy Ike, Reefer, Beno or Kwikfish, then add split shot six inches apart on the monofilament, starting 18 inches above the plug, in quantity and size sufficient to cause the plug to sink at an extremely slow rate.

Fished 12 to 20 feet deep in the early morning and evening hours, these banana-shaped plugs waddle temptingly through fresh-run schools of fish and draw sudden, hard strikes. Boatmen stroke v-e-r-y slowly on their oars, to maintain a slight upstream pace or, in the case of slow-moving water and opposing wind, downstream trolling also will deliver. In midday, action slacks off, but additional fish can be hooked by dropping the plugs down 25 to 45 feet deep and continuing the slow trolling speed.

Sharp hooks are critical in this method of fishing. There is no weight near the plug to help set your barb, and your line is sometimes nearly slack. Most fishermen will prop their rods at a high angle, in view of the oarsman or electric motor operator, so that the first downward jerking action of the rod tip can be seen and the rod instantly seized and the fish struck. When a school of steelhead comes into lagoons or river bays brash, bright and belligerent, this type of fishing can be wild and fantastic.

SIDE-PLANERS

Fishing with a "poor man's drift boat"... using a side-planer to tow a steelhead plug out to fish-holding water, is another excellent method of angling that will allow you to place a lure in harm's way.

Recently my angling partner and I "got some smart pills" when we closely witnessed the effective technique and good fortune of a fisherman who worked his

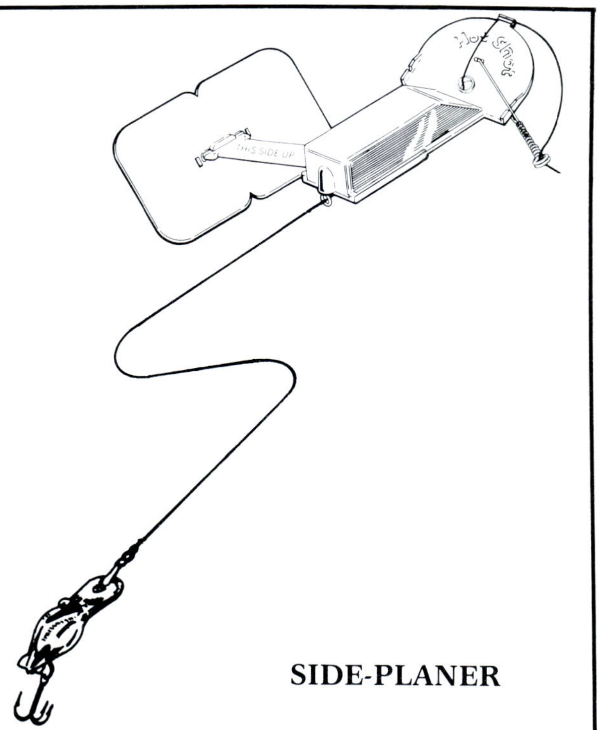

SIDE-PLANER

side-planer and U-20 Flatfish rig from the bank opposite us and above the "Big T" juncture of Washington's Snoqualmie and Tolt rivers. It had been really tough fishing for a week or two, and the rivers were skinny and clear, causing us to fish very light lines and small drift rigs to generate only a single fish all morning. When we saw this angler approach the river with his heavyweight tackle we had a chuckle at the "nummy" who obviously was going to scare half to death any steelhead hanging off the mouth of the Tolt River. At least, we chortled and slapped until that newly-arrived fisherman battled and beached two steelhead in about 25 minutes!

The side-planer is rigged by sliding it onto a main line testing about 15 pounds or more breaking strength, adding a good quality, large barrel swivel on the end of the line, and then attaching a Hot Shot or other diving plug to the other end of the swivel on a three- to four-foot leader. The Hot Shot Side-Planer is designed so it can be assembled for either right or left-handed operation. Snap the side vane into the proper configuration for the current flow where you are fishing and feed the plug and about 12 to 18 feet of leader and line to the river. Then loop the main line around the side-planer's front guide/trip arm and lever the guide arm into locked position. Lower the side-planer carefully into the current and work it and the trailing plug out and across the river by alternately releasing line and raising your rod tip, thus allowing your plug and planer to swim its way across the river.

When a steelhead unloads on the plug, line tension and the force needed to unlock the trip arm often is sufficient to sink your hook into the fish's lips. Being an unbeliever, fourth belt, I advocate smacking that steelhead one more time to be sure it is going to stay on the hook!

The *Luhr Jensen Hot Shot Side-planer™* is a one-of-a-kind, extremely easy to fish and versatile aid to steelheaders. Made of light and very durable plastic, it adds little weight to my steelhead vest, so I pack one, rigged with a Pirate pattern Hot Shot plug, any time I'm fishing steelhead with other than ultralight equipment.

BANK PLUGGING

Effective spots to fish plugs from the bank are where substantial feeder streams or rushing brooks enter the main river, from midstream in wadable rivers, or from islands or points of land where the current directly below you will force your plug underwater and give it the desired pumping, darting action that attracts steelhead strikes.

Most steelheaders prefer to use at least 10-pound test mono in this type of fishing. Tie directly to the screw eye of the plug, using a loop knot, or with a strong, secure knot attached to the positive closure snap that normally comes with the plug. (Note that these snaps have rounded ends that will permit plugs to have free-swinging action sideways, as well as vertical movement.) The action that proves most productive in plug fishing is a throb, throb, throb pulsation that is interrupted only rarely by the plug taking a brief sprint to one side or the other. Watch your plug in the water near you to see that it is swimming properly and keep an eye on your rod tip as you're working the plug downriver to be sure it continues the same nodding motion.

Your plug can be tuned to run straight and fish better if it is a brand that allows the screw eye to which your line or snap attaches to be turned or bent. A plug that continually dashes to the right or turns slow circles to the right, for instance, can be adjusted to run a true course by turning or bending the eye slightly to the same direction. Make minute changes and keep testing how the plug tracks in the water until you get it tuned properly. (Then guard that particular plug from accident, borrowers or being banged about or stepped on. A true-running diving plug that heckles steelhead into hitting is a prized possession and frequent plug users often have pet plugs that have accounted for dozens of steelhead.)

It is not necessary to cast your plug, and advisable not to if any wind is coming at you. Wind does strange things to the plug in mid-air, making it veer, sky and tumble end-over-end, which often catches your line on the hooks, negating the plug's fishability. Instead, let out approximately 15 to 18 feet of line to begin with, then very slowly move your rod tip as far to the left as you can reach, then equally slowly as far to the right as you can stretch. This allows your plug to wobble back and forth across the river and clamber over rocks and gravel bars in search of resting steelhead. Hold the struggling plug in one area for a minute or two, then slip another two or three feet of line off the reel and repeat the side-to-side rod maneuver. (Using your longest rod will allow you to cover more water in this type of plug fishing.)

Light-liners generally have best success by casting plugs and retrieving them. Basically, light-line plugging is done in river situations where there is very little current. Deep pools of good size are ideal, as steelhead hooked in these long, slow spots often will slug it out, rather than running downstream. Also, you have more and better control of how the plug is fished, as well as being able to direct your casting efforts toward hooking specific steelhead. Of course, this assumes you are fishing transparent water, where you can see the fish either suspended or holding near bottom, or spots where you have had solid evidence steelhead lie there.

PLUNKING

It's relatively simple to change from casting or hotshotting plugs to another mode of fishing these deep-diving fish finders. A steelheader can take it easy on the bank, after rigging up and casting his tackle for plunking, and let the plug do all the work.

You'll need a pyramid sinker heavy enough to anchor the terminal end of your line on the edge of a good current flow, a split ring, stopper, or wire spreader about 16 to 18 inches above the sinker, and medium to heavy fishing tackle. Cast the bare line and sinker to the position you want to fish, next to the main current, and let the sinker settle. Next, take a two-foot leader having your plug on one end and a positive closure snap on the other, snap it on the line and drop it into the water below your rod tip. Current will cause the leader and plug to slide down your main line until it reaches the stopping point. It's fishing while you sit back and pour your coffee, build a warming fire or converse with other nearby steelheaders.

A screeching reel and bouncing rod can be trusted to alert you to strikes, but some steelheaders rig further "early warning" signals on their plunking rods, such as a small, bright bit of cloth, piece of reflector tape, or a tiny, clip-on brass bell.

If you carefully read your regulations to see how many lures you may legally fish with at one time, you might want to add more spice to your bottom gear by attaching a bait-laden leader to the line below the stopper point before pitching your pyramid sinker into the river. A bobber/bait, or bobber/bait/yarn combination often is used as the bottom attractor in such rigs, while the plug serves either as main course or flagman for the steelhead dinner traffic. Also, a whirling Spin-N-Glo is another good option for plunking on a separate leader below a plug.

Plunkers normally will use light, breakaway leaders between the sinker and swivel at the terminal end of their line. When a sinker becomes irretrievably hung, and must be broken off to resume fishing, only the sinker is lost, freeing all the other gear to be fished again.

Two-lure rigs work best with leaders of different lengths separated by stops placed far enough apart on the line so the two leaders won't tangle. If you're planning to put this much gear in the water, you're also well advised to install heavier line on your reel so that you can handle heavy bottom sinker, lures and a battling steelhead. Most fulltime plunkers will spool at least 17-pound to perhaps 30-pound test mono on their reels, and leaders range from 15 to 18 pounds breaking strength.

Vary your plunking lures for best results. One day you might fish cluster eggs and a Corky, the next try a Spin-N-Glo and the following day a plug, or plug and lure/bait selection. Once you have found a rigging combination that produces strikes from a particular spot or school of fish, stick with that offering until the steelhead demonstrate your welcome mat is wearing thin by refusing to take it any more.

Preparing for a day on the Kilchis River, Oregon.

Chapter 10

Steelhead Fly-Fishing, Flies and Tactics

By Frank Amato

One of angling's greatest pleasures is to hook a steelhead with a fly. It is also one of angling's more difficult challenges, because to do so takes a fair amount of fishing experience, knowledge of fish run timing, water reading ability, wading prowess and the ability to fly-cast well. Plus, you'll need a thorough understanding of your tackle – especially your fly line and how to manipulate it in the water – and you have to be lucky too, in that the fish decides to take your fly...a fish that is not encouraged to do so because of the scent of bait, but one responding out of curiosity, amusement, reflex feeding action or plain annoyance.

Many steelhead are taken on the fly each year on the West Coast. I would estimate that at least 50,000 summer-run steelhead are hooked and far less winter fish. Why more summer fish? Simply because of colder water temperature and stronger flows in the winter. In water measuring 50 to 65 degrees, steelhead become more aggressive in checking out angler's offerings... whether flies, baits or hardware. In this temperature range steelhead also fight better. Summer-run steelhead often will come willingly to the surface or just under it to latch onto a fly. You can fly-fish for winter steelhead with surface or near-surface flies but go strikeless for many, many days unless an unusual warming of the water takes place.

As you can see, for consistent winter steelhead success with the fly you need a well-sunk, slow-moving fly fished near the bottom.

For summer fish you have three options: first, a deep-sunk fly, as in the winter season; second, a fly just under or in the surface and third, a fly on the surface. We will explore all of these options, but first let's discuss some basic tackle requirements.

WADERS

You need chest waders. Fly-fishing for steelhead demands proper angler positioning in the stream and that often means deep wading. With casting or spinning reels, hip boots will do because the reel is capable of long casts easily made. Most fly casts are from 30 to 70 feet...a fair distance, but not if the fish are 10 feet beyond your longest cast. Waders allow you to thoroughly work the water and, in addition, wading is an art in itself, very satisfying on hot days and having the added advantages that wading makes your body lighter and increases fishing time by eliminating fatigue caused by gravity.

Wading means that you will come in contact with lots of rocks, most of which are slippery, especially in summer. Thus, your waders should be equipped with felt soles or some other form of traction device. In addition, a wading staff is very handy and it will almost ensure that you don't slip and take an unwelcome dunking that could spoil an otherwise fine morning.

ROD

A No. 7 rod will handle 95 percent of the steelhead you hook. I often use a No. 4 for fish from 4 to 10 pounds. In those rivers where fish range in size from 10 to 25 pounds (mainly in British Columbia and Idaho) I use a No. 6 or No. 7.

For the most sensitive and satisfying fly-fishing, your rod should be composed of graphite, will cost from $50 to over $100 and be at least 8½ feet long. I prefer 9 to 9½-foot rods, although I also love my little No. 4, an 8-foot rod which has taken over 100 fish to 15 pounds. However, a longer rod gives you much better line control when mending the fly line to restrain the speed of the fly in the water.

REEL

Your reel should carry from 60 to 100 yards of 30-pound test backing line plus the fly line. A good quality reel will cost from $40 to $100. I prefer fly reels with rim control, because you can palm the reel's rim and thus create the correct amount of drag at precisely the right moment when playing a lively, running, jumping fish. Other acceptable fly reels will have built-in drags but they are less fun to operate in the heat of battle. You should have a spare spool for an extra fly line of a different type. For instance, one weight-forward floating line and one fast-sinking tip line.

You also will want to carry in your fishing vest a leader clipper, hook file, fly box and extra leader equipment. Very small pliers also are handy if you are using barbed flies.

LEADERS

For most steelhead fly-fishing, the tippet generally should test from 6 to 12 pounds. For the floating line/wet fly I use an 8- to 12-pound tippet. Steelhead normally are not leader shy unless they have been kegged up in one run and many fishermen have been casting to them in clear water conditions.

Use as strong a leader as the water, weather conditions and time of day will allow. You will work for your fly-hooked steelhead, so why use a light leader when a stronger one will do? A stronger leader will not readily weaken from chafing, will make it easier to pick out wind knots and, if you happen to have a wind knot (an overhand loop in your leader caused by the fly slowing, then passing through the forward part of the leader), you probably still will land the fish. Also, stronger leaders allow you to play a fish more quickly and, if it is wild, release it in better condition to continue its important spawning journey.

Your leader also should be a stiff type of nylon. Limp nylon is not as abrasion-resistant and when wind knots form, they are much harder to take out. I always tie my own leaders, starting with a 5-foot piece of 25-pound test monofilament, 2-foot piece of 15-pound and then a 2-foot piece of 6-, 8-, 10- or 12-pound test for the tippet. Use either a Blood Knot or a Surgeon Loop to easily and efficiently tie your own.

To tie the fly to the leader, use a Double Turle Knot. This allows the leader to come directly out of the eye of the hook so there is no hinging effect.

SUMMER STEELHEAD FLY-FISHING METHODS

It will be best for you to begin fly-fishing for steelhead in the summer because your success will be greater due to lower water flows and higher water temperature, thus allowing you to find the fish more easily. And, the steelhead will be more aggressive and active. Wading also will be much easier.

Finding the fish (winter or summer steelhead) means doing your homework. First, select a stream or streams having good numbers of fish returning in the period you will be able to fish. Then try to time your trip to the stream during the month or several-month period which seems to be the peak.

FLOATING LINE WITH WET FLY

The easiest way to take a steelhead on a fly is to use a weight-forward taper floating line. If you are using a No. 7 rod, then purchase a No. 7 or No. 8 line. Do not underweight your fly rod by selecting a line less than the manufacturer's suggestion. This will make casting difficult. I generally prefer to overweight my rod by one line size...thus a No. 8 line for a No. 7 rod. The extra weight will work the rod a bit more, feel more comfortable and cast nicely.

I am assuming that you already know how to fish for steelhead with a casting or spinning rod and thus know how to read the water to narrow down the search for the fish. Generally, most steelhead will be found near the head of a riffle or in the tailout area of the run which then leads into fast water and perhaps another riffle. Steelhead like water two to eight feet deep with a riffly to smooth surface appearance and moderate to medium-quick flow. Avoid dead water and very deep water.

You also should be wearing a pair of polarized sun glasses, which cut the sun's glare on the water and allow you to see much better. Sometimes it is possible to spot fish this way, but they might be spooked by your movements and need a 15-minute rest period. I nearly always have polarized glasses on. In addition to helping spot fish, they protect the eyes in windy casting conditions and prevent eye strain and headaches.

Your leader should be about nine feet long and taper to a 6- to 12-pound test tippet selected according to water clarity, sunlight and average fish size. Depending on water clarity, suggested fly sizes will range from No. 2 to No. 8, with 4s and 6s being the most productive. Check the end of this chapter for suggested fly patterns. Dark fly patterns should be used on cloudy days and in shadows, and bright patterns in sunny weather. If you are sure fish are present, try both light and dark patterns.

Wade into the stream at the head of the riffle or tailout and cast about 15 feet downstream at about a 45-degree angle. Continue working out line in one-foot increments at the 45-degree angle until you have lengthened your line to a comfortable casting distance of anywhere from 35 to 70 feet, depending on the size of the river. At this point do not let any more line out. Simply continue making each cast the same length while stepping down the run about 18 inches after each cast. This allows you to methodically work all the holding water with your fly.

As you make each cast you must mend your fly line to prevent the fly from swinging through the water too fast. Steelhead like to take a near-surface fly that is not being dragged. To slow the fly down, flip your fly line upstream as soon as you have completed the cast. Depending on the water current you might have to mend the line once or several times to maintain the proper speed. This near-surface method works well once the water temperature is between 55 to 65 degrees. I would estimate that about 70 percent of all summer-run steelhead are hooked in this fashion.

Oftentimes your fly is virtually in the surface film and you can see the steelhead boil as it takes the fly and turns. Do not strike until the fish is felt on the reel. Most takes will be very hard and strong because the line is directly to the fish and the fish reacts immediately when feeling the prick of the hook.

Because of the strong strike, it generally is not necessary to strike the fish again...or at least not until it stops after a long run or many jumps. However, since such a strike can put extreme stress on your leader it is absolutely necessary to check your tippet every so often to make sure it doesn't have any wind knots. A wind knot cuts the strength of your leader in half. Thus an 8-pound tippet becomes 4 pounds and a strong take will leave you with a broken leader. It happens so quickly it is amazing. You do not even feel the take that strongly. The resistance of the fly line in the water is about all the leverage a steelhead needs to pop a leader having a wind knot.

THE PLUCK OR TOUCH

Most of the time when a steelhead takes the near-surface wet fly it does so with a jolting strike. But not always. In colder water (from 50 degrees down to the high 30s) steelhead will not take nearly as strongly; the colder the water the slower the take. They also will have a tendency to follow the fly in, near the

Low tech and high tech. Steelhead can be caught with a wide range of gear. The tin can becomes a spinning reel and one can work a wobbler deep and well. The fight is exciting, possibly even more so than taking a steelhead on a fly rod. This hatchery fish succumbed to a Patriot.

shore, so you should not pull your line up quickly to cast again; let it hang below you for a few moments and even give it a twitch or two.

When using the floating line/wet fly method, sometimes you will feel a slight touch or pull as the fly swings in the mended arc. This probably was a steelhead that followed the fly and attempted to inhale it or suck it in rather than aggressively grabbing it. Fish can either aggressively approach food or they can inhale it by forcing water through their gills to draw suspended food into their mouths.

The floating line/wet fly method essentially is done with a tight line. If a fish attempts to suck the fly in, all you will feel is a slight pull or pluck. When this happens you should immediately mentally mark the spot on the shore and change your fly to a size smaller and darker and repeat the cast. Many times the fish will come right back and take it aggressively. If it doesn't, after several casts begin moving down the run again, because the fish probably has changed its position and might take farther down. If the fish doesn't come back and you finish the run, then start down it

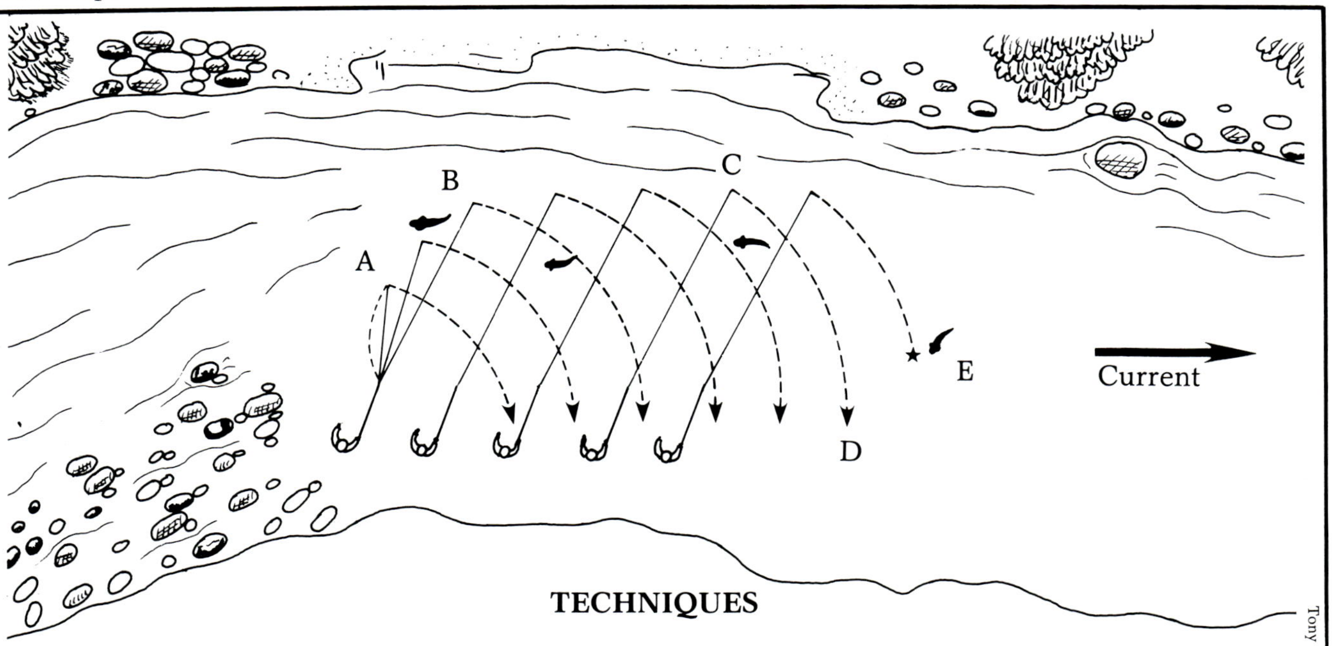

TECHNIQUES

WET FLY WITH FLOATING LINE OR FAST SINKING TIP LINE. RIFFLING HITCH TIED WET FLY WITH FLOATING LINE. DOWNSTREAM BUSHY DRY FLY WITH FLOATING LINE.

Make first cast to point A. Without moving, cast several more times, lengthening the line by about two feet with each cast until a comfortable amount of line is out, about 45 to 70 feet. Now you are at point B. As each cast is made mend the line upstream to keep the fly from travelling too fast. If you are using a dry fly or the riffling hitch, however, let the fly swing through the water more rapidly. After each cast, move one to three feet downstream before the next cast. Fish will often see the fly as far out as you can cast and then follow it for up to 20 feet or more before taking it. This is especially true of summer steelhead in water above 55 degrees. In colder water fish will often take at point D after having followed the fly for many feet. Wait several seconds after the fly has stopped below you before you begin to cast again. The colder the water the slower the fly should be worked.

RIFFLING HITCH KNOT

ALWAYS TIE RIFFLING HITCH KNOT ON OPPOSITE SIDE OF FLY.

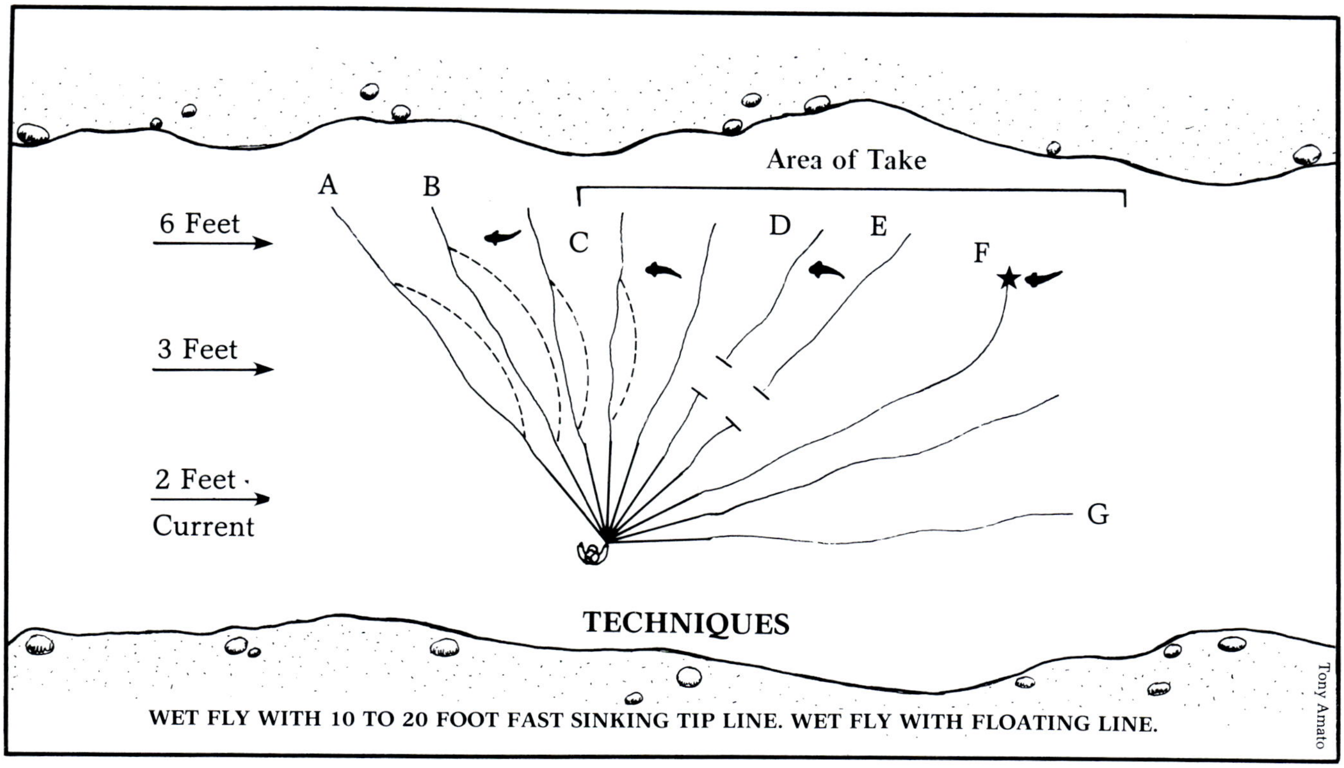

With either dry floating line or fast sinking tip line, cast upstream and quickly mend your fly line either up or downstream to take line tension off the fly, thus allowing it to sink quickly and deep. At point C the fly should be travelling near bottom in about six feet of water or more depending on the speed of the current. From point C to F is the normal taking range. At points D and E line can be fed out to extend the fly's drift in productive water. At point F the fly will slow and begin to tighten against the line and travel toward shore while lifting from the bottom. This is a very good time to receive a strike. At point G let the fly hang for several seconds before starting the next cast. Cold water steelhead will sometimes strike here.

Work an upstream cast dry fly very carefully with a long, small diameter leader. Cast upstream and, as the fly floats back, gather line in until the fly is opposite you. At this time you can either cast again a bit farther out or allow the fly to float on below your position by feeding out the same line you just gathered in, all the while trying to keep the fly floating without any leader or line drag.

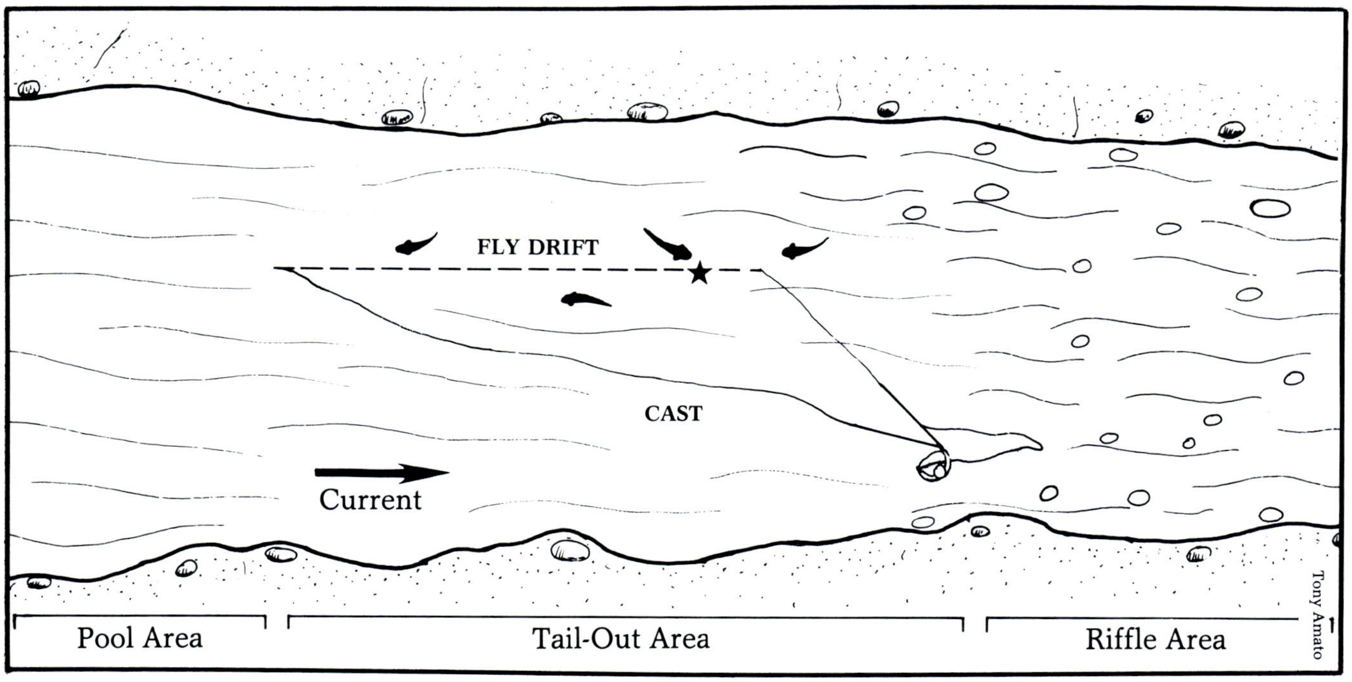

again about 40 feet above where it first plucked. Chances are better than 50 percent that it will take.

SURFACE FLY METHODS

Riffling Hitch: In some summer and fall situations a fly being worked on the surface of the water with a half-hitch around its body will move fish when other methods fail. Cast the same as you would when using the floating line/wet fly method. Then mend as soon as the fly comes tight to your line. It will pop up and start skating in and on the surface. It is very easy to visually follow the fly at this point and you can witness scenes never enjoyed by other steelheaders.

Steelhead will slash at the fly and you sometimes can see them come to it with their mouths open and partly out of the water. Don't set the hook or you will pull the fly from the fish's mouth. Wait until you feel the fish, let it run and then come back firmly. You also can leave about a foot-and-a-half of loose line between your reel and casting hand, which you can release from the fingers when a visual take is noticed, thus allowing the fish to take the fly and turn, securing the fly in the hinge of its mouth.

When tying the riffling hitch, tie the half-hitch knot off the opposite, or backside, of the fly so that it will work to your side of the river. This method works very well in some situations and, because it is visual, in that you can follow the fly, it provides some wonderful experiences.

You can use most of the standard wet steelhead fly patterns with the riffling hitch method. Fly color does not seem to make a great difference in the results. Sizes 2, 4 and 6 flies all work well.

When you are fishing riffly or tailout water that you are fairly certain holds steelhead, but they either have not moved or have refused the floating line/wet fly method, then it is time to try the riffling hitch. This method will work on summer steelhead, especially in the fall and early winter down to temperatures of 40 degrees, but only if the fish are one to four feet deep.

Dry Fly: Summer steelhead sometimes will take a true dry fly...one that is cast upstream and allowed to drift with the current. They will be more receptive to this approach in streams that have a good amount of insect surface activity. Again, you should be fairly certain that fish are present when you use the upstream dry fly, either by having just stealthily observed them or by having had consistent success in the run on previous trips.

The dry fly (suggested patterns listed at the end of this chapter) initially should be chosen on the basis of either past experience or according to the size and type of insects on the water when you are fishing. Dry fly patterns in sizes No. 6 and No. 4 generally are used. Smaller flies down to No. 12 also will work in some situations.

With the dry fly you work upstream, covering the water closest to the shore with short casts, and then working out about two feet more of line with each successive cast. Do not begin wading upstream until you are casting about 30 to 45 feet of line.

Steelhead will take the dry fly by turning and following it, sometimes for as many as 10 to 20 feet. When the fish takes your fly, do not strike immediately. Wait about a second and then lift the rod in a striking motion once you think the fish has turned back upstream, thus ensuring a solid hook-up.

For dry fly fishing the leader should be at least 10 feet long and the tippet material from 4- to 10-pound test, depending on the water clarity and whether there are shadows on the water, clouds or clear sky. The brighter the conditions, the smaller diameter the leader should be.

The rise will vary from a quiet sucking in of the fly, as a larger resident trout might do, to a splashy follow and then a very visible take, leaving one almost spellbound. An interested steelhead often will follow the fly several feet and then return to its holding spot after refusing the fly. It might do this several times. Be patient and work the fish slowly. Try changing fly sizes, shapes and colors. You might even have to rest the fish for 15 minutes or so if it fails to follow the next several casts or fly changes.To fish dry flies for summer steelhead takes an intimate knowledge of the water at hand, excellent casting ability, lots of patience and, yes, some luck!

Damp Dry Fly: Once a dry fly drifts downstream and comes tight against the line, technically it then becomes a damp dry fly. A pure dry fly floats with the river current. A damp dry fly is one that is purposely held and worked against the current and thus is downstream from your casting position. The current is pushing against this fly and occasionally it will dunk under the water's surface for a moment or two before bobbing up again.

The damp dry fly method accounts for several thousand fish each summer. I would estimate that the true upstream dry fly method accounts for at most one to two thousand fish per summer...and possibly far less. Dry fly patterns are listed at the end of this chapter. Pattern sizes vary from No. 10 to No. 2, with No. 4 and 6 being most frequently used.

The damp dry fly method is not very effective until the water warms to at least 50 degrees, although I know of fish that have been taken on this method in water as cold as 37 degrees. The damp dry fly method is best from midsummer on into early winter wherever summer steelhead are found on the west coast. It is fished in riffles and runs, as well as in tailout situations.

The fly should be thoroughly dressed with a good fly floatant to make it as water resistant as possible. The same casting and wading approach should be used as in the floating line/wet fly method. However, there are subtle differences, because the object of the damp fly method is to not only bring the fly across the water in a slow arc, but also to have it riding high on the water's surface.

In riffly water this is not always possible to do because the current sometimes will drag the fly under and, when this occurs, it sometimes is necessary to pull the line quickly and then release it, allowing slack, to let the fly pop to the surface again. Steelhead often will take the fly when it is under the surface – which is fine – but the true object of the damp fly is to bring the fish to the surface so you can see the splashy take.

When using either the riffling hitch or damp fly technique, as well as the pure upstream dry fly method, part of the angler's reward is in seeing the fly and watching its progress through the water. One very important aspect of seeing the fly is watching the effect your mending of your fly line has on the fly itself. Too severe a mend will cause the fly to jump upstream. This is not necessarily a bad thing, for fish sometimes will come charging to the fly after having been surprised by its darting movement. However, as a general rule you should bring the fly through the water smoothly on the first cast and give it some movement on the second or third casts to the same spot. This variation would be for runs where you are quite certain there are fish and which you consequently want to work very slowly.

When a steelhead takes the damp fly, don't strike. Let the fish's hurried movement and weight pull the hook tight in its jaw, mouth corner or roof of its mouth. Once you feel the weight, then strike smartly but not overhard. Fly hooks penetrate well if they are sharp and the line also is straight to the fish, so the hard strike you would make if you were drift fishing with bobber or bait, thick No. 1 to 2/0 hooks and, in addition, bellied line to contend with, is totally unnecessary and could cause you the loss of some fine fighting action.

The clearer the day, the higher the sun (until midday) and the brighter the water, the less steelhead will be inclined to take any type of surface fly. If the sun is coming straight down the river and the fish are facing into it, it is next to impossible to get a steelhead to come up to or even near the surface for the fly. I have hooked approximately 2,000 summer steelhead on the fly and cannot remember taking even one when the sun was directly upstream and shining into the fish's face. (I have taken many with drift gear or on hardware in this same situation.)

When the sun is overhead, at an angle, or to either side of the fish, then you sometimes will have action. As the sun falls behind the fish your chances improve. Now the fish has excellent sight and will be willing to dash to the surface to take the fly. The darker it gets, the more comfortable the fish becomes and the more aggressive. Cloudy summer and fall days are excellent. On sunny days, mornings until 10 a.m. and from 4 p.m. until nightfall are best. Shaded areas will produce well on sunny days.

Working a fly far off so as not to disturb the steelhead in this small, clear water stream.

OTHER FACTORS TO CONSIDER WHEN USING A FLOATING LINE AND THE WET FLY, RIFFLING HITCH, DRY FLY OR DAMP DRY FLY TECHNIQUES:

Why does a steelhead take the fly? There are several possible reasons, all related to the fish's mood and curiosity. To satisfy curiosity and test the object of its interest a fish has four senses: sight, smell, touch and hearing (or the sensing of vibrations).

A fly has virtually no smell and produces little if any sound. It is almost a purely visual item that appears to be alive in the water and substantially different from most things the fish sees, as a steelhead concentrates its eyesight near or along the bottom. When a fly swings overhead, it is very unnatural in that it appears to be alive, because it is swimming at a different rate than the current's speed. Also, it is fairly colorful. If it is alive, it probably is good to eat, and if it is not darting erratically, it probably will be easy to catch. But steelhead generally do not feed actively in fresh water. Occasionally, you will find bits of food in their stomachs, but this is the exception. So why do they strike if not driven by hunger? No one can answer this question absolutely, but here are my theories:

I think some steelhead simply are curious and take the fly in their mouth to inspect it. At other times I think they really do take the fly with the idea that it is food and they want to eat it. I think they also may take it out of annoyance, especially if it has repeatedly been put past them (this is especially true of the sunk wet fly, as we shall see later). But most of all I think they take a fly out of reflexively learned behavior, a trait learned throughout their lives, of moving quickly to take food items. A steelhead is the sum of its experiences...avoiding predators and being first in line when it comes to eating. This means moving fast; reflexive action. Just as we do some things instinctively, the steelhead does the same.

MENDING SUGGESTIONS

When mending the fly line, most of the time you will want to mend upstream to slow the swing of the surface or near-surface fly. However, there are times in slower water currents where it is best to mend downstream to pick up the speed of the fly. When using the riffling hitch or damp dry fly techniques, this forward mend, speeding up the fly's movement, sometimes will provoke a strike when the upstream mend, which slows the fly, doesn't work.

TWITCHING THE FLY

I normally let my wet fly swing in a steady manner. However, if you are certain there are fish present, and they have not responded, vary your drifts by slightly twitching the fly as it comes around. You can do this to good effect with the riffling hitch, damp dry fly and upstream dry fly as well.

TYPES OF STEELHEAD

There are basically two different types of steelhead: winter runs that come into natal streams from December until May to spawn within several weeks to a month or two of their arrival, and summer steelhead that come in from the ocean from late April until October and spawn the following spring. On the Pacific coast from central California to southern Alaska there are thousands of streams with steelhead and their life histories, migration times and average size vary greatly. Thus, to become an accomplished steelhead fly-fisherman it is necessary to learn about the variations in run timing, size, best water levels and clarity for the stream or streams you plan to fish.

One of the most helpful books is *"Steelhead Flyfishing and Flies,"* by Trey Combs. This excellent book goes into methods, fly patterns and biology like no other book. It is the basic reference. Another invaluable book for steelhead fly-fishermen is *Dry Line Steelhead*, by Bill McMillan. It also is excellent concerning techniques and understanding fish runs.

WORKING THE FLY DOWN DEEP

In colder water – below 50 degrees – more consistent success is obtained by sinking your fly down near the bottom, because the colder the water, the less steelhead are inclined to come near the surface.

Dry Line Deeply-Sunk Wet Fly: In using a dry line to fish a deeply-sunk fly (generally, steelhead will be found next to the bottom in water from two to eight feet deep), use a heavily weighted fly and a long leader of 10 or more feet with a 9-to 13-foot rod for better line control. Cast upstream at about a 45-degree angle to shore and try to mend the fly line in such a way as to release tension on the fly, allowing it to sink to within inches of the bottom. When the fly is parallel to you, feed some fly line through the guides to give slack to the fly so it will drift as long as possible near the bottom. If the water is not overly deep and swift you can obtain a good drift this way.

If the line starts tightening quickly, give it a smart strike with your rod...it could be a fish or you might just have hung up on the bottom. Make sure you check your hook point to ensure it is razor sharp after each snag. Because of the softness of the fly rod and the belly in the line it is necesary to set the hook firmly when using this technique. Much of the time steelhead will take the fly gently, so determining when to strike is difficult.

Fast-Sinking Tip with Wet Fly: There are lines now available which have been designed especially for working a fly deep for steelhead and salmon. The Teeny Nymph lines are excellent, as are certain Scientific Angler and Cortland fly lines. I would suggest that anyone interested in fishing wet flies deep for winter or summer steelhead ought to visit the nearest fly shop and ask for specific recommendations about the wet fly lines available.

Good wet lines for steelhead generally have about 60 to 80 feet of floating running line which can easily be mended for line control, in conjunction with from 10 to 25 feet of very fast sinking line which has powdered lead worked into it.

The major challenge in working a fly deep for steelhead is current movement. If not handled properly your line will be dragged by the current, thus dragging your fly through the water too quickly.

When casting a sinking tip line, use a short leader of about three or four feet maximum. The object of the sinking line is to get the fly within a foot of the bottom very quickly and to keep it there as long as possible as the current takes it downstream. The slower the water flow the easier it is to accomplish this objective. The sink-tip line normally will sink faster than the leader and fly, which is why the leader must be only four feet long or less. The sinking portions of fly lines generally are dark brown or dark green and thus normally do not spook steelhead.

When casting with the sinking line, cast upstream of your position and, as soon as the line settles on the water, mend the floating line out to the current to reduce line pull on the sinking part of the line and to allow it to sink more quickly. Sometimes a forward mend will work and other times a modified roll cast is best. The slower and the more uniform the water's flow, the easier it will be to work the fly line to allow for a deep, slow drift of the fly.

Once you have become comfortable with the fly line and casting and mending it, then the next step is to extend the fly's drift by feeding fly line that you have pulled from the reel and hold coiled in your hands. With practice you can extend the effective fish-enticing range of the fly by many feet on each cast.

Fishing the wet tip line with floating running line is much more demanding than angling with a pure floating line and is not nearly as much fun to cast. But, in many situations it is without a doubt the most efficient way to fly-fish for steelhead.

In general, from the end of October until the water warms again to over 50 degrees the following summer, you should be relying mainly on the wet tip line.

I like to use very fast-sinking wet tip lines that have from 10 to 20 feet of sinking line followed by floating line. Some fishing situations and rivers will demand longer wet tips, others shorter. That is why I suggest you contact a fly shop in your area to seek out firsthand advice concerning the stream you will be fishing and the best time of year, which dictate methods.

Flies to use when fishing deep for steelhead include almost all the patterns listed for the other types of steelhead fly-fishing except for the dry fly patterns. Dark flies will work just as well as bright flies in most cases. The important thing is the presentation...slow and deep. On waters that have been hit hard by other fishermen using everything from bait to bobbers to hardware, especially try dark patterns. There is a good chance that the fish are very jaded and will show curiosity toward an unthreatening fly that looks insect- or fish-like and is not loud and blaring like bright yarn, bobbers and hardware.

FLY PATTERN SUGGESTIONS

Dry flies for steelhead damp and dry fly-fishing can be used from Size 4 to 12. Suggested patterns: October Caddis, Steelhead Caddis, Grease Liner, Steelhead Bee, Steelhead Muddler, Wulff series dry flies, Black Irresistable.

Wet flies for steelhead for use with floating line methods such as the riffling hitch and wet fly techniques include: Brad's Brat, Fall Favorite, Skunk, Max Canyon, Purple Peril, Skykomish Sunrise, Green Butt Skunk and Juicy Bug. For winter and deep water fishing try some of these patterns: Babine Special, Black Boss, Glo Bug (various colors), Silver Comet, Polar Shrimp, Teeny Nymph (various colors), Winter's Hope, Paint Brush, Thor, and the Skunk. Also, you can use any of the wet flies listed above.

Eric Owen with wild Deschutes River summer steelhead about to be released.

Chapter 11

Boats and River Courtesy

Steelhead boats offer anglers the freedom of fishing any spot on the river regardless of thick brush and trees on the bank or a proliferation of No Trespassing signs that blocks foot traffic along the stream. It's said that, about 90 percent of the steelhead in a river generally are in 10 percent of the water. If those limited pieces of river don't happen to be reachable from roads or public accesses, boats are the answers to questions of how to get to where the fishing is best.

Many types of boats are satisfactory for steelheading on your home river and others you know well. The two most popular craft you will see are sleds and drift boats in varying sizes from 13 feet long to 18 feet, plus a few 20-foot or larger sleds. These are special craft developed on the west coast by and for fishermen. They are ideally suited for steelheading, are safe, roomy and a pleasure to use in fishing. However, many steelheaders also take to their favorite rivers in alternate choices that are adequate fishing platforms costing much less than the new price of a drift boat or sled.

I scurry around on my pet stream in a 10-foot fiberglass cartopper that is wide and stable, but I fish in it mostly alone (I'll take no more than one lightweight angler with me) and I never attempt to anchor. A 10-horsepower outboard planes this boat just fine with a little starting run and I can tackle some excellent holes that not only are far apart but are virtually untouchable by bank anglers.

Other anglers do well with similar cartoppers, trailered boats that range between 12- and 16-foot hulls, medium to large rubber rafts/boats (there's a difference) and a few intrepid anglers occasionally fish from canoes or kayaks. All of these craft can be used to pursue steelhead but you must be aware that prams, canoes, rafts and skinny cartoppers are easily upset and, being light in weight, also have a tendency to slide out from under you if you try to stand to fish. In addition, they all share one common problem which you normally can overlook on still water but not on rivers, all of which have tremendous hydraulic force although they may seem deceptively gentle.

Almost every one of these small boats has an anchor loop or eyebolt at the front, outside the boat, about a foot down the keel. They are, in my opinion, unsafe to use in the best steelhead boat position...anchored on the edge of a good run of current. Imagine if you will what can happen when the anchor gets hung on bottom and the strongest, biggest member of the fishing party gets right up in the nose of the boat to pull that sucker loose...the prow dips, water pressure catches inside the front, and you crash dive swiftly, borne down by the current!

My recommendations for small boat steelheaders are, that you know your river well before you put your boat in it and, instead of anchoring, either beach the boat and fish the honey hole from the bank or make several floats over the sweet spot and repeatedly cast to or boondog the best water. Walk a pram, cartopper or canoe around the tough spots, use a guide rope to line it down to safer water, or drag/carry it around the rough stuff. Every boat fisherman, and especially each occupant of a cartopper, rubber raft, canoe or kayak, should wear a U.S. Coast Guard-approved flotation device at all times.

JET SLEDS:

Sled is the term given to a long, low, flat-bottomed type of fishing boat that has a rakish upsweep at the prow and is both oared and powered by an outboard (sometimes inboard/outboard) motor ranging from 35 to 150 or more horsepower. Modern sleds range from

13 to 22 feet long and most of them now are made of aluminum, but you still may see older plywood sleds working the drifts on many rivers. These innovative craft are controlled while drifting from the middle of the boat with 9- to 12-foot oars. Heavy anchors are suspended at the prow by means of a bracket plate having a pulley wheel and rope arrangement that permits hand-hoisting the anchor in most sleds, cranking a hand winch from the rowing position in some or, in a few instances, powering the anchor up with a small electric winch. One or more seat top serves as a lid for a fish box or tackle storage area and there quite often may be a watertight, lockable front storage compartment for cameras, raingear, engine tool kit, extra flotation cushions and lunches.

Sleds can fish up to five anglers in comfort, speed them to the best angling spots upstream or downstream several miles from the launching point and, once limits have been taken or, in case of emergency need, can zip back to the ramp in minutes. They are shallow draft craft that seemingly can run on wet gravel under the guidance of an expert operator.

Outboard motors are by far the top choice of sled boat owners and all but a few sleds are designed to accept these motors on the transom. A few sleds, however, mount the outboards inside, in a well several feet from the rear of the boat, and other fishermen (generally owners of larger, 18- to 20-foot sleds) operate with inboard/outboard motors that take up the same space.

Rocky, snag-laden rivers of the west coast have spawned use of an attachment called a jet pump that replaces a standard outboard motor's lower housing and propeller. Most sleds you see on our western rivers have pump drives. The jet pump unit projects slightly below the boat's bottom and provides forward and reverse drive by means of a shiftable gate that controls the directional flow of the expelled water. There are sacrifices of neutral gear and of power (about 27 percent) involved in the changeover from propeller to pump, but these are more than offset by the ability to go almost anywhere there is a thread of water.

Jet boats skim and bounce over rocks, logs and gravel bars that would quickly eat a prop's shear pin at the least or possibly damage propeller blades or lower drive unit. Skilled river jockeys have been known to approach a scarcely-wet clay, sand or gravel bar, slack speed just enough to roll a wall of water over the bar and by pouring on the coal ride their own wake into otherwise inaccessible steelheading water.

Jet sled owners often use a small trolling motor – either gas or electric – to fish with, particularly when hotshotting plugs.

Bill Herzog displays a fresh steelhead taken with a plug from a drift boat.

DRIFT BOATS:

Rowing dories and skiffs have long been in use on both of the American continent's coasts, in rivers as well as on salt water. Pictures of east coast Grand Bank fishing in the 1700s and 1800s show dories that appear to be the models from which west coast fishermen adapted the particular styles of drift boats known as MacKenzie and Rogue River models. Resembling a banana sliced lengthwise, flat-bottomed, stable, deep and wide, today's western drift boats are as agile as waterbugs on our steelhead streams. Many have fish boxes under the rower's seat or at the rear. The high prow is an excellent location for lunches, spare gear and rainwear, and many drift boats have a watertight, lockable compartment there.

Most drift boats measure 12 to 17 feet long. Fiberglass drift boats are the most common, followed by wood, then aluminum, however, this order varies from area to area. Sharp at the prow and nearly so at the stern, these shallow-draft craft are held from proceeding downstream, rather than rowed down, by oarsmen facing downcurrent and stroking Viking-like blades 9 to 14 feet long. Oared prow first, or held by an anchor lowered from the stern, drift boats will pause at productive or likely runs and holes to sample in each the steelheading possibilities between morning launch point and afternoon take-out on their one-way trip downriver, or can be beached at good holes that merit serious, long-time casting.

Some few drift boats have widened sterns or motor wells that allow outboard motors to be used for upstream transportation. At best a compromise, the motor well version occupies a large area of interior space and adds balky weight to the rower's task. Drift boats designed to operate with outboards on their sterns present some operators with "good news, bad news" choices... to power with a motor that will dependably "chug" upstream at a slow but safe and comfortable pace or to hang enough horses back there to scream upstream like a jet sled.

The second choice might be a very risky option because of the drift boat's width and curvature of its bottom, and the fact it will be running on only a third of its length. This hikes the front of the drift boat high in the air, so that the high-powered outboard operator can hardly see around the boat to avoid rocks and floating debris. In addition, with the nose of a planing drift boat high out of the water, it could be prey to gusts of wind and current changes that would suddenly turn the banana into a turtle! (Sure, it's obvious this would be dangerous but I have seen these "accidents on their way" standing on their tails on upstream runs!)

Sliding seats allow the oarsman or guide to better balance his boat. Generally, the two passengers standing or sitting up front and facing downstream are the only ones fishing while in motion, although the rower may trail a boondogging line. In some areas, steelheaders use heavy drag chains instead of an an-

An early native summer-run steelhead.

chor, to slow their float and hold the boat correctly pointed downstream while all aboard fish. Drift boat anchors are lowered from the rowing position via a rope and pulley that drops 10- to 35-pound anchors from a bracket on the stern of a drift boat. The rope is caught in a V-lock or by a movable eccentric cam to hold the desired anchor length. It's a common practice to anchor up at the head of a productive hole or drift, fish that area, then pull the anchor and drift downstream 30 to 50 feet, dropping anchor again to fish out the next stretch, and so on...

Jet sled and drift boat operators alike should know the water they will encounter before embarking on their first river run down a new stream. The peaceful flow you see from the highway may turn into rampaging rapids in another half-mile. Fish the river first with a guide or with a friend who will point out the problem areas and dangers to avoid. If you are uncertain about how to run through a particular corner or boulder bed, beach the boat and walk down to the area and give the water and your possible course careful consideration. You will find boat operation on western rivers safer, and save a lot of hard and fast rowing, if you continually observe, and attempt to remember, landmarks to spot where deadheads and snags lurk, ragged boulders rise near the surface and eddying currents lie in wait to jerk you around.

In addition to their use as transportation from hole to hole, as anchored platforms from which to fish middle and far sides of the river and as the means to fish stream stretches not accessible to bank anglers, jet sleds and drift boats permit boating steelheaders to enjoy two methods of fishing difficult to perform from the bank. These are *hotshotting* and *boondogging*.

Hotshotting got its name from steelheaders who dubbed the practice of backtrolling, or pulling plugs, after the original Eddie Pope Hot Shot plug (now made by Luhr Jensen), the lure that scored phenomenal catches of steelhead and other fish when the method was first devised. Guides depend on hotshotting to produce steelhead when the fishing gets tough and for beginning anglers, and most private boaters carry with them at least a small number of plugs to permit varying their fishing approaches. Steelhead appear to be irritated or infuriated by a plug dancing in front of their noses and often will savagely attack this diving, bright-colored, wobbling invader of their territory. Many other plugs (see chapter on plugs) beside the Hot Shot also are effective lures for steelhead, but the generic term has clung to the method.

The hotshotting system is relatively simple. Drift boat or sled fishermen pay out 30 to 60 feet of 12- to 20-pound test line bearing plugs, and snug down the line drag on their reels to a point where striking steelhead can take line, albeit grudgingly. Their rods are stuck in rodholders or propped inside the boat and only picked up after a thumping, jarring strike. Starting at the head of a run, drift or hole, the boat is oared or powered so that it works slowly from side to side of the fishable water and then is allowed to slip downstream a foot or two and the side-to-side maneuver continued. Nearly all of the fish-holding water can be probed with the plugs and, if there's any steelhead in the river, the hotshotting method generally is very successful at causing them to hit the lures.

Boondogging draws its name from a walk or hunt through the "boonies" with the family dog trailing behind, sniffing at all the interesting cover. Steelheaders practicing this system will do best by keeping their boat crosswise to the river current while trailing bait/bobber drift rigs as they drift downstream. Here, jet sleds have an advantage over drift boats, since they are able to quickly run back upstream to boondog again through a stretch delivering fish or strikes that were missed. Sinker leads used in boondogging are cut to a length and weight sufficient to keep the upstream lures/baits following directly behind the boat, providing instant striking capability. Rods normally are kept in hand by the anglers so they can be best attuned to the riverbed rhythm of their terminal tackle.

Boondogging is an excellent fishing method often chosen by drift boat steelheaders who want to make good time over the last few miles of river but still be fishing, or for sled boat anglers who find biting fish in a long drift that can be tackled several times through use of their motors. Cartop craft also are fine choices for boondogging and can provide memorable experiences for a single angler. Often, when fishing alone, I have had excellent luck and enjoyable fishing by hooking a striking steelhead, then tucking the rod between my knees while oaring, or keeping light reel tension on the fish while motoring to a gravel bar or beach and playing out the steelhead from the shore. Netting a steelhead from a boat alone, or when you tie into a real hummer of a fish can be – as the old Chinese saying puts it – "very interesting!"

STEELHEAD GUIDES

One of the best investments a beginning steelheader or angler visiting an unfamiliar river can make is a day or weekend trip with a steelhead guide. Guides are on the water day after day and are aware of the best fishing holes and drifts, the time of day steelhead become active biters in these spots, kind of bait or color of lure the fish take best and where you should be standing or anchored to put your hook on the steelhead's nose.

Many big west coast rivers have nearby guide services and both winter and summer trips can be arranged. Check with your area fish/wildlife agency to obtain a list of guide associations, and talk to friends who have taken trips with specific guides, in order to assess their equipment, experience and success. Guides generally have a favored method of fishing, but will arrange to fish almost any other way if you set it up with them prior to the trip. For instance, some guides will cheerfully plan fly-fishing-only trips, while others make a standard practice out of supplying all the fishing tackle and baits needed to dredge bottom for steelhead in bait-fishing style.

Be sure to reach an understanding with any guide you contact as to costs, number of fishermen in the day's party, what he will be furnishing and what you are expected to bring. (I've had some bacon, toast and egg breakfasts on gravel bars and I've heard of at least one steak/champagne deluxe trip!) You might possibly have a choice – with the same guide – of taking either a drift boat or sled trip, as some guides have both options. When the fishing's at its peak, or if the weather is dour and gloomy, a sled trip would be my top pick. If good weather prevails and the forecast is balmy, a guided drift boat trip can be a grand day's adventure, as well as a learning experience.

You'll be responsible for bringing your raingear and any cold weather clothing needed, all the accessories needed for your style of fishing, generally your lunch and refreshments (and cameras if you want a record of the river journey). The guide will take care of all boat needs, landing net, fish whacker and cleaning knife. He may clean your fish for you, might pack along a big coffee jug or cooler of canned liquids and may furnish the bait, depending on the local practice and his individual habit.

Besides paying close attention to what and how the guide rigs to fish, and the manner in which he suggests you fish it, it will reward you to study the water he chooses to fish. Ask him why he works over one spot longer and more seriously than another...what makes it a better steelhead lie? Most guides are such dedicated anglers themselves that they'd be on the water fishing if they were not there earning an income from their service. As such, I've never run into one who wouldn't share information and knowhow with his passengers, and most guides gladly use their experience to tutor their clients on the stream conditions, fish habits, and their views on presentation, all of which affect steelheading success, as part of their function. Very few guides can or will guarantee you will catch fish on a trip with them, but they try very hard to hook you into steelhead. Guides generally are a gregarious, helpful, open breed of sportsmen with whom it can be a pleasure to fish.

RIVER COURTESY:

River courtesy is an essential part of today's crowded steelheading conditions. There are 50 anglers now to every single bank fisherman of 35 years ago and 25 boats ply a stretch where two may have rowed in yesteryear seeking steelhead. Many new steelheaders are youngsters or wives, with families of up to three generations taking a common interest in fishing together. Their steelheading forays, regardless of catch success, can be rewarding outdoor experiences. In order for each of us to best enjoy sport fishing for this grand gamefish and to allow others to achieve equal satisfaction from their recreational angling, a code of ethics has evolved within the steelheading fraternity.

Regulations cannot be written to enforce steelheading ethics. They have to come from inside a true sportsman. The code does exist, however, and reaches from lone anglers to gravel bars loaded elbow-to-elbow with steelheaders. It also is shared and stressed within clubs, groups and families of anglers. Ethics are an amalgam of good sportsmanship that encompasses fair pursuit of steelhead through following written regulations, fish limits, lawful gear and any local or posted rules, extend to honoring the rights of other fishermen and river users to a share of not only the bank or river stretch but the time for fishing the good water, and most of all include respect and consideration for individual steelhead, the species, and the habitat in which it dwells.

River courtesy also is based on common sense, practicality and tradition. It creates pleasurable comraderie on the river and a mindbank full of treasured remembrances. Sharing a cup of coffee and the latest fishing information on the river bank with friends and fellow anglers, helping to net or beach a steelhead, coaching a beginner or stream newcomer, exchanging catch reports from boat to bank and drawing richly from the outdoor experience can, like Clint Eastwood puts it, *"Make my day."* Lack of river courtesy, on the other hand, can quite easily spoil an otherwise-beatific day despite your catch success, and could be hazardous to your health.

Let's look at some of the precepts which ethical, courteous steelheaders honor, some of the basics that promulgated them and a few illustrations whose merits you may judge for yourselves. For my own fishing I've condensed them to three easy-to-observe concepts with which I am totally comfortable.

1. Fish legally.

Regulations and fishing laws are for the protection of the resource and to provide equal opportunities for everyone to participate in recreational fishing. Just as you would want every other fisherman to allow you to enjoy the best that sport fishing offers, give them the same chances by respecting the rules that preserve the fish and fishing.

2. Share the water fairly.

Start at the head of a hole or drift and work toward the tail. Why? Especially, if steelhead cannot see for about 20 degrees to either side behind them, why would you take a position above them? It is because there is less chance of spooking them with your line or bait/lure passing over them before it is properly presented on the bottom, as well as being far easier to trick them into taking your hook if the lure comes downstream ahead of the line and rigging. A fisherman approaching an unoccupied run may of course angle any part of the water he chooses, but if other anglers are working the run, he should wait his turn at the water in the run's head...and it helps gain acceptance into the rotation if he politely asks the top couple fishermen, "Mind if I get in here and follow you down?" Do not wade into the water just above or below another angler. He may be fishing short to a steelhead you might spook by stomping into its lie area. Look to see where others' lines are cast and drifted and try not to cross their lines so that you create a tangle. Long-lining from the head of a drift clear to the tail can produce a lot more than steelhead strikes if there are half a dozen anglers below you who also would like to fish where you are hogging the water. (It's always a good idea to start your own fishing close to the bank, there just may be a steelhead hanging right at your boot toes in the nearby water.)

Fishing licenses, boat permits and guide licenses do not mean you own any chunk of watery real estate unless it's specifically deeded in your name. On the bank, take your turn, move on to let another come behind you, and take care to fish with the same tempo and tackle as that used by others on that stretch (to prevent tangles of line and tempers). If in a boat, pull your fishing gear out of the water while passing bank anglers, go behind them if it is possible, or as far from them as they might conceivably cast. Leave them undisturbed in the tiny fraction of the river you don't need with all the rest of the river to fish. This simple courtesy may save hard words, rock-throwing incidents and physical damage to your towing vehicle and trailer, while winning friends among bankies who can be sources of information or future passengers.

The courtesy of drift boats leaving water for bank anglers to fish and sleds yielding to drift boats is out of consideration for the mobility of each. Bank anglers have only the immediate water in front of them to angle, drift boaters can tap all the river between Point A to Point B downstream, and sleds can run up and down at will to any productive spots.

3. Treat the river as you would your living room.

If every steelheader were equally as mindful of his actions and language in Nature's living room as in his own all of our stream banks would be beautiful, clean, totally enjoyable places to visit.

You'd probably appreciate very much more having your nine-year-old offspring or your fishing companion wife learn that a steelhead that just threw the hook was a lucky lunker! rather than a effing S.O.B! or much worse, delivered in stentorian splendor sufficient to carry 200 yards up and down the river. It is vital we involve our children and families in steelheading for tomorrow's support of wild fish and hatchery programs to ensure the future of recreational fishing. Repeat trips get harder to arrange after their ears have been trashed by such barrages. In addition, private property now accessible to fishermen might be closed by owners sensitive to earthy education of their youngsters and guests.

Trash should never be littered on the banks and in the river. We're a plastic age people, it's true, but the plastic we leave behind will outlive us all because it is less biodegradable than we are. Bags, six-pack carrier rings, monofilament, empty lure packages and abandoned bait containers are not only eyesores but dangerous to many forms of wildlife that might ingest parts of them or become entangled and trapped, losing their lives by slow starvation or succumbing to predators in their helplessness. A can or bottle carried to a fishing hole weighs a lot less to pack out when it's emptied, so if you don't make it a practice to stuff it in the cushions of your living room sofa, don't jam your dead soldier between rocks or toss it in the bushes.

Treat a captured steelhead with respect for its beauty, battle and rareness. Free or retain it with due care. Proper handling will increase its chances of survival if released and its quality on the dinner table if your catch is kept.

River courtesy is that simple...obeying regulations, fairly sharing the water, respect and consideration for others and for steelhead and the habitat.

January day on the East Fork Lewis River, Washington.

Chapter 12

Field Care, Cleaning and Cooking Steelhead

West coast steelhead are, in my estimation, magnificent fish in appearance, battling ability and as tablefare. Newly-arrived from the Pacific Ocean, their gun-metal backs and alabaster bellies have a glistening, saltwater sheen that sparkles in the daylight. When only a few days from salt water, the lines between backs and chromium sides seem as though etched by an engraving tool. Whether fat as footballs, long, deep and strong hens, or male fish with shoulders, prime, bright steelhead have power and energy you have to hook into to believe! I admire all gamefish, sometimes for different reasons than appearance, but these torpedos with tigers in their tanks get my "10" rating for beauty as well as brawling ability and are my favorite species to catch and...yes, to eat.

Anglers who fish with me, and with whom I will fish more than once, handle captured steelhead with care, humanely dispatch fish that are slated to be on their dinner menu, observe all fishing regulations and respect the need to release wild steelhead (having no fin clip at all) to build up gene pools of this hardy coastal breed. There are some acrobatically inclined, hard-charging hatchery fish, too, that because of their seemingly desirable traits of pugnacity and sheer defiance I feel should be released to fight again another day.

The first thing I believe a sportfisherman should do when bringing in a steelhead is to look around him to see where the steelhead might be landed with the least damage to its scales and the protective coating on its skin...its defense against viruses and infections. I suggest the second thing a steelheader do when playing a good fish is to determine: To keep or release? Then, once the steelhead is brought close enough to check it in the water for any missing, clipped fins, the fish should be played to a finish as soon as possible.

If you are going to release a steelhead the sooner you do so the better chance of survival it will have. A hard battle creates a build-up of *adrenalin,* one of its body chemicals, which can cause asphyxiation of the steelhead after release if the struggle is overlong. Second, the hooked steelhead will emit *pheromones,* which chemically scream DANGER! to every other downstream fish. Play one for a long while and you may not catch another fish from that run or hole. Third, the heightened chemical levels brought about by the struggle might detract from the flavor of a fish retained for the table.

Bring the steelhead to you as quickly as it is willing to come quietly and, if it is to be freed, grasp the hook firmly with a needle-nose pliers or surgeon's forceps and reverse it with a short, firm shake. Your leader also can be cut, burned through with a cigarette's glowing tip, or snapped to let the fish swim free...hooks other than stainless steel soon will be rubbed out or, acted upon by the acidity of the fish's mouth, will erode away. A spent, tired steelhead should be held gently, with your hands under chin and belly, and rocked back and forth slowly in the water until its gill action can be jump started and it can swim under its own power.

A fish to be kept for kitchen use will taste much better if it is dispatched immediately upon removal from the river and bled by cutting one or two gill arches. After a merciful thwack of your pacifier across its ears has stilled the fish, insert the tip of a knife into the gills and draw it through. Its muscles will clench enough times to pump out most of the blood that can spoil its meat for delicious eating.

Fermentation of a steelhead's body juices – especially the gills, blood and innards – will start within an hour of its death, and sooner if the weather is hot. If you can do so, remove the gills and internal organs within 10 or 15 minutes after landing a steelhead and you'll wind up with much better-tasting meals. Use the tip of a sharp knife to cut just through the belly skin – being careful not to slice into any egg skeins – from the anus to the pectoral fins, do a Y at the pectorals (who wants to eat fins?), then slice the skin shield between the lower jaw and gill plate along the pale lower gum line you will find. Clip the gills at the roof of the mouth, grasp the jaw shield and gills and pull firmly toward the tail. Gills, pectorals and yuckies all should peel out at once. Immediately and carefully separate the egg skeins from the other organs and set them aside. (This is where the small plastic bags come in handy for packing egg skeins separately from the fish, and they and the fish are best kept on ice in a cooler.)

There's a soft, broad band of blood-filled kidney tissue against the backbone and under a thin sheath of intestine that should be removed next. Take the front edge of this sheath between thumb and forefinger at the head end and pull the sheath from front to rear. Next, split the kidney's thin cover with your knife tip. You can press a thumbnail into the body cavity at the rear and run it forward smoothly to remove most of this kidney tissue...it will require two strips, one on either side of the backbone. Some sheath knives favored by steelheaders come equipped with a spoon projecting rearward from the hilt and are ideal for this job.

Wash the inside and outside of the fish to remove blood and grime, and keep it as cool as possible until you get it home. A cooler with bagged ice works very well, or a double plastic bag arrangement with ice in one bag and the fish on top of that in another bag so that your fish cannot lie in any water. (Do not use a plastic bag without ice, as it will function like a small bake oven to speed up the fermentation process.) If you have no cooler or ice with you, the next best thing is to keep the fish in the shade or dig a trough in gravel or dirt, wrap the steelhead in cloth, and cover it over so the sun can't warm it. A last resort is to hang the fish in a tree where it is exposed to a cooling breeze, or even if the breeze is warm, air current will remove surface moisture and leave a glazed finish on the meat (in winter, this is the easiest way to keep steelhead fresh and, depending on the temperature, near-frozen).

Beginning of Vancouver Island wilderness steelhead stream.

When you reach home with your field-dressed steelhead there are only a few cleaning chores left. Wash and scrape all blood, bits of kidney tissue, gills, and intestinal skin from your catch. Use the tip of a sharp knife to twist into the last few pockets in the spinal column near the tail...they always seem to have a few bits of kidney tissue or blood clots in them. Many steelheaders prefer to scrub or scrape the mucous coating from the steelhead's skin to reduce the chance of it flavoring the meat. Scraping can be done with the edge of a dull knife held at 90 degrees to the skin, pressing slightly as you scrape from head toward tail. A stiff brush kept for this use also is worked from head toward tail to scour the slime coat off. Both operations are best done under gently running water.

Determine whether you are going to leave the head on or not, as is best in baking, or if the steelhead is to be filleted, cut into rib steaks, chunks for your smoker, broiler or boiler, for pickling, poaching, frying, or strips to be breaded and deep-fat fried. Cutting works best for me on an old, large breadboard.

If the whole fish is to be baked, double-bag it and store it in your freezer until ready to use it. For fillets, I find it easiest to place the fish on one side, then insert a sharp, long knife through the fish from anus point to back, making sure the knife blade faces tailward and rides over the backbone. Slice to the rear, but stop your blade short of coming out the skin at the tail (unless you plan to barbecue, in which case you want to leave the skin on, so cut the fillet clear through at the tail). Then bring the blade back and reverse the edge so that you can cut forward to the head, using the head as a handle to hold and turn the fish.

Cut through the ribs and then upward through the skin when you reach the head. Flop the steelhead over on the other side and repeat the process. To best remove the skin, grasp the steelhead by the tail, lay one fillet skin-side down on the cutting board, and insert your knife blade between the skin and flesh on the down side. Use a shallow angle, and press lightly toward the cutting board as you smoothly push the knife away from you and toward the front of the fillet, while pulling slightly on the tail. Turn the fish and strip the skin from the second fillet, then discard the stripped skeleton and skin and wash the two fillets.

For rib steaks, position a headless, unskinned steelhead upright on your cutting board, with belly flaps outspread. Cut ½-inch to ¾-inch vertical slabs, with knife blade between the ribs, from the front of the fish to the dorsal fin. This will give you five to nine fish steaks, while the section left, dorsal to tail, makes an excellent roast.

For deep-fat fried, or pickled steelhead, filleted and skinned meat is sliced into pieces a bit larger than your thumb, taking care to remove as many bones as possible while doing so. Place in freezer bags a sufficient quantity of deep-fry chunks for one family meal and store these away in your deep-freeze. Do any pickling immediately after cleaning fish, while the steelhead meat still is fresh.

BROILED STEELHEAD: One of the easiest and most delicious ways of preparing steelhead is to broil it, either as fillets with skin left on, or as steelhead steaks. Pat the steelhead meat dry with a paper towel, then place on a buttered broiling pan, sprinkle with lemon pepper or lemon juice, dust the meat with parsley bits and tarragon and they're ready to pop into a pre-heated broiler. Fillets with skins on are not turned and take about eight minutes to cook. Baste once or twice with melted butter. Steaks are cooked 3-4 minutes on each side, and basted with butter after being turned. Serve piping hot with your choice of fish sauce or dressing. G-o-o-d!

BARBECUED STEELHEAD: Fillets or steaks can be gourmet delights when properly barbecued. Light your grill and prepare an aluminum foil tray to keep the juices from dripping into the hot coals. Prepare a sauce of 2 1/2 tablespoons vegetable oil, 2 1/2 tablespoons brown sugar, 8 to 10 ounces of cheese-tomato sauce, 1 lemon squeezed into sauce pan, 1/4 teaspoon dry mustard, dollop of Worcestershire sauce, and 1/2 teaspoon oregano and let this mix simmer for about 7-9 minutes. Have on hand some grated Cheddar cheese, chopped parsley and sesame seeds. Brush on the sauce mix, sprinkle on the sesame seeds, and cook for 12 minutes, basting two to three times with the sauce. Sprinkle or spread the grated cheese on the fish and continue cooking another 5-8 minutes without further basting. Put the parsley in with the sauce mix and place fish and sauce on the table together. Dig in!

BOILED STEELHEAD: Skinned fillets or chunked steelhead make superb meals easily and quickly prepared. All you need is to add a cup of tablesalt to 6-7 quarts of water in a large cooking pot and bring the water to a boil. Fold the steelhead into a ball shape in cheesecloth or dishtowel, tie a stout cord at the top of the wrapped bundle and lower it into the boiling water. Clap on the lid and boil for about 50 minutes. Spread lemon slices, celery and carrot sticks around the fish on a large platter, set out your own or a commercial fish sauce, favorite white wine and French bread or bread sticks, and you've a meal fit for a king.

DEEP-FAT DELIGHT: You can debate the merits of fat-fried steelhead cooked in a shallow pan versus the deep fryer as much as you want...just call me in to judge the results! This is my favorite way to indulge in the rewards of my catch. There are wide choices of fish batters on the market and every cookbook will provide recipes for egg/milk mixes to enhance the fish flavor. I like 'em all, but am especially partial to a beer batter devised by my Ontario, Canada fishing buddy Robert Dias and I've never tasted better.

Heat your cooking oil, dip the steelhead chunks into your chosen batter, drop them into the fryer for about 4-5 minutes, then pluck them out to sit on paper toweling and drain until cool enough to eat...nothing could be simpler or taste better. If you use king-size toothpicks to spear them from a shallow fryer, have a choice of hot and plain fish sauces in which to dip them, and a bowl of pineapple chunks, melon chunks and sliced and diced apples nearby for dessert. Scrumptious!

CHERIE'S PICKLED STEELHEAD: Here's a recipe for pickling steelhead or salmon that's well known along the Columbia River. It was taught by longtime Stevenson resident and fisherman Stan Szydlo to his daughter-in-law, my angling partner's wife. Fillet your fish, leaving the skin on, and layer them in a large stone, porcelain or glass crock, skin side down. Sprinkle each layer very lightly with sugar, then cover the layer with rock salt. Place the top layer skin side up in the crock and cover generously with rock salt. Cover the crock with a clean cloth and weight the fish layers down with a clean brick or rock on a dish (do not use a metal weight). After at least 30 days, take fish fillets out and soak them overnight in cold water, cutting fillets into bite-size chunks.

Prepare a brine mixture of 1 cup vinegar, 1 cup water, 3 teaspoons pickling spices per quart. Slice onions to add to brine. Pack the fish in clean jars and add cold brine. Layer the fish and sliced onions. Store jars in refrigerator and use within four months.

SMOKING STEELHEAD: Cut steelhead fillets (skins on) into as many pieces as you can get three to five inches wide and long. A brine mixture of one cup of barrel salt (not tablesalt) to one quart of water is a good measure commonly used to flavor smoked steelhead, but some anglers also have brown sugar or molasses formulas that produce smoked steelhead to their individual taste. Immerse the chunks of fish for 8-12 hours, then pluck them out and rinse clean of brine, spread the pieces to dry where they will not be in contact with each other, and give them an hour, while cranking up your smoker.

One key to achieving well-smoked fish is to allow plenty of air space between pieces of fish on each smoker shelf so that your heat and smoke can spread and penetrate all pieces evenly. Use alder, hickory, apple or maple wood chips, or a mixture of these, for best results. Smoking should take about five hours, but you may want to check on the heat level and current results about every hour. Smoked fish can be kept in a refrigerator below 38 degrees for a week or two, or can be frozen in airtight cold storage bags and kept for a couple months. Done properly, smoked steelhead has a distinctive flavor that needs no sauces or added flavoring when eaten. It can be eaten as is or warmed to serving temperature in a microwave.

Rogue River, Oregon wood drift boat about 1939.

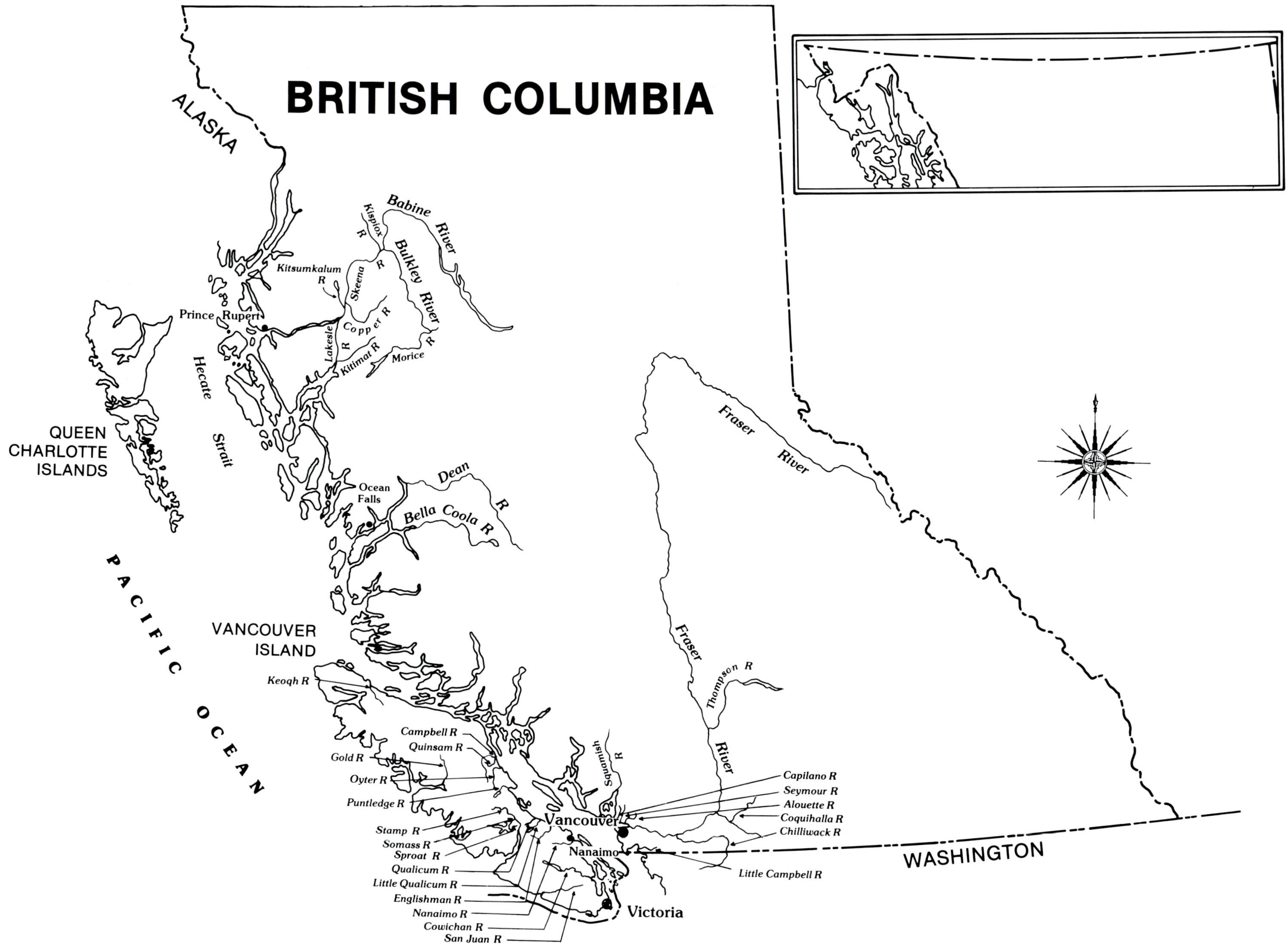
BRITISH COLUMBIA
ALASKA
Babine River
Kispiox R
Bulkley River
Kitsumkalum R
Skeena R
Copper R
Lakesle R
Kitimat R
Morice R
Prince Rupert
Hecate Strait
QUEEN CHARLOTTE ISLANDS
Ocean Falls
Dean R
Bella Coola R
Fraser River
PACIFIC OCEAN
VANCOUVER ISLAND
Keogh R
Fraser
Thompson R
River
Squamish R
Campbell R
Quinsam R
Gold R
Oyter R
Puntledge R
Stamp R
Somass R
Sproat R
Qualicum R
Little Qualicum R
Englishman R
Nanaimo R
Cowichan R
San Juan R
Vancouver
Nanaimo
Victoria
Capilano R
Seymour R
Alouette R
Coquihalla R
Chilliwack R
Little Campbell R
WASHINGTON

Chapter 13

British Columbia

Scarcely enough adjectives exist in the English language to appropriately describe the wealth of outdoor grandeur in the Canadian province of British Columbia – awesomely lofty mountains, plunging canyons, beautiful sun-swept ocean beaches and singing rivers – but the "Super Natural" appellation on all provincial literature comes close.

British Columbia is BIG...its 952,000 square kilometers, for comparison, is more land than possessed by any U.S. state except Alaska. A rough translation of size is 366,266 square miles, containing rain forests and contrasting sun belts, six distinct mountain ranges covered with Western red cedar, Balsam and Douglas fir and hemlock, nearly 17,000 miles of saltwater coast- line and perhaps 200,000-250,000 kilometers of fishable rivers, over 20,000 kilometers of which (more than 200 streams) hold steelhead. Few B.C. streams have large populations of steelhead, however, because they may be low in nutrients, cold, or have waterfalls near the sea.

British Columbia has produced steelhead among the largest on the Pacific coast. While many streams hold only 4 to 9-pound fish, some consistently yield such huge wallhangers that anglers can legitimately hope a new world record steelhead may come from B.C. waters. Giant rainbow trout are much more than myths in British Columbia. The record Gerrard rainbow trout (strain of Kamloops and a cousin to the steelhead) is a 52-pounder that was taken from Jewel Lake. Californian Karl Mausser still holds the flyrod record of 33 pounds for a 1962 Kispiox River steelhead and the 1952 rod-and-reel Kispiox River steelhead catch of a 36-pounder by Chuck Ewart is the official record.

However, on Sept. 12, 1976, a cock (male) steelhead weighing 37 pounds, 8 ounces was reported caught from the Babine River by millworker Ted Lowley, witnessed by a local conservation agent and the catch was noted in veteran steelhead fisherman and observer Lee Straight's Vancouver newspaper column. Topping all other unverified entries is the 1968 mention in OUTDOOR LIFE by legendary angler Joe Brooks of a giant steelhead taken in a net by Babine Indians...a fish weighing 47 1/2 pounds!

If you'll accept hearsay, other British Columbia steelhead larger than the official record supposedly have been caught. Bob Hooton, Anadromous Fishery Biologist in the Babine-Kispiox-Skeena area, told us, "Yes, we are aware of steelhead larger than 36 pounds that have been caught and released, or netted in Indian fisheries and, in one instance, a 37½-pounder illegally taken during closed season by a rod and reel fisherman."

British Columbia steelheading is managed by the Wildlife Branch of the province's Ministry of Environment, Lands and Parks, Parliament Buildings, Victoria, B.C. V8V 1X4. Anglers, both resident and non-resident, 16 years of age or older must have a current year, basic angling license to fish non-tidal waters. Residents over 16 years old pay $10 for a 6-day license and $17 for an annual license. Citizens of other Canadian provinces pay fees of $8 for 6-day and $16 for annual licenses, plus a $5 surcharge on each. Non-residents are charged $28 for an annual fishing license or may opt for a 6-day license at $16. A surcharge of $5 is used to support the Habitat Conservation Fund.

In addition, steelhead permits allowing a harvest of hatchery steelhead or the rare chance to claim a wild fish must be purchased at $7 for residents and $17 for other Canadians or $42 for non-residents of Canada. A "Classified Waters License" is required (see fee schedule) for anglers on many of the province's productive, wild and picturesque streams heavily impacted by fishing pressure. The number of anglers allowed to fish them is limited, to preserve wilderness character and ensure survival of large, trophy quality steelhead.

Wild steelhead caught from British Columbia waters generally must be released, under specific river regulations that may allow only hatchery fish to be legally retained. Any rainbow trout greater than 50 cm (20 inches) in length, nose to tail fork, in waters where anadromous 'bows are found is considered to be a steelhead. Many sportsmen voluntarily choose to release legal wild fish and hatchery fish (having a healed scar marking a missing adipose fin) as well. In some cases (see regulations) single barbless hooks, bait bans and no-boat restrictions must be observed, so it is essential each angler read and comprehend the most recent "British Columbia Freshwater Regulations Synopsis" available free from the B.C. Environment offices.

Steelheading success runs high in British Columbia, which accounts for visiting anglers comprising 10 to 12 percent of the total number of licensed steelheaders. Summer-run steelhead are best taken from June through October and winter fish, the more numerous, generally appear in catches from mid-November through March. In the 1983-84 season, 98,622 fish were caught by 20,576 anglers; in the 1984-85 season 23,336 fishermen caught 147,838 steelhead and in 1985-86, 145,344 steelhead were caught by 25,619 rodsmen. All but yearly averages of 13 to 15 percent of the wild fish and 25 to 43 percent of hatchery steelhead caught were released, either according to regulations or anglers' personal wishes, as indicated by annual steelhead harvest analyses (which were conducted by telephone survey after each season) compiled by Susan J. Billings of the Fisheries Management Section.

This huge province is divided into eight management regions, of which the three interior areas...Region 4-Kootenay, Region 7-Omineca-Peace and Region 8-Okanagan have no, or extremely few steelhead. On the other hand, the remaining five regions on the western side of the province yield steelhead to more than half the anglers who fish for this prized species of Salmo gairdneri.

Here are the major steelhead waters:

REGION 1–VANCOUVER ISLAND

Twice-blessed, by virtue of having two coasts, 280-mile-long Vancouver Island has many excellent steelheading streams. Much of the fishing can be reached from public lands, but some access is through private property and permission to fish is essential. Fly fishermen enjoy winter and summer catches, as do drift and bait anglers (among whom the dew worm or night crawler rates highly) and hardware users fishing spoons, spinners and plugs.

BIG QUALICUM RIVER: Enters the Strait of Georgia midway between Nanaimo and Courtenay and is crossed near the mouth by the Island Highway (No. 19) slightly north of tiny Dunsmuir. The Qualicum is fed by Horne Lake, as well as by Hunts Creek, which begins on the eastern slope of Mt. Mark. The flow from Horne Lake is controlled by a Fisheries and Oceans dam, and this river suffers little from flooding or siltation, often being fishable when other streams are running high and discolored.

Estimates of the annual catch on the Qualicum range from over 1,000 to 2,600 steelhead and 25 to 30 percent of these are retained. Summer anglers are limited to catches below the E & N Railway bridge in the period May 1-June 15. A fall closure or fly-fishing-only season may be declared by emergency regulation for protection of spawning coho salmon. Best fishing is near the hatchery in man-made holes and pools, but the lower, tidewater stretch is private Indian land. Hiking anglers or pedal bikers may use the several miles of Fisheries road alongside the river for access, or may trek downstream from a point near Horne Lake reached via the Horne Lake Caves Park route to reach interesting natural pockets, runs and pools on the upper Qualicum.

CAMPBELL RIVER: Legendary stream made famous by Roderick Haig-Brown's studies and stories. The Campbell traces a path from Strathcona Park past Elk Falls Park, where Elk Falls blocks anadromous fish, eastward through the City of Campbell River to flow beneath Highway 19 and into Georgia Strait past the equally-renowned Tyee Spit where giant salmon of 50 to 80 pounds have been caught. The once-free Campbell now has three dams on its upper reaches, above Elk Falls.

The Campbell was, in the past, best known as a winter steelhead stream delivering 1,100 to 2,400 fish of which 350-500 might be kept. A summer-run hatchery program of steelhead enhancement appears to have been very successful in the Campbell, though, and a June-October fishery is becoming increasingly productive, to the delight of shirtsleeved fly-casters.

Fly-fishing-only is permitted from Elk Falls to 200 meters (marked by a powerline crossing) above the Quinsam River mouth, and there is an Aug. 15-Nov. 15 fishing closure between signs 200 meters apart at the John Hart Power Station. Float fishing with bait and drift angling with bobbers, yarn/bait rigs and casting lures are productive methods for taking steelhead in the Campbell below the Quinsam.

There is excellent access on the lower Campbell River for both bank and boat anglers. The end of the public road system is extended by MacMillan Bloedel Limited logging roads past Elk Falls Park, and maps for recreational users are available upon request to their Vancouver head office.

COWICHAN RIVER: Highly popular and heavily fished, the Cowichan River is approached off the Island Highway (No. 1 at the lower end of the island) at Duncan, the midpoint between Victoria and

Nanaimo. It drains huge Cowichan Lake eastward into the Strait of Georgia through Cowichan Bay and Satellite Channel. Highway 18 – Lake Cowichan Road – is the major route from Duncan, but other roads and footpaths provide excellent access to the river's fine angling.

The Cowichan yields 4,200 to 6,600 fish annually, by harvest estimates, with the bulk of these gamesters being caught in the winter season, December to March. An excellent fly-fishing stream, the Cowichan also produces extremely well for drift rig anglers.

Anglers must carefully read the regulations on the Cowichan, as it has restrictions intended to protect not only spawning steelhead but to preserve a good brown trout fishery and coastal cutthroat stocks.

ENGLISHMAN RIVER: Tumbling down from Mt. Arrowsmith and Mt. Moriarty (Moriarty Creek), the Englishman River reaches the Strait of Georgia below Parksville, passing under the Island Highway south of that city. Four-wheel vehicles can easily transport steelheaders upstream good distances on rough roads following both banks to share catches of 1,300 to 2,200 steelhead each year.

Sixty percent of the steelhead appear to be wild fish, but a strong hatchery program is boosting the numbers of hatchery fish encountered in the Englishman each year. The river regulations show a fly-fishing-only section from Englishman River Falls to Morrison Creek.

GOLD RIVER: This superb westside stream and its tributaries (Heber, Ucona and Upana) provide wilderness quality steelhead fishing for between an estimated 6,500 and 8,900 steelhead yearly, with the lion's share being wild fish.

Highway 28 from Campbell River passes through Strathcona Provincial Park and follows the headwaters of the Heber downstream to the town of Gold River, about a 60-mile trip. This route also provides access along the lower Gold River from that point downstream to where the Gold enters Muchalat Inlet. Logging roads take you north along the upper Gold River and track the Upana, while the Ucona is reached south of Gold River by another logging road. Access generally is limited to weekends and holidays on the logging company's active private roads.

Both summer and winter steelhead mount the Gold River all the way into Gold Lake, but falls on the Upana and Ucona block passage for migratory fish, leaving only short distances above their junctures with the Gold as productive fisheries. The Muchalat River mouth marks the upper deadline for fishing on the Gold, and the Muchalat itself is closed, but supplies winter steelhead that add to the Gold River catch.

Drift anglers do well on the Gold River with winged bobbers, float bobbers and suspended flies/jigs, chewy artificials and cluster eggs (when permitted). Much of the Gold River is in steep mountainous area, limiting access to fishermen willing to hike, scramble and climb to reach canyon pools, runs and drifts.

KEOGH RIVER: This river's headwaters begin in the highlands west of Port NcNeill and it flows northwest to enter Queen Charlotte Strait southeast of Fort Ruppert. A good winter run of wild steelhead may be equally balanced in some years by returns of hatchery fish, with the estimated yearly catch bouncing from 400 to 1,000 steelhead.

No fishing is permitted within 300m below the lower fish counting fence near tidewater. The Keogh is exempt from a bait ban, and roe or dew worms are effective, as are bobbers bearing attractor scents. 1993 regs call for steelhead release.

LITTLE QUALICUM RIVER: Enters the Strait of Georgia near Dashwood in the Qualicum Beach area. Highway 18 crosses the river at the mouth, and Routes 4A and 4 will lead you to Little Qualicum Falls Park below Cameron Lake, which the Little Qualicum drains. A natural waterfall blocks upstream passage of fish into the lake. Access is good at several hike-in spots along this short, but productive river.

Estimated annual catches vary from 1,400 to more than 2,300 winter steelhead fought annually, of which two-thirds generally are wild fish. A few summer fish have reportedly been caught. No fishing is permitted between Kincade Creek to Little Qualicum Falls and there is a Sept. 1-Nov. 30 fly-fishing regulation, but the Little Qualicum is otherwise exempt from a bait ban. Some drift fishing rewards are garnered by Little Qualicum anglers, but most fishermen familiar with the stream use float bobbers having tempting roe, shrimp or dew worm baits hung beneath them.

NANAIMO RIVER: A heavily-fished and popular stream, the Nanaimo River passes under the Island Highway south of the City of Nanaimo, then flows into Departure Bay about 9.3 miles below the ferry landing. It is fed from tributaries, starting high on the slopes of Mt. Hooper, which create the Nanaimo Lakes and then join to become the mainstem Nanaimo, which continues east to the island's inside coastline.

Harvest analyses estimate 1,000 to 1,800 winter steelhead subdued annually in the Nanaimo, with wild fish accounting for all save a scant hundred strays or remnant wild spawners. Drift rig anglers using winged bobbers and soft-bodied lures share the angling action with baiters employing shrimp, roe and dew worms.

Access is relatively abundant and easy on the lower river section below the Island Highway. Steep ravines and plunging slopes upstream of this point limit fishermen to a few good pools and runs per hiking approach, then a return to the all-weather road to the lower of the Nanaimo lakes, which follows the river's course on the north shore, and another hike-in trip to more rapids and deep lies. No fishing is permitted between the powerline crossing at the Bore Hole upstream to and including the North Nanaimo River.

OYSTER RIVER: Spidery fingers of the Oyster River pluck tiny rivulets from Mt. Adrian and the Forbidden Plateau, gathering size and strength. The mainstem flows sinuously eastward, reaching the Strait of Georgia below Kuhushan Point. The river glides under the Island Highway a short distance north of Miracle Beach Provincial Park.

A late-run, March/April winter steelhead stream, the Oyster is reviving from logging operations and mining explorations that often still leaves it in silt-laden, mucky condition. Intensive study and stocking in the early 1980s jacked catches from a few hundred annually in the late '70s to 600-1,200 in recent years. About 75 to 80 percent are wild fish. Still troubled by floods and siltation, the Oyster can be subject to closure (see regs), but local efforts to save and enhance the steelhead runs have shown promise.

Excellent access to the upper Oyster River is had by taking MacMillan Bloedel's Iron River Access Road which follows upstream along the north shore, or to the lower river via public roads north of Courtenay.

PUNTLEDGE RIVER: A short river, the Puntledge leaves Comox Lake and flows east to join the Courtenay River at the north side of Lewis Park in the City of Courtenay. Mainly noted as a winter fishery, the Puntledge has a little-known, almost overlooked summer steelhead run best fished in August and early September.

Fishermen can easily reach the Puntledge's banks from city routes, then trace its course upstream to the power dam above Bevan. Past harvest analyses show 500 to over 1,200 steelhead caught annually in the mid-1980s, the bulk of which were wild fish. 1993 regulations call for steelhead release, as well as cutthroat trout release, and anglers are cautioned to observe several "no fishing" areas identified in the regulations booklet.

QUINSAM RIVER: Threading its way from high country eastward, the Quinsam River pauses at each of the Quinsam lakes before continuing onward to feed into the Campell River about two miles above the Campbell's mouth. The lower Quinsam is readily reached by logging loads owned by Crown Zellerbach, and the MBL main haul road pursues the upper river and tributaries, affording hike-in opportunities.

Enhancement plants from the Quinsam hatchery have revitalized the early winter (December-February) steelhead runs and anglers have made estimated catches of 1,400 to 2,300 fish annually. The Quinsam is exempt from a bait ban. No fishing is permitted from signs at the powerline crossing above the Quinsam Hatchery to Cold Creek, below the hatchery.

SAN JUAN RIVER: A lower island westside rarity, the San Juan River and tributaries are best reached off logging roads leading to Port Renfrew from Koksilah River Provincial Park. The San Juan River and adjoining streams have a winter fishery producing from December through March. The upper deadline of fishing is the Fleet River mouth and fair steelheading for an annual catch of about 400-plus fish extends downstream to where the river's fresh flow meets the salty Strait of Juan de Fuca.

SOMASS RIVER: Formed by the Stamp and Sproat rivers, the Somass River offers excellent steelheading on its relatively short course before entering Alberni Inlet at Port Alberni. Anglers have very good access from Highway 4 and Sproat Lake Road, as well as from boat launches at Port Alberni.

Summer steelhead appear in the Somass from early August through October and winter steelheading peaks December-February. Harvest estimates range from 1,100 to more than 1,600 fish caught, with slightly more wild fish than hatchery stock making up those numbers. The Somass is exempt from a bait ban.

SPROAT RIVER: Given new life by strong hatchery plants, the Sproat River is edging back onto steelheaders' calendars by virtue of annual catches of a few hundred fish in 1983-84 climbing to over 1,000 fish in 1985-86.

Highway 4 crosses the river below the Sproat Lake outlet and Sproat Lake Road nudges the river from the south. No fishing is allowed between the lake's outlet and a point (signed) 300 meters below Highway 4 from June 15 to Nov. 15.

The bulk of fishing is from the middle of November to early April for hatchery steelhead, but some August-October summer-run angling has delivered fair catches.

STAMP RIVER: One of the premier streams of British Columbia, the Stamp River yields an estimated 7,000 to 10,000 steelhead each year to winter and summer steelheaders. The hatchery-wild fish ratio is about 2:1 in harvest analyses. Exempt from the bait ban, the Stamp is an excellent producer on roe and shrimp baits. Often crowded in August-September when the Chinook salmon hatchery run is returning, the Stamp can deliver enjoyable fly-fishing on the upper river and in hard-to-reach spots. Float-fished baits also garner strikes, and some fish are taken on spinners and spoons.

Beaver Creek Road takes you northwest from Port Alberni to Stamp Falls Park, a mandatory take-out spot for rafters fishing upper sections of the Stamp downstream to this dangerous falls. The park is a good center for upstream and downstream angling, or for wintertime fishing on the upper Stamp and the Ash River, one of the Stamp's main tributaries, but which has only a few steelhead. Logging roads No. 74 and 73 reached from Great Central also provide access for hiking to the south bank of the Stamp.

REGION 2 – LOWER MAINLAND

ALOUETTE RIVER: Heavily affected by urbanization, the North Fork Alouette and Alouette River are easily reached by following Highway 7 (Lougheed

Hwy.) east from Vancouver across the Pitt River, then choosing an arterial above the Dewdney Trunk Road, north of the Fraser River in the Pitt Meadows Municipality east of Vancouver. The south fork of the Alouette is the outlet of Alouette Lake, on which there is a B.C. Hydro dam. A good road from Haney provides access to fishing spots. After the two forks meet, the Alouette wends westward, flowing into the Pitt River, which melds with the Fraser River at Douglas Island.

Bank access is limited, due to increasing private ownership of property that in many cases extends to mid-river, but wading anglers and hikers who explore out-of-the-way areas find the Alouette River system is making a remarkable recovery from its steelheading doldrums of the 1970s when only a few hundred steelhead were counted. Annual hatchery plants of 20,000 to 25,000 smolts for the past eight years and wild fish release regulations have boosted harvest estimates since 1984-1986 winter seasons to 1,400 up to 2,800 steelhead brought to hand each year, with December through February marking the peak of best fishing.

Anglers have had success with imitation roe, tiny drift bobbers, yarn ties, dark pattern flies, small spoons and spinners and, when regs permit, roe or shrimp bait. Drifting bait, weighted flies or jigs under float bobbers is an excellent approach to taking Alouette fish.

The Alouette system can muddy very rapidly after steady rains and it is often out of shape for fishing. The opposite face of the coin is prolonged periods of low flow, which make steelheaders search their tactics bags to induce strikes. Periodic closures on specific areas of the Alouette and North Alouette are listed in the regulations synopsis.

CAPILANO RIVER: Motorists crossing the Burrard Inlet on Highway 1A/99 to North Vancouver enroute to the Horseshoe Bay ferry might catch a glimpse of the angling action occurring below them on the Capilano River, a close-in steelhead stream that delivers 500 to 1,400 fish annually to a large number of anglers.

The Capilano yields winter steelhead from December to March, and a small run of summer fish may best be taken from July to October. A short (5-mile) river, the Capilano has a bait ban from Aug. 1 to Oct. 31, a period when heavy salmon migration occurs, and anglers must further observe no fishing signs posted at the footbridge near the upstream fish counting fence and the tidal boundary of the B.C.R. bridge.

CHEAKAMUS RIVER: The Cheakamus River is approached from Vancouver by driving about 35 miles north on Highway 99 to Squamish, above which

Bulkley River, B.C. big water with fish that range from four to over 20 pounds.

point the Cheakamus joins the Squamish River, with the mingled waters shortly reaching Howe Sound. Fed by tributaries flowing west from Garibaldi Park, the Cheakamus has fair spot access from the road system on the east bank and good walking access along the B.C. Railway on its west bank.

Winter steelhead are on tap from December to May, with runs peaking in March and April. Noted for the occasional 20-pound steelhead it can yield, the Cheakamus produces from 600 to nearly 2,000 wild fish, according to harvest analyses, and a scattered few hatchery fish.

There is a Dec. 1-May 31 bait ban, and no fishing is permitted from Mile 56.6 (the B.C.R. bridge) to the B.C. Hydro Dam about 2.5 kilometers above Cheekye.

CHILLIWACK-VEDDER RIVER: Located approximately 65 miles east of Vancouver, the Chilliwack-Vedder River is easily reached from highways and roads on either bank, with 10 to 12 miles of fine pools, runs and drifts readily accessible. This lightly populated area of the Fraser valley permits good upstream/downstream passage of anglers and the river is an extremely popular one.

Harvest estimates show from 8,000 to over 20,000 steelhead caught annually, one-quarter to one-third of which may be hatchery fish. No fishing is permitted above, and including, Slesse Creek, and below Slesse Creek the river is closed between May 1 and June 30. Best fishing generally takes place from December through April. Large fish, some weighing to 20 pounds, can be caught, but the bulk of steelhead taken will range from 9 to 12 pounds.

COQUIHALLA RIVER: The Coquihalla River tumbles south through a steep and narrow valley from near Merritt to Hope, where the mainstem Coquihalla pours into the Fraser River after flowing about 25 miles through rugged, mountainous country. Logging, mining and repeated crossing of the river by a gas pipeline nearly eliminated the Coquihalla's highly-regarded but limited summertime steelheading 25 years ago, but careful nurture of the remaining broodstock and years of closure brought renewed vitality to this small river and its delicate fishery. A new major highway (Coquihalla/Merritt Hwy.) is being constructed to join the two population centers now, though, and a period of siltation and reduced fry survival may be anticipated. However, after nature washes the limited amount of spawning gravel clean again, the highway should improve the fishing access now gained from the old road structure.

Although harvest estimates seldom credit the Coquihalla with more than 400-500 steelhead caught annually, and the majority of the steelhead normally weigh only from 4 to 7 pounds, the upper river still is a favorite of summer fly-fishermen, who enjoy a July 1-Oct. 31 fly-fishing-only, catch-and-release season. Long whitewater rapids, with few pools and pockets for resting lies, limit the fishable sections of the upper river, but the lower river delivers some winter steelhead from December through April.

Anglers are advised to read the Coquihalla regulations very carefully for bait ban periods, "no fishing" areas and specific seasonal closures, such as steelhead release and bait ban below lower tunnel June 1-July 31.

FRASER RIVER: Huge when it reaches Vancouver and the Strait of Georgia, the 785-mile-long Fraser River has its origin in snowmelt off Robson Mountain, the highest point in the Canadian Rockies. The upper Fraser flows northwest to Prince George, then turns sharply south-by-southeast to Quesnel and Williams Lake, and is traced by Highway 97. Then the river veers southwest, away from the highway, crossing the Fraser Plateau to Lilloet, where Highway 12 joins its course to Lytton and is then replaced by Highway 1 to Hope.

Noted for fine bar and river mouth steelheading, the Fraser is valued more as a steelhead "highway" for fish heading to other rivers than as a quantity producer. It does, however, deliver 500 to 800 steelhead annually to anglers, most of which are caught between the river mouth (tidal boundary is the C.P.R. bridge at Mission) and Hope. Regulations for 1993 show steelhead release is required Jan. 1-June 30, and no fishing is allowed from signs 6.5 km south of Boston Bar to signs 2.8 km south of Hells gate.

Baits drift-fished, plunked or fished under float bobbers will deliver strikes from Fraser River steelhead, as will spoons, spinners and plugs. There also are fly-fishing opportunities on some of the less-used lower river sections. Predominantly an early winter fishery, steelhead mount the Fraser in increasing numbers from November, peaking in February, to April.

(LITTLE) CAMPBELL RIVER: A short, tidal stream just north of the U.S./Canadian border in the Municipality of Surrey, the fishable portion of the Campbell is a bare 5 miles long. Yet, annual catches range from 700 to 1,000 steelhead registered in the harvest analyses. Tidal boundary is the Burlington Northern Railway Bridge and no fishing is allowed above the Bamford Bridge (12th Avenue). There is an April 1-June 30 fishing closure below 12th Ave. on this small, but productive stream.

Bait – roe, worms and shrimp – are the best producers in the Campbell, with flies, spinners and plugs accounting for a small number of fish, and best fishing is on an outgoing tide. Both slack water and equally slow fishing is created when tidal gates block incoming salt water tides from entry into the flat farmlands.

SEYMOUR RIVER: Public access on the Seymour River, located in North Vancouver, is diminishing, but this 9 1/3-mile stream offers up 1,000 to 1,200 steelhead annually to fishermen who know or can find fishing spots on its banks. Tidal boundary is the

C.N.R. Bridge and no fishing is permitted between signs in a 330-meter section of river above and below the pipeline bridge near the Greater Vancouver Water District gate. (Inquire locally for permits to enter the Water District.)

The Seymour hosts winter fish and some summer steelhead.

SQUAMISH RIVER: About 35 miles north of Vancouver, reached via Highway 99, the Squamish River is then tracked nearly to its headwaters by a good gravel road and some paving.

A large river, the Squamish yields some big steelhead in annual catches that vary widely from 500 to 1,500 steelhead. There is excellent streamside access, with good casting room. A bait ban must be observed Dec. 1 to Sept. 30. Winter steelheading is best from February to May.

REGION 3 THOMPSON-NICOLA

THOMPSON RIVER: The only major steelheading river in the southern interior of British Columbia, the Thompson River is famed for quality fishing experiences highlighted by large steelhead averaging in the mid-teens.

From 12,000 to 5,000 steelhead are estimated as an annual catch, with the peak of angling occurring October-December, although steelhead are found in the Thompson from September until May. No trout under 35 centimeters in fork length may be taken, and there is no angling allowed from a boat.

Fishable from its junction with the Fraser at Lytton for approximately 65 miles to below Kamloops Lake at Savona, many of the Thompson's holes are readily accessible from the highway. Perhaps the best-known area of the Thompson is the Spences Bridge section at the junction of Highways 1 and 8, easily reached from Merritt.

Fly tackle, spoons and spinners, or standard drift gear all are successfully used to battle the Thompson River's legendary steelhead giants.

REGION 5 – CARIBOU

BELLA COOLA RIVER: A coastal stream that enters Fitz Hugh Sound via Lebuchere Channel and past King Island, the Bella Coola River can be reached by following Highway 30 about 300 miles west from Williams Lake or by fly-in airplane arrangements.

There are steelhead in the Bella Coola and its tributaries (of which the ATNARKO is the best known and most productive) from September to June, with the best fishing from October to April. The Bella Coola will yield an average 1,500 steelhead annually, according to harvest analyses of 1983-86. Often, the river may be silty from late spring and summer runoff.

Steelhead are taken on spoons, bobber lures, bait (bait ban in effect May 1-July 15) and flies. No angling is allowed from power boats, which may be used for transportation only. All trout taken from the Bella Coola and tributaries must measure 30 centimeters or more in fork length.

DEAN RIVER: Reached only by boat or air, the lower Dean River enters the Dean Channel at Kimsquit, while the upper Dean may be approached from Highway 20 about 200 miles west of Williams Lake at Anahim Lake.

The Dean is noted for its excellent fly-fishing. When and where they are legal, spoons, spinners and bobber lures also can be effective. There are many specific regulations peculiar to the Dean River and its tributaries, however, that anglers should read before fishing, pertaining to single hooks, bait ban, fly-fishing sections and dates and boat use.

Dick Lawson returns Morice River, B.C., summer steelhead to river.

This river is an exceptional steelhead fishery that yields from 3,500 to 8,300 steelhead catches each year. Increasingly heavy use has prompted its designation as a special fishery for which anglers will be required to purchase a Classified Waters License in addition to their annual basic fishing license and steelhead permit. As of 1993, anglers must write the date and water name in ink on the back of the Classified Waters License, guided anglers will return completed licenses to the guide and non-guided anglers must keep their licenses for a year. To preserve its unique wilderness experience, management biologists and enforcement agents will closely observe the limited Dean fishery and may recommend further strictures.

REGION 6 – SKEENA

BABINE RIVER: The upper Babine River, below the outlet of Babine Lake, holds exceptional steelhead angling for fish that may average in the mid-teens, and often produces catches past the 20-pound mark. A minimal number of hatchery fish are included in the 1,300 to 3,500 steelhead counted as caught over the past few seasons.

A supreme fly-fishing stream, and also productive at times for anglers using spinners, spoons and drift lures, the Babine can best be reached via the Yellowhead Highway (No. 16) from Prince George, departing that route at Smithers, to Smithers Landing on the lake. Boats or a short road and foot trails will take fishermen downstream to the better upper river angling areas. The fishable length of the Babine is about 50 miles through wilderness after leaving the lower Babine Lake area. Some fishing reached by boats in the lower Babine takes place above the junction of the Babine (between the towns of Kispiox and Hazelton) with the great Skeena River. Best fishing for the Babine's wild, summer-run steelhead is in September and October. Anglers are cautioned to identify the "no fishing" sections and dates in the regulations synopsis before fishing the Babine.

BULKLEY RIVER: One of the most readily accessible Prince George-to-Prince Rupert area steelheading streams, the Bulkley is closely followed almost its entire length by Highway 16. Catch estimates range from 3,200 to 4,500 steelhead in recent harvest analyses, with all but a few fish being wild steelhead.

Most of the better angling is found between Houston and Moriceton, readily reached off the Yellowhead Highway on the north bank, while the C.N. Railway traces the river on the south side. Late

This heavily damaged, bright summer steelhead was caught by Marty Sherman, Editor of *FLYFISHING* magazine. The question arises: How much pain do cold blooded animals experience?

August and September are the peak months of the Bulkley River steelheading season. Flies, spoons, spinners and drift bobbers take the largest number of Bulkley fish. The Bulkley has much excellent fly-fishing water.

There is a bait ban restriction in all months save July, and fishermen should note and observe boat fishing regulations as given in the synopsis.

KISPIOX RIVER: Current holder of the province's record for biggest steelhead, a 36-pounder, the Kispiox River is one of the larger tributaries to the Skeena. Road access to the lower Kispiox is off Highway 16 at New Hazelton then through Hazelton and Kispiox, where a rough road leads on upriver.

A shallow, rocky river, the Kispiox has many pools and pockets that can be very productive of steelhead from 9 to more than 20 pounds, with a few larger fish pushing 30 pounds. The annual catch estimates range from 800 to 1,900 steelhead.

Ideal water for fly-fishing, the Kispiox also can be tackled with spoons, bobber/yarn lures and spinners. No angling from boats and a bait ban are two Kispiox restrictions, while there also is a steelhead release regulation for the periods Aug. 15- Sept. 30 and Nov. 1-Dec.31. September and October are the best months.

KITIMAT RIVER: A small stream found south of Terrace via Highway 57, the Kitimat River flows from the east to meet the highway about half the distance between Terrace and Kitimat.

Strengthened by hatchery releases, the Kitimat River should deliver fishing challenges for 700 to over 1,000 steelhead annually. All wild steelhead must be released and there is a bait ban from May 15 to Aug. 31. The region-wide 1993 quota of two hatchery steelhead per month does not apply in the Kitimat. Anglers using bait when legal, bobber lures, hardware and flies, will find willing steelhead from late November through March.

KITSUMKALUM RIVER: Flowing east from an upcropping of the Coast Mountains, the Kitsumkalum tumbles into Kitsumkalum Lake and then emerges again running southeast to join the Skeena River near Terrace. Departing Highway 16 at Terrace, a paved road leads north along the Kitsumkalum's east bank to Rosswood, on the lake. A restricted logging road follows the western bank of the river beyond the lake.

Approximately 26 miles of readily accessible river may be tapped for increasingly good steelheading that has seen wild fish catches estimated at 1,100 fish in the 1983-84 season swell to nearly 2,000 in 1985-86. Steelhead will appear in the river from late July on, and fishing continues good through March.

LAKELSE RIVER: Drains Lakelse Lake (8 miles south of Terrace on Highway 37) north-northwest into the Skeena River. This short river can produce estimated catches of 1,000-1,300 steelhead annually. Fishermen should read the regulations very carefully for bait ban, fly-fishing, single barbless hook and steelhead release period information.

MORICE RIVER: Noted for the occasional big steelhead sagging scale needles past the 20-pound mark, the Morice River is a 50-mile stream that drains Morice Lake north to join the Bulkley near Houston, on Highway 16. Very easily fished from a good gravel road to Morice Lake that closely follows much of the river, the Morice holds good steelheading from September through November. The steelhead season basically extends from July 1 to Nov. 30 and there are specific regulations in the angling synopsis to which anglers must refer before determining which tackle and fishing area they will utilize. The Morice has much excellent fly water.

SKEENA RIVER: The great Skeena River is second in length within the province only to the Fraser, and likewise serves best as a huge migration route for anadromous fish mounting to tributary streams. However, steelheaders have begun probing the secrets of taking Skeena fish from the mainstem and catches have steadily risen from 2,200 to over 4,500 fish in the mid-1980s.

Often silty because of run-off from feeder streams, the Skeena's chancy fishability is balanced by ready access off Highway 16 from Terrace nearly to Prince Ruppert. It is exempt from the spring closure and offers steelhead fishing year-around, with the most productive period occurring from late September through February. Bait, bobber lures, spoons, spinners and plugs may be the best angling choices, although catching the river in clear condition may yield steelhead taken on bright flies.

Boat anglers fishing the Skeena should use 14-foot or larger craft adequately powered to handle the heavy currents and eddies to be encountered.

ZYMOETZ (COPPER) RIVER: The Zymoetz River joins the Skeena east of Terrace, flowing under Highway 16 to make the junction. A yearly analysis of catches shows 1,050 steelhead battled in 1983-84 increasing to over 2,600 in 1985-86.

There is a bait ban on the Zymoetz, and anglers are advised to check the specific area closures shown in the regulations synopsis. The Zymoetz is a good fly-fishing river in September and October, but rain will muddy it.

QUEEN CHARLOTTE ISLANDS

Fine steelhead fishing can be found on the major islands – Graham, Moresby and Louise – of the Queen Charlotte Island chain, 60 miles off the coast from Prince Rupert. Short streams as a rule, catches of steelhead brought in on high water from rainstorms are the key to October to May fishing success. Most productive streams are Copper Creek and the Deena, Mamin, Pallant, and Yakoun rivers, each of which can yield 400 to 800 fish yearly, with the Yakoun zooming to 3,600 steelhead in the 1984-85 harvest analysis and 3,900 the following season.

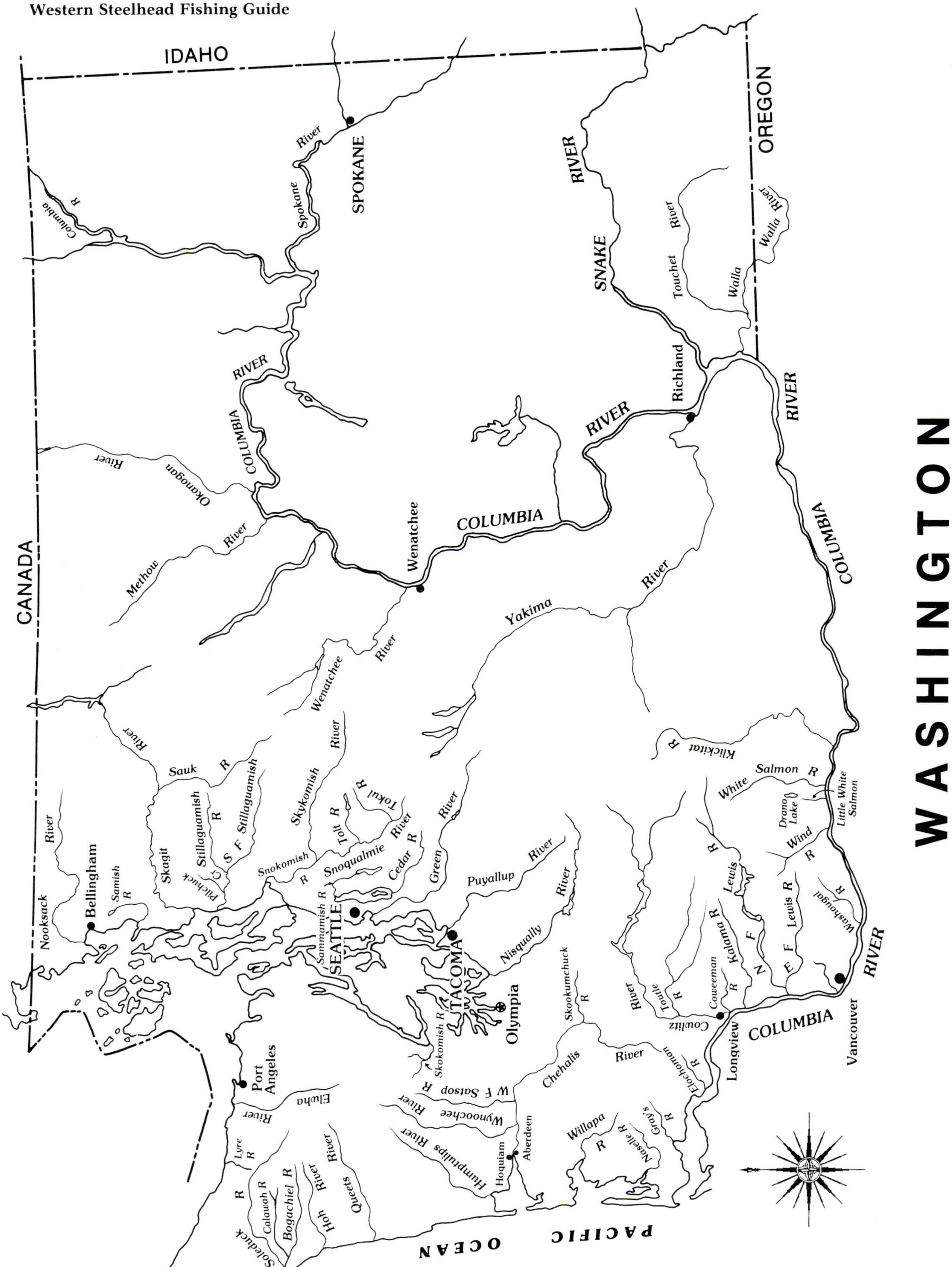
WASHINGTON
IDAHO
OREGON
CANADA
PACIFIC OCEAN
SPOKANE
Spokane River
SNAKE RIVER
COLUMBIA RIVER
Columbia R
Touchet River
Walla Walla River
Richland
Okanogan River
Methow River
Wenatchee
Wenatchee River
Yakima River
Klickitat R
White Salmon R
Little White Salmon
Drano Lake
Wind R
Lewis R
E F Lewis R
N F Lewis R
Washougal R
Kalama R
Coweeman R
Toutle R
Cowlitz R
Vancouver
Longview
Elochoman R
Grays R
Naselle R
Willapa R
Chehalis River
Skookumchuck R
Aberdeen
Hoquiam
Humptulips River
Wynoochee River
W F Satsop R
Skokomish R
Olympia
TACOMA
Nisqually River
Puyallup River
Green River
Cedar R
SEATTLE
Sammamish R
Snoqualmie River
Tolt R
Tokul R
Skykomish River
Snohomish R
Pilchuck
S F Stillaguamish
Stillaguamish R
Sauk R
Skagit River
Samish R
Bellingham
Nooksack River
Port Angeles
Elwha River
Lyre R
Soleduck R
Calawah R
Bogachiel R
Hoh River
Queets River

Chapter 14

Washington

Washington is a wide, rectangular state of 68,192 square miles, in which the broad, central Columbia Basin and the state's larger eastern half are buffered from Pacific Ocean rains first by the Olympic Mountains and then, after a narrow latticework of metropolitan development, fertile valleys and some prairie, again by the soaring peaks of the Cascade Range. A network of rivulets emerges, from snow-clad mountain heights bearing fir, spruce, hemlock and cedar trees, to become thin, swiftly-growing creeks that burgeon into tumbling rills and broader rivers to provide more than 50,000 miles of fishing opportunity.

Steelhead angling draws from 45,000 to 100,000 adherents yearly and past catches have registered from 125,000 to nearly 250,000 sea-going 'bows annually listed in the *"Summary of Summer-Run and Winter-Run Steelhead Trout Sport Catch in Washington."* Management of freshwater species by the Washington Department of Wildlife (600 Capitol Way N., Olympia, Washington 98501-1091) arbitrarily divides Washington steelhead into summer-run fish that return from May through October and winter steelhead that come back to their natal streams from November to April. (The Washington Department of Fisheries manages foodfish, including salmon.)

The rod-and-reel sport-caught record summer steelhead is the larger of the two, a giant of 35 pounds, 1 ounce caught Nov. 23, 1973 from the Snake River by Gilbert Pierson. Gene Maygra hoisted a 32-pound, 12-ounce steelhead from the East Fork Lewis River on April 14, 1980 to claim the wintertime steelhead record.

Heftier fish reportedly swim the state's rivers every few years. A friend swears he observed the weighing of a 38-pounder released back into the Snake River, and another story persists of two lunker bucks of 40½ and 42 pounds that were recycled from the Cowlitz River Salmon Hatchery back into the Cowlitz below I-5. But, the bulk of Washington's steelhead normally will weigh from 5 to 12 pounds, a standard hatchery size fish that crowds into rivers from early December through February. In February and March, natives show in catches and can range from 8 to 25 pounds. Summer fish are in streams from June to October.

Indian tribes are promised by treaties the opportunity to take 50 percent of the steelhead returning to many Washington rivers and a few streams are plagued by increasing seal and sea lion numbers. Few Washington rivers can sustain the netting, predation and tremendous increase in angling interest over the past 15 years by relying on reproduction from wild steelhead alone and a strong, continuing program of hatchery plants and several years of fin restriction measures have brought new promise to the state's steelhead streams.

All persons 15 years of age or older must have a fishing license to legally angle in Washington and, regardless of age, any fishermen seeking steelhead also must possess a steelhead permit (punchcard) on which catches are immediately recorded after a fish is retained. The daily steelhead bag limit is two fish, with an annual limit of 30 steelhead.

Specific regulations on some rivers require the release of wild fish, identified by an unclipped adipose fin. All hatchery fish have either a clipped adipose fin or a clipped ventral fin (and sometimes both) and the fin area must have a clearly healed scar. Steelhead punchcards must be returned to the DOW within 30 days after the April 30 closing of most rivers to steelheading, while fishing licenses are for the calendar year.

Some steelhead streams remain open every month

of the year; many end their season at the close of February or March. A few streams have April 15 or 30 closing dates. Anglers may fish for steelhead 24 hours a day, except where specifically prohibited by regulations. Phosphorescent, fluorescent or luminescent finishes may be used on lures, but no lights may be shone on the water you are fishing.

1993 costs were: resident annual fishing license $17, or $29 for a combination hunting/fishing license. Non-residents will pay $48, for an annual fishing license, or $17 for a 3-day fishing license. The steelhead permit is $18 for all anglers.

Steelhead have a two-pronged entry into the heartland of Washington. The Strait of Juan de Fuca and Hood Canal drain the Olympic Peninsula streams into salt water and the Strait leads into Puget Sound, a gigantic intrusion of salt water into the northwestern quarter of the state that allows anadromous fish to reach hundreds of large and small streams on the west slopes of the Cascades. In the southwest corner of the state, the mighty Columbia River provides another passageway that permits steelhead to fin three-quarters of the way across the state between Washington and Oregon, climb fish ladders at a series of dams and either mount Columbia Basin rivers or veer east to swim up the Snake River into Idaho.

The state of Washington is divided into six management regions, each of which has steelheading opportunities. Here are the major steelhead rivers:

REGION 1 – SPOKANE

SNAKE RIVER: Flowing out of Idaho along the borders of Oregon and Washington, the Snake River turns sharply west at Clarkston and plunges into the 2,000-foot deep Snake River Canyon. From the canyon to Lyons Ferry, Washington steelheaders generally are limited to boat fishing, with few bank access spots except at the mouths of rivers. However, steelhead catches are on an increase in this area, with 3,000 to 5,000 summer-run fish counted in the past few years' catch summaries.

Open to fishing all year around, the Snake is CLOSED to taking steelhead over 20 inches in length from June 1 to Aug. 31 and wild steelhead must be released in the period Sept. 1-Mar. 31. Anglers holding a Washington fishing license may probe the Idaho side of the mainstem Snake by boat in a reciprocal arrangement, but may not fish from the opposite state's shore or in sloughs or backwaters of Idaho. Only one daily limit of fish may be taken, regardless of whether more than one state's license is purchased.

Best fishing in this section of the Snake is by trolling from boats, using big-billed, deep-diving plugs such as the Hot Shot, Tadpolly, Hawg Boss, Wiggle Wart, Flatfish, Hot'N Tot and any of the alphabet plugs...Big O, Big N, etc. Drifting with baits such as roe, shrimp or nightcrawlers also can produce strikes.

TOUCHET RIVER: Run-off from Blue Mountain area tributaries is the lifeblood of the Touchet and the pendulum effect high or low water has on this small stream can swing catches of 250-300 steelhead per year to a high of over 500 fish.

The Touchet enters the Walla Walla River about 12 miles above that stream's junction with the Columbia at Walulla. It is open from June 1 to April 15 for taking hatchery steelhead over 20 inches in length. All wild steelhead must be released.

Shrimp, cluster eggs, nightcrawlers and grasshoppers are prime baits for drift-fishing the Touchet. Steelheaders also will use drift bobbers, spinners, spoons and flies to tackle some of the Touchet's steelhead. Best fishing is in March. A good gravel road follows the Touchet from the town of Touchet nearly to Eureka.

WALLA WALLA RIVER: From 600 to 1,600 winter steelhead are plucked from the Walla Walla River from October through April each year, with the peak of angling mid-December through January. The river is traced from Wallula to Walla Walla by Highway 12 and byroads west of Walla Walla offer some access.

Steelhead over 20 inches in length may be taken from June 1 to April 15 and all must be hatchery fish having a healed clipped-fin scar. Anglers have good success trolling plugs from boats, although many other fishermen plunk from the bank or drift-fish baits and bobber lures for their catches.

REGION 2 – EPHRATA

COLUMBIA RIVER: Inland steelheaders annually tap the Columbia River between Highway 12 at the Tri-Cities – Pasco, Kennewick and Richland – and Bridgeport, in the north center of the state, for 8,000 to 12,000 summer-run steelhead. Catches above Highway 12, the lower section of river in this region, are strongest in July and August, while October is the best time to be fishing the Columbia above Wells Dam.

Some of the most productive steelheading will be at the mouths of feeder streams, with boaters and bank anglers sharing the action. Sand and gravel bars and beaches along the river sprout rows of plunking poles when the steelhead are moving through. Drift-fishermen mostly bump bottom for catches, although increasing numbers of steelheaders are switching to float bobbers with suspended baits or jigs under them to fool their quarry. A small number of Columbia River Basin fishermen take their catches on spoons and spinners.

All wild steelhead hooked in this region must be released.

METHOW RIVER: Asleep for many years as a steelheading stream, the Methow River has rebounded into contention as one of the top 10 summer-run rivers in the state, yielding from 3,000 to 4,800 steelhead each year. It begins high in the Okanogan National Forest and cascades down to Winthrop beside Highway 20. From Winthrop to its junction at Pateros it is closely followed by Highway 153.

Methow River steelhead can be caught from late September to November before the river ices up, and good numbers of fish are taken after ice-out from late February through March. Bank anglers will do well with float bobbers, side planers and bait or lures, spoons and spinners. Boat fishermen make their catches best with plugs, although sometimes in spring they can trick steelhead with everything from trolled flies to marshmallow baits!

Only marked hatchery fish may legally be retained.

OKANOGAN RIVER: A quiet resurrection has taken place on the Okanogan River, with mid-80s yearly catches mounting to over 1,000 steelhead from this north-central stream that flows out of Osoyoos Lake to join the Columbia below Chief Joseph Dam.

Hatchery fish are the only steelhead that may be kept. Access to the river may be gained off Highway 97 and/or sideroads that track and bracket the Okanogan River from Fort Okanogan to Oroville. Bank anglers should have best success with drift bobbers, bait, hardware and flies.

SNAKE RIVER: The short stretch of Snake River in this region yields from 450 to 800 steelhead annually, taken between its junction with the Columbia to just below Lower Monumental Dam. It is big, slow water between Ice Harbor Dam and Monumental, which produces best for anglers using trolled plugs and drift-fished baits eased along above bottom or suspended under float bobbers.

Both banks of the river are tapped at several points by county roads, providing some bank access for plunkers. All of the steelhead retained must be hatchery fish.

REGION 3 – YAKIMA

COLUMBIA RIVER: From McNary Dam to Highway 12, the Columbia yields from 400 to over 700 hatchery steelhead annually, with all wild steelhead being released in this area.

There is good bank access in the Tri-Cities area from both sides of the river and plunkers score well, as do drift- and float-fishermen. Boaters have the best luck pulling plugs and drift-fishing baits or bobber rigs.

WENATCHEE RIVER: Wenatchee area steelheaders and visitors generally pull an average of about 800 hatchery steelhead from the Wenatchee River between its mouth and the Icicle River Road Bridge at Leavenworth.

Access is off Highway 2 which, in its descent from Stevens Pass, seldom departs from the river's edge. Good drift-fishing with bait or bobber rigs can be had in the Wenatchee-to-Cashmere area and at Peshastin. Spoon and spinner tossers also will take a share of the steelhead and some fly-fishing is available when the river is running clear. Best months for these far-swimming summer steelhead are November and December. The Wenatchee is closed to taking wild steelhead and the wintertime season ends at the close of March.

YAKIMA RIVER: Open to fishing year-around from mouth to 400 feet below the Prosser Dam, this stretch of Yakima River is closed to steelheading from April 1 to May 31. It may be fished June 1-March 31 from Wapato Dam to Roza Dam, with ONE hatchery steelhead the daily bag limit. All wild steelhead must be released in these two areas. Baits, bobber lures, floating bobbers and jigs, flies, hardware and plugs account for 450 to 1,250 hatchery steelhead a year from the Yakima. Boaters, too, do very well drifting the Yakima by back-trolling plugs, anchoring and drift-fishing, or by floating downriver while shortlining plugs such as the Flatfish, Guppy or Kwikfish on drift rigs lightly weighted with pencil sinkers.

No baits or boats are permitted on the Yakima River from Roza Dam to 400 feet below Easton Dam. All wild steelhead must be released in this area.

Yakima steelhead can appear in late September, but the peak of steelheading will take place from mid-October into February.

Bill Stinson with winter steelhead from Lewis River, Washington.

REGION 4 – SEATTLE

CEDAR RIVER: This tiny stream begins in high wilderness west of the Pacific Crest Trail and about midway between Stampede Pass and Snoqualmie Pass. Temporarily trapped in Chester Morse Lake behind a double-dam system, the Cedar remains relatively clear in winter, often fishable when other area streams are running mud.

Steelheaders have a split season in which to try for 350-600 winter fish and a handful of summer-run strays or remnant natives. From mouth to Landsburg diversion dam, the Cedar is open June 15 to Sept. 1. At best, 25 to 35 steelhead may be taken in this summer period. From Dec. 1 through February, however, bright and sometimes exceptionally big winter steelhead test the tackle of area anglers. The peak month for fishing the Cedar alternates between January to February.

Fishing from any floating device is not permitted on this suburban, highly wadable, narrow river, and steelheading is not allowed between 7 p.m. and 5 a.m. because of past snagging problems. Access is relatively good in the heart of Renton from city streets and byways. Highway 169 closely follows the Cedar through the Maple Valley to the town of that name and on to Summit, where a north turn onto the Landsburg Road again crosses the river.

Anglers have to balance their gear carefully... light lines and leaders will gain fishermen more strikes, but TOO light can be disastrous when tangling with a rambunctious 16 to 20-pounder! A good choice of line/leader weights for drift fishermen might be 10-pound main line and 8-pound leader to fish shrimp, cluster and single eggs or night crawlers. Small Lil' Corky, Okie Drifter, Fenton Fly, Mou-Jo or Cheater bobbers with a tuft of yarn on the hook shank also prove effective for Cedar steelhead. There are a few areas where a fly-fisherman will enjoy casting, but much of the Cedar is lined with small alder and willow growth, or brush.

Slightly heavier tackle is suggested for the Cedar below Landsburg, due to the very "grabby" rocks you'll encounter there. Access is by foot from railroad tracks following the river on the north shore or working through brush on the south shoreline.

GREEN (DUWAMISH) RIVER: One of Washington's finest steelhead streams and a perennial contender for the Number 1, 2 or 3 spot on total annual catches, the Green River drains westward from the Pacific Crest Trail, above Lester, to flow into Howard Hanson Reservoir. It is open to fishing for steelhead from June 15 to March 31 from mouth to Tacoma Headworks Dam. Anglers are cautioned, though, there are specific, large areas below and above the Soos Creek salmon hatchery that are closed to fishing in September, October and March. See your regulations.

The Green is an excellent spoon river, especially from Soos Creek upstream through Palmer. Stee-Lee, Ottogator, Otto's Ace Bait, Krocodile, Wonderlure, Hot Rod and like lures all tempt strikes, with good patterns being the hammered nickel/spot or center slash/orange edge models. Baits and bobbers fished on drift rigs are the most heavily used, however. The lower river, from Auburn to the Duwamish double waterway mouth, is slow and meandering, with best catches generally coming from popular plunking areas. The upper Green, below the Tacoma Headworks Dam, is a series of deep pools and runs connected by thin riffles.

Efforts to establish a summer-run fishery in the Green are showing bright yearly dividends of 1,200 to 2,000 steelhead best caught in June and July. Winter steelheading's prime time on the Green River peaks in mid-January, with the annual frostbite season good for another 4,500 to 7,000 fish ranging from 5 to perhaps 25 pounds. Wild fish, as well as hatchery steelhead, may be retained in the daily bag.

Summer anglers may fish from boats and other floating devices, while Green River steelheaders are limited in winter (after Nov. 1) to using boats only for transportation between fishing spots. There is little need for floating craft, however, as numerous public access points, highways, roads and fisherman trails line the Green from its double mouth in the Duwamish area around Harbor Island in Seattle through the heavily populated Green River Valley to Flaming Geyser Park near Black Diamond. Above Flaming Geyser, the Green River Gorge below Palmer is best fished from hike-in spots that are approached from the east bank.

NISQUALLY RIVER: The Nisqually River begins high on Mt. Rainier and wriggles west out of Pierce County into and across Thurston County on its way to lower Puget Sound to mingle with the salt water in Nisqually Reach. A long, large stream that changes from brawling down mountainsides to peacefully rolling through the miles of soft delta west of I-5, the Nisqually River is a late-winter favorite of southern Washington anglers.

Approximately 2,000 steelhead are plucked from the Nisqually annually, with March and April being the prime months to fish it. A good way to sample its angling is to drift the river from McKenna to the Handicap Access at Old Nisqually near I-5. Many fishermen stick to the lower river spots, where there is fair public access. The steelhead season is open from June 1 to the end of February from the mouth to LaGrande Dam, and through April 15 from the McKenna Bridge downstream. Many plunkers and bank anglers seldom leave the lower river in a winter's angling.

However, other successful fishermen obtain a fishing permit (free) from the Range Control Officer at giant Fort Lewis Military Reservation (which lies along many miles of the Nisqually's north shore and overlaps the river for several miles on the south shore) and cast from bank spots reached through the military reservation or from offroads leading to the river from Highway 510, which skirts the reservation and river from Old Nisqually to McKenna. Summer anglers can forge upstream to the LaGrande area via Highway 7 from Tacoma or Piessner Road and Weyerhaeuser log roads on the south bank.

Shrimp and cluster egg baits, bobbers, bobber/yarn rigs and yarn ties are the most common lures used on the Nisqually. Fly-fishermen sometimes score well in the upper river or on the float trips from McKenna to Handicap Access. Good catches are made by drift boaters backtrolling plugs.

NOOKSACK RIVER: Spidery threads of water escape the glaciers on the north face of Mt. Shuksan and west and south slopes of Mt. Baker to become the three tributaries of the Nooksack River by the time they reach Deming. The mainstem river then flows northwest to Lyndon, near the U.S.-Canadian border, before dipping southwest again to greet the salt water of Rosario Strait at Bellingham.

Open to steelheading June 15 to March 31, the Nooksack and tributaries are together capable of producing from 700 to over 2,000 winter hatchery steelhead. All wild steelhead must be released in this system and anglers also should note they may not retain ANY steelhead over 20 inches in length during the June 15-Oct. 31 trout season in the South Fork Nooksack. There also are motor restrictions in winter on the three tributaries.

Many public access areas on the river are easily reached from Highways 542, 539, 544 and 9, from which main routes a network of sideroads leads to the main Nooksack River.

Visibility is the key to good Nooksack River fishing. Due to glacial melt which keeps the Nooksack murky in summer and early winter, your best fishing is early in the day, and the cold of late February and March produces the best water conditions and traditionally the most steelhead catches. A rich, translucent green color in deep pools and runs will aid anglers to coax Nooksack steelhead to grab bait and drift bobber lures. Most of the popular fishing spots can be fished with hip boots or high paks, as the narrow width of the Nooksack makes it advisable to stay out of the water for fear of spooking the fish.

South Fork Nooksack steelhead spots can be tapped from byroads off State Highway 9, or by following Saxon Road upstream. The Middle Fork Nooksack is tracked from Kulshan upstream by the Mosquito Lake Road. Anglers may reach the North Fork Nooksack off Highway 542 above Deming.

PILCHUCK RIVER: It's easy to miss the tiny Pilchuck River from Highway 2 east of Snohomish...if you're not watching for it, you can zip over the brushy banks and 15-foot wide stream without even knowing it is there. Wrestle with a 15-pound, ocean-bright and

Don Roberts displays a fine summer run steelhead which he is about to release.

frisky Pilchuck River steelhead just once, though, and you'll make it a point to find and fish the stream in January, its peak month.

The Pilchuck's fish fortunes rise to over 1,000 and fall to less than 300 winter steelhead caught in poor years, but some knowledgable anglers always try it early in December, seeking the handful of 20-pounders that sneak out of the Snohomish and fin upward to near Granite Falls before swinging southeast to spawning areas in this tricky little rivulet that rises from the snowfields on Mt. Pilchuck.

Open for a steelheading season that runs only from Dec. 1 to the end of February, from its mouth to the Snohomish City diversion dam, the Pilchuck is followed and repeatedly crossed by the Snohomish-Machias Road and then Russell Road to Highway 92 and Granite Falls, which seldom are out of sight of the river and along which are many pull-out parking spots and public access areas that permit anglers to reach the fishing.

Pocket, slot and small pool fishing you'll experience on the Pilchuck is best handled with a medium-length rod and mono about two to four pounds heavier in breaking strength than you would first estimate. Pilchuck fish are fresh from their short trip up the broad and gentle Snohomish and often, when hooked from the narrow, twisting curves of the Pilchuck, seem determined to put several bends of the bank between themselves and you...or even go back to a more-friendly ocean!

Esther Poleo (right) and her sister Aura, display two bright winter steelhead of hatchery origin.

Shrimp, roe clusters, single eggs or nightcrawler baits with light pencil lead drift rigs are favored for Pilchuck River steelheading. Most anglers rig these with a couple strands of orange or chartreuse yarn tied in and may also add a drift bobber to help keep their gear from hanging bottom. A spoon or spinner fisherman will also draw strikes from Pilchuck River steelhead, especially when the water is up a foot and slightly colored.

PUYALLUP RIVER: One of Washington's premier steelheading streams in the 1940-50 era, and yielding over 18,000 steelhead in its peak recorded season, the Puyallup River currently surges from a low of 2,000 winter steelhead to more than 10,000 (1984-85) in a good year. All are winter fish, with summer-runs contributing so few steelhead you could count them on your digital extremities.

The Puyallup is open June 1-Jan. 31 from its mouth to the Electron power plant outlet and from its mouth to the Soldier's Home Bridge at Orting Feb. 1 to March 31. The lower river from the city of Puyallup to its entry into Commencement Bay at Tacoma is channelized and heavily silted. Above Puyallup, however, there's an entirely different river that has deep holes and green glides that spell "fish" to anglers either floating or fishing from both banks.

Highway 410 traces the lower river along the south bank from Tacoma to Puyallup, where arterials and sideroads provide downtown access. Highway 162 and offshoots tap the Puyallup from the center of the city to Orting. There are no developed launches, but you'll often see drifters who have found rough put-in spots working their way downstream.

Since the Puyallup River originates high on the west glacier slope of Mt. Rainier, warm temperatures can turn the stream rich brown and soupy in a few hours. Cold days and early morning hours are the best times to try for steelhead with orange, hot pink, lime, red, peach fluorescent and chartreuse/red winged or round bobber/egg/yarn combos in the lower river, best fished on drift rigs, although some plunking produces well. In the clearer upper river, spoons often entice bright battlers, as will spinners and, from boats, back-trolled plugs.

SAMISH RIVER: Small, easy to overlook, but often productive, the Samish River rises north of Wickersham and east of Lake Whatcom. It dips southwest first and then loops back north to Samish Bay near Edison. Steelheading begins to perk in December, comes on strongly in January, its peak month, then simmers down through February to its March closure. Along the winter way, from 600 to over 1,400 steelhead may be hoisted from the Samish's pasture-fed, teak-colored waters.

Only a dozen or two summer-run steelhead surprise trout fishermen during the June 1-March 31 season, and all wild steelhead hooked from Feb. 1 through March 31 must be released. The river is open from the mouth to Old Highway 99 bridge, then a closed area from Old 99 to a Department of Fisheries rack and open again above the rack to the Hickson Bridge. Highways 9, I-5, 11 and 237 all cross the Samish and numerous smaller roads provide easy access to the banks of the tiny stream.

The soft banks of the Samish are thick with alder and willow, and the narrow streambed often is studded with downed trees and rootwads that furnish good cover for steelhead but are tough to fish among and around. The best bet is to go to heavy main lines of 15-to 18-pound test and leaders nearly as strong. Drift rigging is the standard gear used in tight runs, pockets and undercut bank holes of this river and bait and bobbers are the steelheaders' top choices on the Samish.

SAMMAMISH RIVER: Joggers and bikers may pause to watch while steelheaders on the mostly urban Sammamish River lean back on their rods to persuade hatchery winter steelhead to come to hand. A truly flatland stream, the Sammamish was dredged and its banks stabilized nearly 40 years ago, leaving a weedy slough of uniform depth that winds slowly from Lake Sammamish to the Kenmore tip of Lake Washington. Since a jogging/bike/hiking trail follows most of the river's length, almost every yard of the river is accessible to fishermen plying its gentle flow in split seasons running from June 1-Aug. 31 and again Dec. 1-end of February.

Access is from Highways 202, 405, 522 and sideroads that brush the Sammamish River on its twisting route through the wide valley from Redmond to Bothell.

Banner years for the Sammamish were 1971-72 and 1972-73, when more than 1,150 steelhead were caught from The Slough, but recent years have seen sea lion and seal incursions into the Ballard Locks area, through which all Sammamish steelhead must pass, that have decimated the runs. Still, steelheaders expect a winter catch of 350 to 500 hatchery fish (all wild steelhead must be released) in a good year.

Small drift bobbers, bobbers and yarn, bait, bait and yarn, and medium size spoons and spinners, best fished on light lines and leaders, will appeal to Sammamish River steelhead. Often, very little, or no, sinker weight is needed with an egg cluster or shrimp bait in the light current.

The slow flow causes many hang-ups, and Sammamish River steelhead are noted for their delicate bite habits, but playing hooked steelhead in The Slough is a ball, as they will leap more freely and often than fish stuck by your steel in deep rivers. Also, the Sammamish remains fishable even when it is two to three feet higher than normal when swollen by rains. It will gradually turn to a rich coffee color that's still productive, while other area streams are chocolate brown and raging.

SAUK RIVER: Big, wide and having many huge boulder beds and deep holes, the Sauk River charges down from the Mt. Baker Forest to meet the Skagit River at Rockport. The upper Sauk is reached off the Mountain Loop Road from Darrington and the lower river is tracked by Highway 530 between Darrington and Rockport.

Once famed for a late March run of huge native steelhead, the Sauk now produces 300 to 600 winter steelhead yearly in a season from June 15 through the last day of February from its mouth to the mouth of the White Chuck River. A catch-and-release only season from March 1-April 30 between the river mouth and bridge at Darrington still permits anglers to wrestle some mighty steelhead, but none may be retained.

Drift bobbers are excellent choices for fishing the Sauk, as are cluster egg and shrimp baits. Narrow, heavy spoons and more standard 1/2-ounce Dardevle shapes also are effective for probing the boulder beds for Sauk River slab steelhead. A good pattern is the Otto's Ace Bait No. 4 hammered nickel with orange flame back and center nickel slash, although chartreuse with red spots also will draw slashing strikes.

SKAGIT RIVER: Perhaps the most renowned and best-known of Washington's steelhead rivers, the Skagit River in its 1960-70 years of greatest production gave up 14,000 to 19,000 steelhead to bank and boat fishermen each season and once topped 34,000. Overall catches have dropped, but this large and popular stream still vies for yearly honors among the top five state streams by yielding 3,000 to 6,000 steelhead, including some summer-runs but predominantly winter fish.

The Skagit originates in British Columbia and is trapped by Ross, Diablo and Gorge power dams before flowing from the North Cascades National Park to find salt water in Saratoga Passage near La Conner-Conway.

Interstate 5 and a network of local roads will lead plunkers and bank anglers to the lower North and South Fork Skagit arms at its delta west of Mt. Vernon. Highway 20 is the route up the north bank of the big river that is liberally spotted with public access points and boat launches. Both banks of the river can be approached between Sedro Woolley and Concrete, while the rugged terrain above Concrete limits all but dedicated fishermen to the north shore, reached from Highway 20.

The wide, deep and strong currents of the Skagit host a large, hard-fighting breed of steelhead best fished for from jet sleds and drift boats. There are guides operating year-around for anglers who drift-fish, hotshot plugs or cast flies to attract the Skagit's steelies. However, bank anglers have good opportunities, also, to hook their share of steelhead on winged and standard bobbers, baits and spoons.

June and July are the best months for summer anglers, while March outranks the December-February catches in most years. There are specific areas closed to fishing late in the steelhead season and varying closure dates, which require steelheaders to carefully read and follow the regulations brochure on the Skagit.

SKYKOMISH RIVER: Fed from trickles beginning on the west slopes of the Mt. Baker-Snoqualmie National Forest, tributaries to the Skykomish River rush through rocky gorges and canyons to become North and South Forks, then join together near Index as the mainstem Sky and surge downward again alongside Highway 2 to meld its water with the Snoqualmie River below Monroe, where the two streams then form the Snohomish.

A highly popular river easily reached from the metropolitan Seattle area, the Skykomish produces 4,700 to 5,800 steelhead per year currently, though it has seen catches much higher. It has ample public access and well-spaced, concrete boat launches that allow angling trips of half-day or day-long duration. There are guides who fish the Sky through the winter season and who will make summer trips by arrangement.

While the steelheading season on the Skykomish is basically from June 1 through March 31, there are area closures, some boat restrictions and selective fishery regulations of which anglers must be cognizant. Read the regulations very cautiously before planning a March steelheading venture.

Skykomish summer-run steelhead are best caught in July and August, while the winter-runs show up most strongly in January. The river is easily fished from the bank at multiple access points and amply rewards drift-fishermen using bobbers or bait, or spoon and spinner anglers. Boaters do extremely well by hotshotting with green and blue metallic finish plugs, as well as others in crawdad and fish scale patterns.

Both North Fork and South Fork Skykomish anglers also take fair July-February steelhead catches, with the North Fork the more productive of the two tributaries.

SNOHOMISH RIVER: A steelhead thoroughfare for entry into the Skykomish and Snoqualmie rivers, the broad, slow Snohomish begins at the junction of the two tributaries under Highway 522 south of Monroe, then meanders northwest to enter salt water at Everett. Much of the river flows through private land that affords little access, but enough steelheaders find their way to its banks to hoist 1,600 to 1,800 steelhead from the Snohomish each year and, when counts at the end of 1988 are reviewed, that total may zoom dramatically as a result of excellent fishing.

Though back roads closely follow the river from Monroe to Snohomish and again from there to Everett, there is little room for parking and fishermen must find access on their own, as there are only a couple small, rough boat launches in addition to a tiny ramp in downtown Snohomish. Anglers can motor up from Everett or drift/motor down from Monroe to fish the middle river with plugs or bait/bobber drift rigs.

Spoons cast to many of the Snohomish's deep holes also account for steelhead catches, as will bait or bobber rigs either cast or plunked from the banks.

June and July deliver the best bite from summer-runs, while December to early February fishermen garner the bulk of the Snohomish winter catches. From Highway 529 to the mouth, the Snohomish is open to fishing year-round, while the upstream portion is open June 1-March 31.

SNOQUALMIE RIVER: From the towering 210-foot Snoqualmie Falls found off Highway 202 between Fall City and Snoqualmie, to its conjunction with the Skykomish near Monroe, the Snoqualmie lays a serpentine track through a broad, farm-filled valley often partly flooded by spring and winter high waters. Run-off from fields keeps the river colored an emerald green in "clear" condition and the prime time to fish the Snoqualmie is when it is dropping from a two to five-foot "pasture puck" brown raise to normal.

Catches of 6,000 to 8,000 steelhead per season in the 60s and 70s have for the past few years dissipated to 2,000-3,400 winter fish from the Snoqualmie and perhaps a couple hundred summer-runs annually, in my opinion largely due to the migration run timing of Snoqualmie fish being early December... the same period when Indian tribal netting in salt water off Everett is most intense.

There are good boat ramps available to the public on this pleasant river, with the ramps adequately spaced for short or long trips. Access to its banks is excellent, also, and the entire river from the Tokul Creek Fish Hatchery to Carnation Research Farms below Carnation is heavily fished by shoreline anglers. For years, a clown pattern Okie Drifter (chartreuse with red spots) was a never-fail upper river producer, but there now is a wide range in bobber styles and colors used. Cluster egg and shrimp or prawn baits trick hundreds of Snoqualmie fish to hooks and boat anglers pulling plugs or lazily drifting downstream while boondogging drift bobber/bait rigs behind them do very well too.

Summer fishing begins June 1 and spots on the upper river from the falls to Fall City produce fair catches, as does the Carnation/Tolt River mouth area. Light tackle produces the best summer results for bait and bobber users, and some fishermen will cast 3/8-or 1/2-ounce spoons to generate strikes. The winter season pumps out the most steelhead from mid-December to late February and ends March 31. Generally, there is a flurry of fishing for heavy wild fish which can yield 20-pounders two to three weeks before the season closes.

STILLAGUAMISH RIVER: Best known for fine fly-fishing on the North Fork Stillaguamish, the mainstem Stilly and South Fork Stillaguamish also deserve their share of good repute. Put them together and steelheaders may currently expect 2,300 to over 3,000 steelhead to be taken annually from this delightful stream. Credit the North Fork for a few hundred July-August steelhead and nearly 1,000 December-March steelhead and divide another 1,400 to 1,600 between the main river and South Fork and you'll have the picture of an evenly-balanced, productive system.

Highway 530 closely follows the Stillaguamish from Stanwood near salt water almost to Darrington, where the North Fork darts upward into the Mt.

Baker National Forest. There are many small pull-off spots for anglers to park, and a couple large public access points. Anglers should note there is a wild steelhead release regulation in place March 1 to Nov. 30 for the North Fork and that, while the main stem and North Fork of the river system remain open to March 31, the South Fork Stillaguamish closes at the end of February.

Popular bobber patterns on the Stilly and North Fork are two-tone chartreuse-and-orange winged and round bodies, or peach, nickelled, pink or lime finish Lil' Corkies. The top spoon pattern of which I am aware has a nickelled finish, with red spots on its back. Boats may be used on the North Fork only for transportation, while fishing from floating devices is legal on both the South Fork and main Stillaguamish.

TOKUL CREEK: This short, shallow stream may be the hottest 100-yard steelhead fishery in the state...if you can enjoy short-line, repetitive dredging of one or two tiny pockets of water while shoulder-to-shoulder with dozens of other rodsmen.

From 500 to 1,200 steelhead per year are plucked from Tokul Creek on an assortment of bobber/yarn or bobber/bait rigs. Most of these are taken from late January through early March.

Tokul Creek is found via Fish Hatchery Road off Highway 202 midway between Fall City and Snoqualmie Falls.

TOLT RIVER: Starting near the northwest tip of the Alpine Lakes Wilderness, the Tolt River snakes its way through deep, brush-filled and rocky canyons, is held temporarily by a Seattle water supply dam, then runs through Weyerhaeuser timber property before reaching the Snoqualmie Valley floor near Carnation and joining the Snoqualmie.

Increasingly sealed off from road access by private property, the Tolt has recently yielded 250-500 winter and summer steelhead to anglers who can find a route to the tiny river's banks. Once there, wading fishermen are relatively free to work upstream or down. One public access at road's end five miles above the town of Carnation allows fishermen to penetrate to the upper river, but the majority of steelheaders devote their efforts to the lower two to three miles.

Open June 1 from its mouth to the USGS trolley cable below the confluence of North and South Fork, the bulk of the Tolt's fish are taken in the December-early February winter season. Several dozen summer-runs may be caught shortly after the June opener, and a scattered few continue to show in July and August. Best lures in summer are miniature bobber/yarn combinations, flies, yarn ties, spinners and small spoons. Bait is banned June 1 through Nov. 30. The Tolt River generally runs low and clear as glass in summer and light tackle is recommended.

In the old days excessive trout limits ensured the slaughter of hundreds of thousands of steelhead smolts migrating to the sea.

REGION 5 – VANCOUVER

BIG WHITE SALMON RIVER: An unusual steelhead fishery, most of the fish caught from the Big White Salmon River are taken from the semi-lake formed at its junction with the Columbia River about four miles east of Bingen. Held by embankments for the S.P. & S. Railroad and Highway 14, this big backwater is deep and cold, a major attraction for upstream-bound anadromous steelhead pointed toward mid-state Columbia tributaries or the Snake River system.

About 3½ miles of the Big White Salmon are open to year-round fishing, from its mouth to within 400 feet of the dam below Northwestern Lake. The lower mile-and-three-quarters is plumbed by slow-trolling anglers inching small boats against the current while towing lightly-leaded Flatfish, Kwikfish and other banana-shape plugs. Fire orange, gold, metallic green and coho scale finish plugs in sizes from U-20 down to F-7 (Flatfish models) are tied directly on the main line, the line weighted with split shot scattered 6, 8 or 10 inches apart so that the plug slowly sinks, and 35 to 40 feet of mono is let out behind the boat.

Oared cartoppers seem to be the best choice for trolling the mouth of the Big White, though larger boats have equal success with electric motors. All steelhead taken from the Big White Salmon are counted as summer-runs and the most of 2,000 to 3,500 annual catches are made in the prime months of July, August and September, although winter anglers continue to take some fish. Wild steelhead must be released May 16-Oct. 31.

Some bank angling access is available immediately below the road and railway bridges at the mouth of the Big White Salmon and fishermen score well on heavy spinners pitched to both rivers' currents. There is parking along north-south Highway 141, which grazes the east side of the popular fishing area, some pull-out spots along Highway 14 and a fairly large daytime access area with restroom facilities on the west shore of the backwater.

COLUMBIA RIVER: From the Megler-Astoria Bridge to McNary Dam near Plymouth in Washington and Umatilla, OR., steelhead fishermen take 8,000 to over 15,000 fish annually from the broad, liquid border between states. Plunkers line popular sand and gravel bars to heave winged bobbers and/or baits to the edges of main currents of the Columbia, then

Jim Bedford tricked this late-winter hatchery steelhead with a small spinner on a stream near Astoria, Oregon.

pour their coffee and settle back into lawn chairs to await action. Boaters also take a good number of steelhead on drift-rigged bobbers and baits, or on trolled plugs.

No steelhead may be kept April 1-May 15 between the Megler-Astoria Bridge and I-5 bridge and wild steelhead must be released in this area from May 16-Oct. 31. From I-5 to the Highway 395 bridge no steelhead may be kept April 1-June 15 and wild steelhead caught between June 16 and Dec. 31 must be released.

Public access is extremely good along the Columbia. There's a latticework of federal, state and county roads that parallel and approach the big river and steelheaders who refer to county and city maps have little difficulty finding fishing spots.

COWEEMAN RIVER: The Coweeman River rises northwest of Elk Mountain in Cowlitz County and zigzags west to join the Cowlitz about four miles below Kelso. From 700 to 1,000 steelhead are caught from this underfished stream per year and banner seasons have in the past yielded double those numbers.

Access to the lower Coweeman is via city streets leading east out of Kelso, but the upper Coweeman is approached only from the Carrolls/Rose Valley Road. One public access area is located near Jim Watson Creek, providing up-down wading access in the upper stretch of river below the angling deadline at Mulholland Creek.

Cutbanks, holes, pockets and deep runs of the Coweeman yield steelhead to anglers fishing bait/bobber drift rigs, spinners and spoons. A fat nightcrawler sifted into likely resting spots often will be warmly welcomed by waiting steelhead.

Steelheading cranks up June 1 and the season expires March 31 for hatchery and wild steelhead alike. Only a scant handful of summer-runs are caught. Late December through February is the peak time to be on this small, but productive river.

COWLITZ RIVER: Leading all Washington rivers in nearly every seasonal steelhead summary since the early 1970s, the Cowlitz River produces 10,000 to 18,000 steelhead yearly, and has recorded as many as 32,000 in one year. This may in part be due to no Indian tribal netting, but a well-planned, effective hatchery program must also be heavily credited.

Open from mouth to Mayfield Dam year-around, the Cowlitz can provide steelhead willing to exercise your rod arm any month of the year, but delivers its largest numbers of summer fish in July and August and winter-runs in December and January. Widespread tributaries grab their sustenance from the slopes of both Mt. Rainier and Mt. Adams before being stalled by huge dams forming Riffe Lake and Mayfield Lake, then rush onward to furnish the incoming steelhead with an aquatic route spiced with the come-hither scent of home stream chemicals.

Bracketed by I-5 and Highways 411 and 506 from its mouth to Toledo, tapped by country gravel routes and Highway 12 zipping upriver to Salkum, the Cowlitz is readily reached by anglers from north, south and east. The big river has more than a half-dozen good concrete public launches staggered at day-trip intervals from Salkum to its junction with the Columbia River below Kelso.

Steelheaders also have ample bank access points and plunkers or drift rig casters probably outnumber boat anglers three to one. However, catches often seem to be split about evenly between boat and bank rods. One of the best ways of fishing the Cowlitz is a tactic called the "drop-back," wherein fishermen anchor up and fish short lines behind their boat, lifting their pencil lead to walk bait and bobber rigs downstream a few feet at a time until a steelhead picks up their hook or the rig won't travel farther. Other boaters do very well by hotshotting plugs of all makes and colors.

Hardware is excellent for enticing strikes from early fall and late winter steelhead, especially long and narrow spoons such as the 1/2-ounce Ottogator and Krocodile. Hammered nickel or brass finishes on these spoons, sporting some spots or slashes of orange or red on their backs, are time-proven steelhead attractors in the Cowlitz.

DRANO LAKE/LITTLE WHITE SALMON RIVER: Short river systems along the Columbia often have the sweetest, richest rewards, and the Little White Salmon River and the tremendous Drano Lake backwater pool at its mouth are no exception. The Little White Salmon squeezes out of the southern tip of the Gifford Pinchot National Forest to contribute its flow to the Columbia at Cook, on Highway 14.

A special rig and sensitive touch pays off best in Drano Lake, which is wide enough so that the outflow moves very slowly toward the big river, causing standard drift rigs to drop to bottom and snag. Instead of pencil lead in surgical tubing or pinched-on hollow core lead, "savvy" steelheaders at Drano Lake use a sliding egg sinker above a barrel swivel and two-foot leader offering bait or bait/small bobber combination. Midway between the swivel and hook, a small trout bobber or large, neutral color Lil' Corky is pegged to the leader.

When this set-up is cast and allowed to settle to the bottom of Drano, anglers begin a subtle, gentle retrieve. As the suspended bait/bobber undulates under the float, passing steelhead are thought to give it rocking action they can't resist...and their bite can take shape as either a gentle nip light as a tiny trout would take or a vicious, line-stripping smash!

Parking is limited at Drano Lake, but there is good access along the west bank. Boaters can put in at a rough launch and do well by trolling plugs at the lower end of Drano and in the northeast corner.

The Little White Salmon River is open June 1-March 31 from mouth to water intake of federal fish hatchery at Cook, and anglers are advised to read carefully the regulations on fishing Nov. 1 to March 31 in the river below the fishway to markers at the hatchery. For the peak of steelheading, try the period from early August midway into September.

ELOCHOMAN RIVER: Almost every Washington angler has heard of the Elochoman River, but only a few thousand fishermen can easily direct you to this little stream's banks. Not hidden...it's just out of the way of most highway travel, about 25 miles west of Kelso via Highway 4. The key to sharing some of the Elochoman's 600-1,200 summer-runs and 3,000 to over 6,000 winter steelhead is that you have to be there when it's hot.

The short stream drains almost due south from upper Wahkiakum County into the Columbia River at Cathlamet and its fish move through quickly. When the bite's on, get there soon or the run will be gone upstream. Highway 104 pokes its way north along the river, leading you to several public accesses, and fisherman trails line other popular spots. Standard drift rigs, floated jigs, spoons and spinners all appeal to Elochoman steelhead.

The Elochoman is open to steelheading June 1-March 31 from mouth to mouth of West Fork. All wild steelhead must be released during the winter season.

GRAYS RIVER: The Grays River arcs downward from the Willapa Hills to ease into Grays Bay and the Columbia River between Megler and Altoona. Fishermen approach this stream from Highway 4, the Ocean Beaches Route, then forge upriver on county and logging roads to fish for 400 to 1,000 winter fish and a minimal number of summer-runs.

Best catches bounce between January and February and yearly totals depend largely upon the stocking program for this river. Fish kept must be hatchery-produced, having a missing adipose or ventral fin, and all wild steelhead must be released.

Bait, bait/yarn, bait/bobber and bobber/yarn drift rigs are tops for Grays River steelheading. Small spinners and spoons also may be worked in its deeper runs and pockets, or teased beneath undercut banks.

KALAMA RIVER: Mt. St. Helen's disastrous eruption fortunately affected the Kalama River only slightly, as this beautiful stream flowing down from the southwestern corner of the National Volcanic Monument area has long been a favorite summer-run and wintertime steelheading stream for Washingtonians and visitors from nearby Oregon.

From 2,900 to 7,700 summer-run steelhead and 2,500-3,000 winter fish may be caught each year from the highly popular, easy to reach and fish southwestern stream. Access is via the Kalama River Road, which departs I-5 shortly above the town of Kalama and climbs eastward along the north river bank.

Open to fishing year-around, there are area and time closures affecting steelheading on the Kalama that are detailed in the regulations booklet. All wild steelhead must be released through Oct. 31 and there is a fly-fishing-only area above Summers Creek.

There is good access, though many private homes line the Kalama's banks and no trespassing signs are becoming more prevalent. Five public boat launches allow fishermen to drift the Kalama from the mouth of the little Kalama River downward and motorized craft are permitted from mouth to Modrow Bridge in the lower river.

Winter anglers generally employ drift gear – bobbers or bait or both – to garner strikes, while summer-run anglers do best with tiny bobber/yarn rigs, flies, small baits, spinners and spoons. The Kalama has many fine pools and runs and lots of boulder beds having large pockets in which steelhead find cool, shady cover. The peak of summer angling occurs in July, while December and January share wintertime honors.

KLICKITAT RIVER: In barely 20 miles of driving on Highway 14 east from Cook to Lyle, anglers heading for the Klickitat River pass from Cascade Range dampness into the welcoming warmth of the Columbia Basin. There, the main Klickitat surges south from the Goat Rocks Wilderness Area to pick up the Little Klickitat northeast of Wahkiacus, then flow into the Columbia near Lyle.

The lower Klickitat, from mouth to the Fisher Hill Bridge, is open June 1 to Nov. 30 and the river 400 feet above No. 5 fishway to its source is open June 1-Nov. 30 for taking hatchery steelhead only. All wild steelhead must be freed in this purely summertime fishery for 800 to 2,000 steelhead taken annually.

Highway 142 closely pursues the Klickitat northeast to the towns of Klickitat and Wahkiacus, providing good access, and the Goldendale-Glenwood Road leads to and along the upper river, while fishermen may also reach the Klickitat via U.S. 97 from the Yakima area by leaving Highway 12 near Toppenish.

Drift boaters may launch at Leidl Campground or Wahkiacus Campground and take their craft out at Wahkiacus (from Leidl) or Turkey Farm Campground, below which point the river smashes over savage falls and powers through sheer rock canyons. The mouth can be fished from motorized boats launched in the Columbia at Lyle.

Best fishing on the Klickitat River is late August through September, a time when cooling night temperatures reduce the amount of glacial run-off that heavily colors the water before noon in June to early August.

Broad, shallow runs, deep slots and some large pools provide the most of the Klickitat's strong, hard-fighting steelhead. On chilly mornings, fly-fishermen working the upper drifts do well, while spoons, drift rigs and bait (including grasshoppers) also account for a good number of Klickitat steelhead. Anglers are cautioned to watch and listen for the possible presence of rattlesnakes among the sun-baked rocks and stones on the river's banks...DOW campground personnel dispatched two in one morning on a weekend when this writer fished the lower river.

LEWIS RIVER: The Lewis River and its North Fork and East Fork, added together, produce 5,000 to 8,000 summer-run steelhead and an average 4,000 to 5,000 winter catch. That's enough to put this shortchanged river system into second or third place among best-producing state rivers if its catches were so totalled. The Lewis River system receives plenty of attention from steelheaders not for numbers of fish alone, but because it holds big, strong steelhead, one of which still is the current wintertime record, at 32 pounds, 12 ounces.

The North Fork Lewis rises on the west face of Mt. Adams, while the East Fork originates in high wilderness north of Lookout Mountain. The main river and both forks are open to angling year-around, with all wild steelhead hooked in the main river or East Fork between April 1 and Oct. 31 illegal to retain.

Though the North Fork is penned by three reservoirs – Swift, Yale and Merwin – the Lewis is a strong, deep and cold stream that breeds powerful fish. Winter anglers are well advised to gear up with heavier tackle in the event they tie into a wallhanger fish. Bait, bobbers, hardware and flies all draw strikes from steelhead in the forks, while boaters do best below I-5 with bright plugs hotshotted on the shoulders of main currents.

Interstate Highway 5 crosses the East Fork and Lewis River near Woodland, and anglers seeking the East Fork upstream lies and pockets will follow the Lewis River Bottom Road out of LaCenter and county roads to Yacolt. Three boat launches on the East Fork Lewis allow floating fishermen to ply their skills and to stop to fish the popular bank spots. Four public boat ramps on the North Fork Lewis allow similar fishing access on that fine stream.

SKOOKUMCHUCK RIVER: Increased numbers of steelhead smolts planted in the tiny Skookumchuck River have prompted a modern-days record catch of more than 1,200 winter-runs taken in the 1986-87 season, a huge jump from the few hundred fish plucked from this Thurston County river in previous years.

The Skookumchuck begins in the orphaned patch of Snoqualmie National Forest between Morton and Alder, and flows to meet the Chehalis River at Centralia. It provides best fishing in the upper river from Bucoda, on Highway 507, about eight miles via the Skookumchuck Road, to the Pacific Power & Light dam holding back Skookumchuck Reservoir.

This is pastureland water having quick, shallow runs, some pocket water and undercut bank fishing, with only a few huge pools to probe. Bait/yarn, bobber rigs and floated jigs and baits are tops for fishing the snaggy, brushy little river. Open June 1 to April 30, the peak time for fishing the Skookumchuck is late in the season, March through April.

TOUTLE RIVER: Slowly rejuvenating after the blow-out of Mt. St. Helens, the Toutle River system had been closed to fishing for several years, but opened again in 1986-87 for steelheading only and now allows taking only hatchery steelhead from any of the mainstem Toutle, North Fork or South Fork. Access is via Highway 504 for the South Fork Toutle and upper North Fork, while Tower Road drops downstream on the mainstem from the two tributaries' junction to Castle Rock.

The destruction of the North Fork of the Toutle River when Mt. St. Helens erupted was devastating. This once fine steelhead river will be recovering for scores of years to come. This is what part of its watershed looked like two weeks after the blast in 1980.

First to respond has been the South Fork, where anglers found nearly 500 willing summer-runs and almost 300 winter steelhead in the first season allowed. The main Toutle and North Fork yielded only scant handcounts of steelhead in each angling period.

The South Fork Toutle is regaining its crystal clarity and fishermen are advised to work it with light monofilament, small baits and bobbers, or tiny spinners for best results. In the North Fork and mainstem Toutle River, siltation, ash and run-off still clouds the water and fishing with medium to large winged bobbers or bobber/bait combinations might be the best approach.

WASHOUGAL RIVER: The Washougal River can be approached from east or west off Highway 14 via Highway 140, which loops from Camas to the junction of the West (North) Fork Washougal and back to Hwy. 14 partway to the town of Skamania. A public access boat launch below the forks and another public ramp about five miles downstream allow enjoyable daylong float trips, and several public access sites and fisherman's trails lead to the productive river's banks.

Craig Lattanzi battles a summer steelhead on the lower Deschutes River

Summer and winter steelheaders ply the Washougal's waters for 1,200-2,700 suntanned steelhead and 1,500 to more than 3,000 winter fish. Open year-around, the Washougal regulations allow only hatchery steelhead to be retained in daily bags taken from April 1 through Oct. 31.

Fly-fishing, or angling with baits, bobbers, and jigs or flies under floats are productive tactics on the Washougal. Summertime anglers take the largest catches of steelhead from June through July, while December produces the best winter bite.

WIND RIVER: The Wind River drops almost due south out of the Gifford Pinchot National Forest to enter the Bonneville Pool of the Columbia River near Carson. Angling success on this fine, but small river varies from a few hundred to over 700 summer-run steelhead annually. (Although open June 1-March 31, all Wind River fish are counted as summer catches.) All wild steelhead must be released June 1-Oct. 31.

Fishing access is via the Wind River Road, which leads past Government Mineral Springs and closely follows the river. Good lure choices for fishing the Wind River are flies, yarn ties, baits such as shrimp or cluster eggs, bobber lures and spinners or spoons. There is one public access boat launch on the Wind, near the mouth at the Department of Wildlife Old Hatchery Site.

REGION 6 – ABERDEEN

BOGACHIEL RIVER: Dashing down from the Olympic National Park, the Bogachiel River carves a twisting, convoluted pathway that first heads northwest toward the town of Forks and then turns southwest to join the Soleduck River about three miles outside the Quillayute Indian Reservation and the mingled Quillayute River waters then pour into the Pacific Ocean. Summer steelheaders pluck 80 to 150 bright and big anadromous 'bows from the Bogie and wintertime fishermen punch 2,200 to over 3,000 fish.

Access to the Bogachiel is achieved via Highway 101, from either Aberdeen or Port Angeles, to the Forks area. From there, the La Push-Quillayute Road leads downriver, while Dowans Creek Road and the county road to the Bogachiel Ranger Station bracket the upper river.

A half-dozen public boat launches afford good access to the Bogachiel River, down to about six miles from salt water, and other accesses furnish bank anglers casting room to wrestle with the Bogachiel's hefty ironheads. The season is open from the mouth to the National Park boundary June 1-April 30.

Boatmen hook many steelhead on plugs with the hotshotting method and more by drift-fishing bait or bait/bobber rigs. The liquid green of the Bogie also yields catches to anglers fishing brightly-colored spoons and twinkling spinners in its pockets, pools and deep runs. January is the strongest month for Bogachiel river catches.

CALAWAH RIVER: Long, pincer-like forks of the Calawah River, a major tributary of the Bogachiel, reach along both flanks of Rugged Ridge in Olympic National Park to feed the mainstem river that joins the Bogie a few miles west of the town of Forks.

Highway 101 crosses the Calawah and county and logging roads permit steelheaders to forge along its banks upstream or down. A good number of the Calawah's 200-500 summer-run catch are banked each of the summer months, while mid-December to early February is the prime time to tackle the river for a chance at 500 to 1,800 winter fish. The Calawah is open to steelheading from mouth to forks June 1-April 30, while the South Fork Calawah season extends from June 1 to the last day of February from its mouth to Hyas Creek.

CHEHALIS RIVER: Steelheaders who ignore the inviting waters of the Chehalis River are missing opportunities of catching 700 to 1,000 winter-run fish. It's easy to consider fishing elsewhere when the Chehalis's major run doesn't show up in strength until the middle of February, but from that point through March, this river can sizzle!

The Chehalis is fed from the low hills surrounding Washington's prairie land in Thurston and upper Lewis counties, then gathers spring-fed creeks and south tip Olympic Peninsula streams in its sedate passage to the Pacific, entering the ocean at Grays Harbor.

Highway 12 traces the north bank of the Chehalis for most of this journey and county roads track and bump into the south bank. Numerous rough and improved boat launch sites stud the Chehalis's path, allowing boat anglers plenty of fishing, and other fishing access points are haunted by bank drifters and plunkers when the word goes out that winter steelhead are in the stream. Bobbers. baits, and combinations of the two work well for hatchery and wild steelhead alike.

ELWHA RIVER: Once one of the most productive streams in Washington and famed for huge salmon as well as hefty steelhead, the Elwha River is now doubly dammed and only the few miles of lower river below Lake Aldwell's dam are open to steelheading from June 1 through April 15. It tumbles north from the Olympic National Park to meet the Strait of Juan de Fuca at Angeles Point.

Fishing success fluctuates widely on the Elwha, with 700 to more than 3,500 winter steelhead biting steel, and 100-400 summer fish hoisted from its deep pools and glides. Access to the head of this water is about three miles north of Port Angeles via Highway 101 and the lower river is reached off county roads.

For bare-knuckle brawls with bright and brash steelhead still having salt water on their tails, try fishing the brackish portion of the Elwha in June and July for a scattering of summer-runs and again in December and January, prime months for winter fish. Bait-casting, spinning or fly-fishing gear all will connect you to some of the wildest steelhead ever encountered!

HOH RIVER: Western slopes of 7,965-foot Mt. Olympus trickle their melting snow water into rivulets that become the mighty Hoh River, which swiftly grows as it churns and chuckles downhill to meet the Pacific Ocean between the Hoh Indian Reservation and Oil City. Unhindered by dams, the Hoh sometimes makes minor shifts in its course through the Rain Forest valley, knocking down small alders and evergreens in one area and creating broad sand and gravel bars in another.

Steelheading season is June 1-April 15 from the Hoh's mouth to the mouth of Mt. Tom Creek and the South Fork outside the National Park boundary. August may be the best month for summer anglers seeking some 400 to 800 fish, depending on rainfall. Best winter fishing for 1,400 to 4,400 steelhead occurs in January. A portion of the Hoh's fish are remnant natives, but the majority of steelhead caught are hatchery plants.

Fishermen can approach the Hoh off Highway 101, which crosses the river south of Forks. The Oil City Road leads from Hwy. 101 to the coast, while the Upper Hoh Valley Road is the upstream route. Good access, and several scattered public boat launch sites permit anglers to tap the Hoh from boat or bank. Best fishing is from boats, with plugs, drift baits or bobbers top choices of most fishermen. Spoons and spinners are good options for fishing the deep pools near the mouth.

HUMPTULIPS RIVER: Ask an oldtimer about Humptulips River steelheading in the 1950s and 1960s and you'll likely spark a nostalgic gleam in his eye and spur tales of seasons that produced 6,000 to 8,000 fish. Current fishing still is good, though not great, yielding 150-300 summer-runs and 1,300 to 2,100 winter steelhead.

The Hump is an easy river to find and to fish. It pours down from the south side of the Olympic National Park, through the Olympic National Forest, to freshen North Bay of Grays Harbor. A fisherman could reach the lower Humptulips via Highway 109, from Hoquiam to Ocean Shores, which crosses the river above the mouth, or take Highway 101 north to the town of Humptulips. From there, the Humptulips Road heads back southwest to the lower river, while the East Fork Road and logging roads forge upriver.

Open to steelheading from mouth to forks June 1-April 30 and with its East Fork and West Fork also

Chuck Schroeder with roe-caught summer steelhead of hatchery origin on Washington's Green River at Flaming Geyser Bridge.

sharing those time frames, the Humptulips' rocky, twisting streambed hosts good numbers of fresh summer-runs from June through July and spreads its winter catch numbers from mid-December to early March.

Most of the public access sites on the Hump also are improved or rough boat launch sites which give entry to the river to anglers floating for their catches, to favorite spots to be thoroughly worked from the bank, or anchored positions in the drifts. Bobber/bait/yarn rigs are prime candidates for eliciting strikes from Humptulips steelhead. Spinners, spoons and plugs also account for catches from this popular steelhead river.

LYRE RIVER: The Lyre River hurries only five or six steep miles from Crescent Lake to the Strait of Juan de Fuca, entering the salt water near Low Point. It is a tiny, rocky, fast and shallow stream that has an impassable waterfall about three miles from the mouth. Steelheading in the lower river section, however, produces 100 to 300 summer catches and winter counts run from 600 to nearly 1,300 bright, and sometimes very big, fish.

Highway 101 is the entry route to the Lyre River area, and anglers will take Highway 112 west from the tip of Lake Aldwell for about 15 miles to reach the Lyre.

Steelheaders tackling the Lyre generally spool on 15- to 18-pound test line and use strong leaders, despite the small stream running clear when other area rivers might be out of shape for angling. Often, steelhead from 14 to more than 20 pounds will jump on a rodsman's hook, then head back for salt water!

Lures most commonly employed on the Lyre are drift bobbers, fished bare or with a bit of yarn, cluster eggs and yarn, or yarn ties. These are dropped into pockets behind boulders or into known or suspected depressions in the swift-moving river's bottom. Regulars who frequent the Lyre move from one favored spot to another, testing each possible lie with a few casts, then move on, searching upstream or down to locate fish.

NASELLE RIVER: Naselle River steelheaders take from 800 to 2,200 winter steelhead and a very few summer-runs each year from this southwestern Pacific County stream. Within easy reach of anglers living in the coastal area from Portland to Tacoma, the Naselle offers excellent bank fishing in the upper river and good trolling prospects from the town of Naselle to the Highway 101 bridge above the mouth of the river at Willapa Bay.

Parpala Road and the Ocean Beach Highway depart Highway 101 on south and north banks of the Naselle and parallel the river to Naselle, affording access. There is an improved boat launch at the town of Naselle. Fishermen heading for the rocky, deep holes and runs of the upper Naselle will follow the Naselle North Valley Road to the North Fork and East Fork conjunction.

Bait, bobbers and bobber/yarn lures effectively fool Naselle River steelhead best in December and January, and anglers working spinners and spoons under and along its underwater shelves and ledges also draw strikes from bright, feisty fish. Trollers do best in the lower river with hotshotting tactics.

QUEETS RIVER: The Queets River is almost completely within the Olympic National Park. It originates high on Mt. Seattle and flows west through the narrow Queets Corridor and then across the Quinault Indian Reservation to the Pacific Ocean . An easily-colored stream, due to being glacially fed, the Queets produces large, strong steelhead that are a delight to battle.

Summer fishermen take a couple hundred

steelhead, most of them caught in July and August, and winter anglers find January and February the top months for a seasonal catch of between 600 and 2,100 steelhead. (Regulations for steelheading within National Park boundaries must be followed.) Most of these fish are taken on the upper river, but anglers who hire an Indian guide and buy a permit to fish the section passing through the Quinault Indian reservation also catch numerous big steelhead.

SATSOP RIVER: Home to a good number of 20-pound and larger steelhead, the Satsop River is fed by forks dropping south out of the Olympic National Forest toward the Chehalis River, joining that stream at the town of Satsop. It is open to fishing during trout season and from mouth to bridge at Shafer Park from Nov. 1 through March 31, while its Turnow Branch and the West Fork Satsop have winter steelhead seasons open Nov. 1-Jan. 31.

Boaters do very well on the Satsop, taking the lion's share of 400 to 900 winter steelhead in February and March. Bank spots are available, as the Satsop has nearly a dozen public access sites, as well as local fisherman spots found by following trails to the river off the Middle Satsop Road, West Satsop Road, Middle Satsop Road or East Satsop Road, a network that permits sampling all the branches in turn. Summer steelhead catches are sparse, and scattered.

SOLEDUCK RIVER: Tumbling down from the north shoulder of Mt. Carrie, the Soleduck River exits Olympic National Park to trail Highway 101 west to Sappho, south to Forks, and then head west to dump into the Pacific at La Push. Boat launches sited from high on the river to Leyendecker County Park, where the Soleduck and Bogachiel meet to form the Quillayute, allow anglers to ply long stretches of this productive stream, plus permitting bank anglers to share the fishing. Log roads are the key to access upstream from Sappho, while Quillayute Prairie Road and the La Push Road are downstream access routes.

Summer anglers pick 400-700 steelhead from the Soleduck, with the most fish showing in June catches. Winter steelheading produces consistent catches from December through March, with an average season totalling between 1,500 to 2,100 fish caught.

The Soleduck is open during the trout season from June 1 on, and the winter steelheading season extends to April 30 from its mouth to the Highway 101 Bridge upstream from Snider Creek.

WILLAPA RIVER: Draining northwest from above Frances in the Willapa Hills, the Willapa River is closely followed nearly to Raymond by Highway 6. Easy to overlook, the small stream nevertheless can produce from 500 to more than 1,100 steelhead in winter seasons that peak alternately in January, February or March.

A winding, brushy stream that crosses quite a bit of private property, the Willapa has only two public access/boat launch sites, at Wilson Creek and in South Bend. Steelheaders in the Raymond or South Bend areas often do well either by plunking or hotshotting, while the upper river's undercut banks and overhanging brush are best fished with bait or bait/bobber rigs.

The Willapa is open to steelheading from the start of spring trout season and again Nov. 1-March 31, while its South Fork closes at the end of February.

WYNOOCHEE RIVER: A prime Aberdeen-area stream, the Wynoochee River can be counted on to yield a consistent 500-800 summer-run catch and 500 to nearly 1,000 winter steelhead. It is open to fishing from its mouth to 400 feet downstream from the bases of dams at Wynoochee and Grisdale reservoirs during trout season, but the winter steelhead season is limited to the river from its mouth to Shafer Creek Nov. 1 through March 31.

Good boat and bank access can be found off Highway 12 north on the Wynoochee Valley Road, which follows the Wynoochee riverbed far upstream past the deadline point.

Plug-pullers generally take a large share of Wynoochee fish, but bobber/bait/yarn anglers also claim good steelhead numbers, with best catches occurring in June and July and again from mid-February through March.

Hatchery winter steelhead caught on drift bobber.

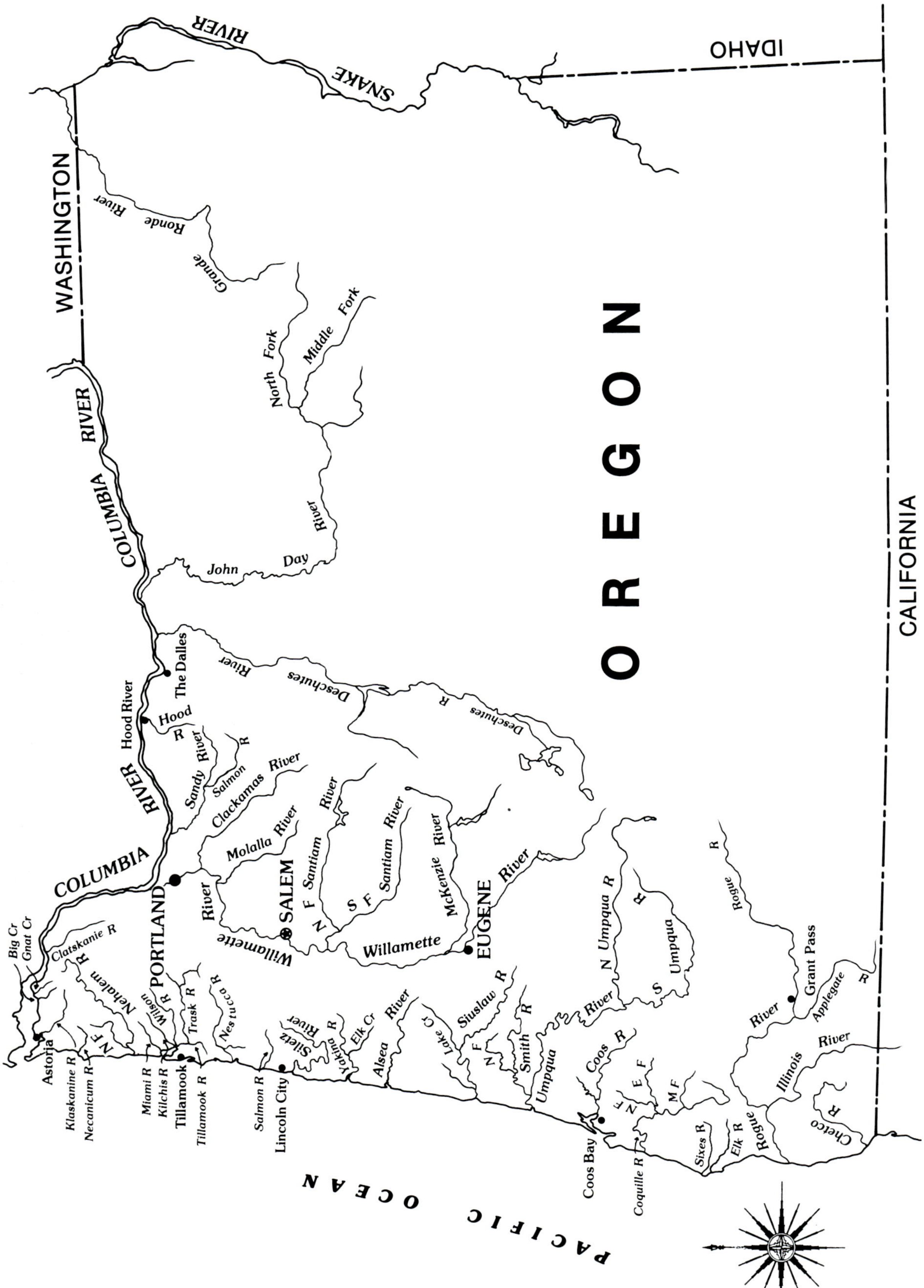
OREGON
WASHINGTON
IDAHO
CALIFORNIA
PACIFIC OCEAN
SNAKE RIVER
COLUMBIA RIVER
COLUMBIA RIVER
COLUMBIA
Grande Ronde River
North Fork
Middle Fork
John Day River
The Dalles
Deschutes River
Deschutes R
Hood River
Hood R
Sandy River
Salmon R
Clackamas River
Molalla River
N F Santiam River
S F Santiam River
McKenzie River
River
Willamette River
Willamette
EUGENE
SALEM
PORTLAND
Big Cr
Gnat Cr
Clatskanie R
N F Nehalem R
Wilson R
Trask R
Nestucca R
Siletz River
Yakina R
Elk Cr
Alsea River
Lake Cr
N F Siuslaw R
Smith R
Umpqua River
N Umpqua R
S Umpqua R
Coos R
N F
E F
M F
Rogue R
Rogue River
Grant Pass
Applegate R
Illinois River
Chetco R
Sixes R
Elk R
Rogue
Coquille R
Coos Bay
Astoria
Klaskanine R
Necanicum R
Miami R
Kilchis R
Tillamook
Tillamook R
Salmon R
Lincoln City

Chapter 15

Oregon

More than 15,000 miles of major rivers await anglers in broad and beautiful Oregon. The western third of the 96,981-square acre state is cool in summer, has mild winter temperatures and receives heavy rainfall on the Pacific Coast-to-Cascades Range forests of Douglas fir and western pine. The eastern two-thirds of Oregon is drier, hot in summer and cold in winter.

Long famous for its big rivers and large steelhead, Oregon's great stream fishing was popularized in the early half of this century by western and outdoor writer Zane Grey, one of the few early fishermen who pioneered fly-fishing and drift trips on many state streams and who for several years had a summer camp on the Rogue River, his favorite.

Oregon has many excellent summer-run streams, as well as a larger number of hatchery-supported winter fisheries. It produced a sport-caught record steelhead of 35 pounds, 8 ounces, a behemoth buck outfought in 1970 on the Columbia River by B. Todd.

Management of Oregon fish is by the Oregon Department of Fish and Wildlife, 2501 SW 1st, P.O. Box 59, Portland, OR, 97207. A valid angling license is required in possession of anyone over 14 years of age to angle for or take any fish for personal use, except smelt. Resident annual licenses cost $14.75, or $24.75 for a combination angling/hunting license, and daily angling licenses are available for $5.75. Nonresident annual licenses are $35.75, $21.25 for 10-day licenses and $5.25 for daily licenses.

All anglers, regardless of age, fishing for steelhead must have in possession a fishing license and a valid, unfilled steelhead/salmon permit tag or daily license. Combined steelhead / salmon permits cost $5.50 and allow 10 fish to be caught, at which time another stamp may be purchased that is good for 10 more steelhead and/or salmon, up to an additional 30 fish. Each fish landed and retained must be immediately recorded on the permit tag and no more than six fish may be kept in any seven-day period. Two steelhead (or salmon or combination of the two) per day may be caught, with a possession limit of six, except where noted by regulation. Also, see regs for recording steelhead released and barbless hook rules.

Oregon also has excellent freshwater fishing for salmon, trout, shad, whitefish, sturgeon, largemouth and smallmouth bass, bluegill, catfish and bullhead, crappie, perch, sunfish, hybrid bass and striped bass.

Visitors to Oregon and anglers fishing rivers well out of their home areas are advised to obtain a copy of the "Official 1993 Directory, Oregon Guides & Packers Association" from P.O. Box 10841, Eugene, OR 97440, and to avail themselves of fishing and river-running guide service for at least one or two trips on a river unfamiliar to them, to avoid dangerous surprises.

Information concerning Oregon angling is available from the ODFW in the "OREGON SPORT FISHING REGULATIONS" pamphlet, with the current booklet effective only for this year's fishing. The regulations are divided into seven geographical sections, plus a Marine Zone for Pacific Ocean, coastal bays and beaches. Only the Southeast Zone has steelheading. Here are the freshwater steelheading prospects in Oregon:

NORTHWEST ZONE

ALSEA RIVER: The Alsea River rises in the Coast Range, east of Corvallis, and eases through Siuslaw National Forest to reach Alsea Bay and the Pacific Ocean after some 55 miles of travel. It is heavily fished by residents of the nearby Willamette Valley, scarcely an hour's drive away, and a strong winter steelhead hatchery program makes the Alsea system one of the most productive in Oregon.

From 3,500 to ver 10,500 steelhead are caught annually from the mainstem Alsea, North Fork Alsea below the Highway 34 bridge and South Fork Alsea below the falls that blocks upstream fish passage. The fishing peaks in mid-December through January and, though a few dozen summer-runs are caught in the late May-Oct. 31 trout season, nearly all Alsea steelhead are banked in the Nov. 1-March 31 winter season. More than a dozen improved and rough boat launches permit boat fishing below Mill Creek, and pull-out spots, public access sites and parks line the popular stream's banks.

Plug fishermen are in the majority on the lower 12 miles of Alsea Bay to the head of tidewater, where some steelhead are taken by trollers working the brackish waters for coho and Chinook salmon. Drift boat anglers score highly with the same lures in the normally slightly-green waters of the middle and lower Alsea River, while bank anglers fishing spoons, spinners, small bobber and bait/yarn combinations, or flies, take upper Alsea steelhead.

The North Fork Alsea below the deadline bridge yields well to bank anglers casting and drifting lures and baits, and is noted for its fine fly-fishing, while South Fork catches add only about 50 to 150 steelhead a year to the total harvest.

BIG CREEK: Clatsop County's Big Creek flows north from near Clatsop State Forest to pour into the Columbia River at Knappa soon after passing under Highway 30. Access to the small stream's banks is north and south from pull-out parking on this route.

The creek is open late May-Oct. 31 and again Nov. 1 through March 31. The largest number of 900-2,100 steelhead annually taken from Big Creek will fall to bait and bobber anglers in January, though December and February also yield good catches. In September, no fishing is permitted downstream from the hatchery rack to the railroad bridge near the mouth.

ELK CREEK: Elk Creek enters the Yaquina River at Elk City after a short run north from the upper tip of the Siuslaw National Forest. It is open to fishing from late May to March 31, producing most of a varying seasonl catch of 250 to 1,000 winter steelhead in December and January.

Best reached from Elk City via a county road pointing toward Harlan, the lower portion of Big Elk Creek delivers fair fishing to bank anglers casting bobber/bait/yarn drift rigs.

CLATSKANIE RIVER: A small, gravelly, boulder-strewn and brushy river, the Clatskanie drops from north of St. Helens to enter the Columbia River north of the town of Clatskanie after passing beneath Highway 30. Its lower stretches are reached off county roads from Clatskanie and by bank anglers seeking the upper river off the Pittsburgh/Columbia City road.

Permission to fish from private property should be sought where much of the stream flows through farmland. Once on the bank, bait and bobber fishermen can expect to take 300-600 winter steelhead, most of which are caught from late December through January. The Clatskanie is open for steelheading from the fourth Saturday in May to March 31.

GNAT CREEK: A short stream scarcely 10 miles long, Gnat Creek rises in northern Clatsop County and flows into the Columbia River east of the town of Knappa. Highway 30 crosses Gnat Creek and affords some downstream access to its banks.

Open only from the highway down, Gnat Creek produces its best Nov. 1-March 31 annual catch of 225 to 500 fish in the period from Christmas to late January, although sporadic catches of summer-run steelhead may be taken June to August after its late May trout season opener.

KILCHIS RIVER: Rising in the Tillamook Burn area of Tillamook State Forest, the Kilchis River is a small stream that flows southwest to enter Tillamook Bay below Bay City. U.S. Highway 101 crosses the mouth of the Kilchis and county and State Forest roads provide upstream access. Quick to clear, the Kilchis often is fishable, especially in the upper, gravel/rock section, when other area streams are running mud. There are several drift boat access sites.

The Kilchis has the potential of yielding 700 to more than 1,100 steelhead annually. Its peak fishing time is December, and the greatest majority of its steelhead are caught in the winter season. Some summer-runs are tricked to the hook in summer, with June and July the optimum fishing times. The Kilchis is open to angling from mouth to North Fork late in May through March 31, except it is closed to adult salmon angling August 1-Sept. 15 upstream from the old Highway 101 bridge.

KLASKANINE RIVER: Astoria area steelheaders have at their doorstep a very productive river system that affords good, easily reached winter fishing. From 900 to more than 2,200 winter fish swim across the Columbia Bar, then veer into Youngs Bay and head up the mainstem Klaskanine, North Fork and South Fork to search out spawning gravel high in the Coast Range northwest of Jewell. Access is off Highway 202 and area gravel roads.

Open late May through March 31, except for the North Fork, where the fishing deadline is 200 feet below the hatchery holding pond fishway up to the hatchery dam, each of the Klaskanine's parts deliver strong January returns to bank anglers. Steelhead mount the Klaskanine early in December, and many of them fall to bank fishermen fishing cluster egg, shrimp, prawn and night crawler baits.

LAKE CREEK: An exceptionally clear stream, Lake Creek rises north of Horton and feeds Triangle

Lake (which functions as a huge "sediment bowl" during high water periods) before dropping southwest along State Route 36 to join the Siuslaw River near Swisshome. It is fishable in most weather short of heavy, hard and persistent rainfall.

Boaters hold an edge over bank anglers in annually hoisting 500-1,600 winter steelhead from Lake Creek from mouth to Greenleaf Creek. Private property limits the amount of bank available to the public, but there are several good boat launches along the stream. Plugs, spinners and bait and/or bobber drift rigs are successfully used on Lake Creek, with the peak fishing period being December through January. The steelheading season runs from late May through March 31, but summer steelhead are rare.

MIAMI RIVER: The Miami River originates in the western edge of the Tillamook State Forest, then flows southwest to Tillamook Bay, sliding into salt water after flowing beneath U.S. 101. It yields 200-700 winter steelhead. Early December hatchery runs are followed in late February and March with some heavy, remnant wild-spawning steelhead that sometimes weigh from 10 to 19 pounds.

The Miami opens in late May and may be fished for steelhead through March 31. Access is good on the upper river, via the back road from Garibaldi to Mohler, with a gravel spur forking east to follow the Miami.

NECANICUM RIVER: The Necanicum River tumbles from the south slope of Saddle Mountain, north of the town of Necanicum, then curls west along U.S. Route 26, following that highway north after it merges with U.S. 101, to reach Seaside, where the Necanicum plunges into the Pacific Ocean. These routes, plus the road to Saddle Mountain State Park and lower area gravel roads, provide good access to the Necanicam, though some posted land near Seaside bars fishing entry. Drift boats can be used in the lower several miles.

Open to fishing late May through March 31, the Necanicum has a very few summer steelhead, catches being scattered from May to August, but it is far better for winter steelhead, which provide the strongest catches in December and January.

There is good fly-fishing on the Necanicum, mainly above tidewater and again for anglers plying the upper river below Saddle Mountain State Park. Drift rig fishermen also score steelhead catches on bait, bobber and yarn set-ups, and plugs account for a fair number of fish.

NEHALEM RIVER: Picture the Nehalem River as a fly-fisherman's 100-mile backcast if he were facing toward the Pacific Ocean at Nehalem...his line rising high to Elsie and Jewell, the bend looping back from Mist to Vernonia and the tippet curling near Timber. That's the course the productive Nehalem follows when it charges down from the northeast corner of Tillamook State Forest.

From 1,200 to about 3,000 steelhead – mostly winter fish – are taken from the Nehalem, the North Fork Nehalem, Cook Creek and Salmonberry Creek, its larger tributaries. The peak of winter steelheading shifts from December to January every few years, with February catches holding strong, but in smaller number.

The mainstem Nehalem is closed Sept. 1-Oct. 31 from Mist 36 miles upstream to the Highway 26 bridge, otherwise it is all open to steelheading from late May through March 31. Salmonberry Creek and Cook Creek from mouth to South Fork are open during the same time frame. There are boat launches on the mainstem river at Lost Creek, Roy Creek, Wheeler and below Nehalem Bridge. Access to the Nehalem, North Fork and tributaries is easily found off Highways 26, 47, 202, 53 and 101 and county roads.

Walt McGovern with a fine winter steelhead caught in Oregon's coastal Wilson River.

Drift boaters have good success with plugs, spinners and baited drift rigs, while bank casters also effectively tease strikes from the Nehalem's winter steelhead with bait and bobber drift rigs. Fly-fishermen often do very well at the mouth of Cook Creek and mouths of other streams entering the main river.

NESTUCCA RIVER: The Nestucca River is one of Oregon's largest and most productive all-year steelheading streams. Summer and winter steelhead catches from this 50-mile-long river average between 5,000 and 11,000 fish each year and the Little Nestucca, which meets its parent at Nestucca Bay, contributes 600 to 1,000 additional steelhead, mostly taken in winter. The Little Nestucca is open only during the late May-Oct. 31 trout season and again from Nov. 1 through March 31 for steelheading.

The big Nestucca rises in the Coast Range and flows west to Beaver, where it turns south past Hebo and Cloverdale to reach the ocean via Nestucca Bay at Pacific City. Anglers must, however, carefully refer to the regulations handbook for hook and finclip closures for salmon, both adult salmon and coho salmon.

Summer steelheading is perking strongly by mid-June and stays hot through the end of July from inner Nestucca Bay for about 20 miles upstream. Winter anglers look for December and January to deliver the largest numbers of steelhead.

There's good access on the Nestucca, with boat launches well maintained at several scattered points by Tillamook County, Oregon Department of Highways, Oregon Department of Fish and Wildlife and sport clubs. Fishermen taking the road from Carlton past former Meadow Lake to Beaver are able to closely parallel the river downstream. The Little Nestucca also is tracked by a good paved road. Highway 101 crosses the big Nestucca above Hebo and passes over the Little Nestucca River at its mouth.

Tadpolly, Hot Shot, Flatfish, Wiggle Wart and Hot'N Tot plugs can upset a lot of Nestucca steelhead to the point of striking, and drifting anglers and bank fishermen also crank in hefty fish fooled with shrimp, prawn, cluster egg and 'crawler baits angled on drift rigs or under floating bobbers. The middle and upper Nestucca are best fished with drift rigs but have many good stretches where fly-fishermen readily take summer-runs on dark or bright pattern flies.

SALMON RIVER: Short, but quick to clear after rains and chockfull of steelhead, the Salmon River is a good bet for Lincoln County steelheaders when bigger systems such as the nearby Siletz or Nestucca are running brown. Open to steelheading from late May through March 31, the Salmon River yields summer-runs in increasing quantity from July on, and turns up all its burners in December and January when its winter steelhead crowd into their home stream.

Easily approached from Highway 18 on the south and a paved road on the north that bracket the lower section of river, the Salmon produces best for bait and bobber drift rig casters, though hardware will hoist steelhead out of the deeper holes and runs and flies can be relied upon for low-water fish.

SILETZ RIVER: Fingers of the sprawling Siletz River reach north of and south to Valsetz Lake in western Polk County to grasp for liquid life and then the Siletz reluctantly wriggles across Lincoln County in growing strength to bequeath its wide waters to Siletz Bay at Kernville.

Sandy River, Oregon, summer steelhead.

One of Oregon's premier steelhead streams, the Siletz is open all year to the North Fork (see special regs concerning the closed falls area) and produces catches of both summer and winter steelhead that together can total from 6,000 to 12,000 bright battlers. The North Fork Siletz to Stott Mt. Bridge (fly-fishing only in the trout season) and South Fork add hundreds more fish in their late May-March 31 steelhead fisheries, and anglers also should look to Schooner and Drift creeks, which enter at the head of Siletz Bay, for more Siletz River steelhead during winter.

Excellent summer steelheading takes place each month of the summer and gets pistol-hot in June through July. Winter anglers take more December fish than any other month, but January often pushes hard for top place. Fishing access is excellent, with Highway 101 crossing the river mouth and Route 229 following the river far upstream to the town of Siletz, where paved blacktop pursues the river to Logsden, then gives over to gravel.

Most of the river is accessible to boat fishermen who float from Logsden downstream, with other access points liberally strewn downstream along the banks. Good plunking spots beckon every few miles and drift rig anglers casting baits or bobber/yarn combinations can find plenty of fishing room a short walk away from crowded access points.

SIUSLAW RIVER: Fishing success on the Siuslaw River and North Fork Siuslaw can vary from about 1,000 steelhead a year to more than 4,300, catch counts which do not include Lake Creek, which is listed separately.

Very few summer-run fish are caught in either river or during the Siuslaw Bay coho salmon and sea-run cutthroat fisheries that peak in early fall, but some steelhead do appear from October on. December and January are the best months to be fishing this river system that lazily winds from west of Cottage Grove along the southwest corner of Lane County to breach a gap in the Coast Range that leads to the head of Siuslaw Bay and the Pacific Ocean.

The Siuslaw and North Fork are open from late May through March 31 to steelheading. Angling deadline on the North Fork is the Meadows Bridge (milepost 11) at Minerva.

Both the North Fork and lower mainstem Siuslaw are prime plunking rivers, having deep pools, eddies and slow loops. There are many boat access points and rough boat slides on the two arms that provide good access to floating and bank anglers.

The Siuslaw picks up speed as you progress farther upstream along Highway 126 to Mapleton and Route 36 to Swisshome and a Forest Service road tracing the north bank of the river to Beecher, Richardson and Austa. Upper river bank anglers may shortcut from Mapleton to Richardson on good highway to reach some fine drift-fishing and fly-fishing holes and runs.

THREE RIVERS: Open for steelheading late May through March 31, this large tributary to the Nestucca River annually yields 1,400 to 2,500 winter fish that fall in greatest numbers for anglers' wiles in December. No angling is allowed from the hatchery weir to mouth from June 1 through Oct. 31.

Three Rivers charges down from the southwest slopes of Mt. Hebo and flows into the Nestucca near Hebo. A good stream for bank anglers, the Three Rivers has excellent gravel beds, rocks and shaded cover. There is a large ODFW access at its mouth.

TILLAMOOK RIVER: The Tillamook River uncoils like a springy leader eastward from near Cape Lookout and then north to slip into the south end of giant Tillamook Bay along the western edge of the town of Tillamook. A slow, quiet stream, it nevertheless delivers good December and January fishing for 400-900 steelhead caught during its Nov. 1-March 31 season above tidewater.

Plunkers and drift-rigged bait fishermen do best on the Tillamook, reaching the river from county roads off Highway 101 south of Tillamook.

TRASK RIVER: The Trask River originates in the southern tip of Tillamook State Forest, where North and South forks join near the settlement of Trask to form the mainstem river. From 1,200 to more than 2,400 steelhead are taken from the river system each year, with the bulk of the fish being caught in December, January and February.

Open all year to Jones Creek Park Bridge and Nov. 1 through March 31 from Jones Creek to the South Fork Wilson River, and in the Little North Fork Jan. 1-March 31, the Wilson River system yields well to light drift-rig and fly tackle in the upper stretches and to plugs, spinners, spoons and baits in the lower river. Plunkers and boaters score best in the slow area below the Little North Fork to Highway 101.

Often muddied, the Trask River is an excellent bait-fishing river. Cluster eggs, shrimp and 'crawlers generate strikes, as will winged bobber/bait and bobber/yarn drift rigs spiced with attractant scents such as Dr. Juice, Berkley Strike or Mike's.

There is very good access for fishermen on the Trask and its tributaries. Highway 1 crosses the lower river a short distance from Tillamook Bay. Highway 101 from Tillamook to Lincoln City also passes over the river and permits upstream access on paved and county gravel roads that parallel the north bank to Trask and up both forks. Boat access and bank angling sites are numerous from the forks downstream to Highway 1.

WILSON RIVER: In easy driving reach from Portland, the Wilson River rises west of Glenwood in eastern Tillamook State Forest. A favorite stream of winter and summer steelheaders alike, the Wilson is studded with many private camping areas, county parks and ODFW public access sites and there are boat guide services available. Highway 6 pursues and crosses the river from its upper reaches to Tillamook.

Open all year to Jones Creek Park Bridge and Nov. 1 through March 31 from Jones Creek to the South Fork Wilson River, and in the Little North Fork Jan.

1-March 31 and Devils Lake Fork (fly-fishing-only) from Nov. 1 through March 31, the Wilson River system yields well to light drift-rig and fly tackle in the upper stretches, and to plugs, spinners, spoons and baits in the lower river. Plunkers and boaters score best in the slow area below the Little North Fork to Highway 101.

SOUTHWEST ZONE

APPLEGATE RIVER: Approximately 1,000 winter steelhead can be expected to be caught annually from the Applegate River mainstem below the Applegate Reservoir dam in its short season from Jan. 1 through March 31. The Applegate River begins in the Rogue River National Forest, flowing from high in the northeast tip to reach the Rogue River west of Grants Pass.

Approaches to the Applegate are from Medford and Jacksonville via Highway 238, which follows the stream to Murphy, and good paved road tracking the lower river to its junction on the Rogue or off Highway 199 at Wilderville, where this route crosses the lower Applegate. Barbless hooks are required.

County areas, picnic sites and campgrounds are the best bases for bank anglers casting drift bobber rigs, baits and spinners, or trying to entice winter-runs to grab a sunken fly.

Sherry Gullings with a hatchery summer steelhead that took a ghost shrimp bait in early May.

CHETCO RIVER: Oregon's southernmost big steelheading stream, the Chetco River, surfaces in the Kalmiopsis Wilderness Area of the Siskiyou National Forest and tumbles about 50 miles over clean, small gravel bottom and through deep gorges to reach the Pacific Ocean at Brookings.

Catches of winter steelhead bounced from a low of 900 in 1983 to 3,500 in 1984, then to more than 5,400 in 1985, with the peak of fishing shifting from December to January to February in successive years. The Chetco River is open to steelheading from late May through March 31, but yields a scant count of summer-runs appearing from July on. (See special hook regs.)

There is good public access available at a number of ODFW fishing sites, Loeb State Park and from Azalea Park. Boat slides allow float trips and guides are available. The Chetco has a good mixture of excellent fly-fishing riffles, long, slow, snag-free runs for drift-fishermen and deep, heavy pools best fished by plugs or back-bounced bait/bobber rigs.

Access to the Chetco is off Highway 101 at Brookings, with a good paved road leading up the river's north bank past Loeb State Park and which gives way to branching gravel roads that chase the river farther upstream.

COOS RIVER: Steelheading steadily improved on the Coos River system in the middle 1980s, largely due to increased ODFW smolt plants and removal of logging "splash dams" on the South Fork Coos River. From a low of 500, catches zoomed to over 4,000 steelhead taken from this coastal stream, with winter-runs peaking from late December to early February producing the lion's share of fish.

The short mainstem Coos River and South Fork to head of tide at Dellwood are open all year to steelheading, as is the Millicoma (North Fork of Coos) River mainstem, while the South Fork Coos from head of tide to Camas Creek Bridge and East and West forks of the Millicoma share a late May through March 31 steelhead season.

Access to the Coos and its forks is off Highway 101 at Coos Bay to Eastside and then paved and gravel roads to Allegany on the Millicoma or up the South Fork Coos. Plunkers do very well in the lower river and drift-rig fishermen casting baits and bobber set-ups also tally good catches.

COQUILLE RIVER: South coast Oregon steelhead anglers are increasingly giving the Coquille River system a "thumbs up" rating for catches that annually place the parent stream (and its North, East, Middle and South forks) among the dozen best rivers in the state. Strong hatchery plants have boosted the South Fork, in particular, with the total Coquille system tally climbing to over 7,500 steelhead in good years.

A network of highways, paved county roads and gravel routes pen the lower Coquille River and provide good access off Highway 101, which crosses the river near its mouth at Bandon. Highways 42 and 42S lead east to Myrtle Point, from which city paved roads radiate north, east and south like wheel spokes to the four forks.

January is the peak time to be fishing the Coquille and its forks, with December and February vieing for second place. The key to steelheading success on this excellent river system is cold, clear weather, as it is quick to muddy. There are boat slides and public access sites available to fishermen on the lower forks and upper Coquille, and foot trails to the riverbank lead through heavy brush and brambles to some fine plunking spots on the lower river.

The South Fork and mainstem Coquille deliver many bright, bouncing steelhead, some of which can weigh to 20 pounds, to spoons and spinners, back-bounced bobbers and bait, or to plugs. Drift-rig anglers will enjoy the generally snag-free, pea gravel runs and glides of the Coos system, while plunkers normally do best in deep holes.

ELK RIVER: Curry County's Elk River flows from the west slope of 4,000-foot-high Iron Mountain and past Humbug Mountain to the north. It reaches the Pacific Ocean after passing beneath Highway 101 midway between Port Orford and Sixes.

A hatchery program supports the winter fishery, which can vary from 250 to 800 steelhead caught, most of which are taken in December and January. The bulk of the fishing is done by float trips from a launch below the hatchery to a take-out above Highway 101. There is little public access on the lower Elk River.

Steelhead fishing season is late May through March from mouth to Bald Mountain Creek. See special hook regulations.

ILLINOIS RIVER: For wilderness steelhead fishing experiences, it would be difficult to ask for more than the Illinois River might provide from Kerby, on Highway 199, to Agness, where the Illinois meets the Rogue River. Only a few miles of the lower river are accessible by road, then there's a gap of more than 30 miles of stream that is only available to boat fishermen, hikers or rafters, until a rough Forest Service road is tapped east of Selma.

Open to steelheading from mouth up to Pomeroy Dam at Kerby all year around, the Illinois best yields its winter steelhead catch of 300-1,000 fish in January, but late rains or fish runs sometimes push the peak of angling into February.

ROGUE RIVER: Perhaps the most storied river on the west coast of the United States, Oregon's Rogue River originates in National Forest wilderness high on the Cascade Mountains Range outside the northwest corner of Crater Lake National Park. Shallow and swift to begin with, it rushes seaward for approximately 200 miles, first southwest to near Eagle Point and then west beyond Grants Pass to sweep north until it can surge and drop southwest again through canyons and gorges from Illahe to Agness and on to reach the Pacific between Wedderburn and Gold Beach.

Highway 101 is your access route to the Rogue estuary and lower Rogue River, and a paved road forges upstream along the river to Illahe. From Grants Pass, paved roads downstream reach to Grave Creek and Rogue River Valley routes repeatedly cross and follow the Rogue upstream east to Eagle Point, then a good highway trails the Rogue past Casey State Park, below Lost Creek Reservoir, north to Union Creek.

Open to year-around fishing from mouth to deadline markers below Cole Rivers Hatchery, the Rogue River offers steelheaders half-pounders in late summer and early fall, then heavier fish in a good October fishery, a premium fly-fishing season Sept. 1 to Oct. 31 between Gold Ray impoundment upstream to Cole Rivers Hatchery, and excellent winter steelheading that holds good opportunity for anglers from December into March. (Anglers are advised that there are several special restrictions listed for the Rogue in the regulations booklet.) Catches in 1983-1985 ranged from 5,600 to nearly 14,000.

Scenic jet boat tours and fishing trips can be arranged from Gold Beach and Grants Pass, and there are several dozens of guides with whom drift fishing trips can be scheduled. Boat accesses, public access sites, state and county parks are numerous along the Rogue and intrepid hikers may reach some of the wilderness area between Illahe and Almeda to fish secluded bank spots. So popular is the Rogue River that access is less a problem than sheer numbers of fishermen...with up to 35,000 anglers a year estimated to test their tackle on the Rogue.

A wide variety of tackle and techniques draws strikes from Rogue River steelhead. Light trolling gear, towed spinners and worms, or flies, will be cracked by feisty half-pounders and a growing number of larger summer steelhead. Back-bouncing single egg, roe cluster, or nightcrawler baits is productive in the lower river, as is hotshotting with large and small diving plugs. Bank and boat anglers take many of their steelhead on drift-rig bait and bobber enticers, while flies, spoons and spinners also account for good late fall and early winter catches.

Almost every bar, riffle and hole on the Rogue River has been given one or more names by past anglers, one of whom was Zane Grey, whose cabin at Winkle Bar still stands. Grey fished and wrote on the Rogue for many summers early in this century and was a pioneer of drift boat fishing, still considered the best way to truly enjoy the fabled Rogue River's steelheading.

SMITH RIVER: The Smith River and its North Fork can yield from 600 to more than 3,100 steelhead annually, with January being the peak month of the year-around season for these productive tributaries to the Umpqua River system.

Arms of the Smith River rise from north of Drain to east of Sulphur Springs and flow west to enter the Umpqua near Gardiner, above the head of Winchester Bay. The mainstream Smith River is tracked from Gardiner upstream by good paved road that eventually leads to Drain. The North Fork lower and upper stretches also have good road access.

Boat slides and rough put-ins on the North Fork allow for drift-fishing, as will boat access sites on the main Smith. Good catches may come from the lower river on drift rigs used with baits or bobbers. The mainstem often becomes heavily colored from hard rains, while the North Fork clears readily and provides good fishing when other nearby streams are unfishable.

UMPQUA RIVER: One of Oregon's three largest river systems, the Umpqua River, North Umpqua and South Umpqua are noted for exceptional steelheading, in which summer-run catches outnumber winter steelhead two or three to one. The mainstem and North and South Umpqua are open to steelheading all year long, but anglers must be aware of area fly-fishing-only and floating device restrictions in the regulations handbook. Fly-fishing can be excellent on the North Fork from July into November, depending upon rains.

Both Umpqua arms rise in the Umpqua National Forest, the North Umpqua gathering its strength from creeks east of Lemolo Lake and the South Umpqua beginning as rivulets on the south slopes of Quartz Mountain. The forks meet the mainstem near Roseburg.

Summer-runs are taken each month from May through October in the main Umpqua, while July, August and September are peak months to fish the North Umpqua. December and January are the top times to fish for winter steelhead on the mainstem and South Umpqua.

Access to the upper Umpqua and lower forks of the tributary arms is excellent off major highways and arterials in the Winchester-to-Canyonville region; Highway 227 and a paved offshoot lead eastward up the South Umpqua and State Road 138 tracks the North Umpqua high into the National Forest and also links Roseburg to the river's mouth at Reedsport via Highway 38 which runs along the main Umpqua River.

There is a string of boat sites accessible to the public on the mainstem Umpqua and guides are available. The lower North Umpqua is best fished from boats, as its banks are mostly private land. Several boat launches permit drifting it from Rock Creek downstream.

WILLAMETTE ZONE

CLACKAMAS RIVER: One of the most popular streams in Oregon and very easily reached from the Portland area, the Clackamas River also is highly productive of both summer-run and winter steelhead. The lower Clackamas, downstream from River Mill Dam, yields over 1,000 fish each of the winter season months from December through March, while the upper Clackamas comes on most strongly in July, August and September, nearly equalling these high catch figures.

Birthed in the Mt. Hood National Forest, the Clackamas gains its growth from liquid fingers reaching toward Ollalie Lake and to Elk Lake. Highway 224 from Gladstone to Estacada follows the Clackamas east into the National Forest, where paved and gravel roads further track the river's banks to headwaters. The river is held by three dams spaced along its winding middle and lower section, then joins the Willamette between Oregon City and Gladstone.

Boat launches are liberally scattered from McIver Park, below River Mill Dam, downstream to the mouth. The lower river is best fished from boats, as public access is generally limited to parks, boat sites, bridges and street ends abutting on the river. Its major steelheading tributaries here are Clear, Deep and Eagle creeks, which are good winter steelhead fisheries. Above River Mill Dam, the mainstem Clackamas continues to provide excellent steelheading abetted by catches from the Collowash River forks.

There are many campgrounds, picnic areas and parks on the upper Clackamas that have fishing access right on or close to the river. Summer steelhead fly-fishermen do well in the rocky drifts, runs and pools of the upper Clackamas and its tributaries. Spoon, spinner and bait fishermen also score good catches.

Open all year to steelheading, the main Clackamas has floating device restrictions and other special regulations that must be observed. Tributaries above the North Fork have a May 22 through Dec. 31 steelhead fishery.

Heavily stocked with summer-run steelhead and having both early and late runs of winter fish, the Clackamas system has a good potential for producing 8,000 to over 15,000 steelhead annually. Ghost or sand shrimp, ocean prawn and night crawler baits, as well as cluster eggs, are good bait choices on the Clackamas. Winged and round bobber lures, with yarn or without, also are popular. Boaters do well with diving plugs, and fly fishermen use a wide variety of dark and light patterns on the Clackamas and tributaries.

MCKENZIE RIVER: Nearly 90 miles long and closely followed to its junction with the Willamette River north of Eugene by State Highway 126 from its origin in Clear Lake, at the northwest tip of Mt. Washington Wilderness, the McKenzie River is best known for its unique strain of redside rainbow trout and as the stream on which McKenzie style drift boats were initiated.

However, this central Willamette Valley stream also has excellent summer steelhead fishing that can provide from a few hundred to 2,000 fish seasonally taken by anglers from the McKenzie, Leaburg Lake and South Fork McKenzie during a late April through Oct. 31 fishery. Some steelhead in the 20-pound range are caught early in the season and similar lunkers show again in catches at the end of October, but the majority of McKenzie River summer-runs will normally weigh between 6 and 10 pounds.

There's excellent access off Highway 126 to the upper half of the McKenzie for bank fishermen seeking to sample its pockets, slots and drifts with fly-fishing, spinning or casting tackle. The lower half of the river is best fished from boats, as much of the streamside property is privately owned. From Blue River to the McKenzie's mouth there are many good boat access sites, but first-time anglers are cautioned that the river above Leaburg is unruly and dangerous until boaters become acquainted with it and guide trips are recommended.

MOLALLA RIVER: Open all year up to Horse Creek Bridge for steelheading, the Molalla River is a prime "late" stream prospect for 500 to 1,200 mostly winter fish, best taken January, February and March. Tributaries also yielding steelhead are the Pudding River, Butte, Abiqua and Silver creeks. The Molalla system is within easy reach of Portland area anglers.

Headwaters of the Molalla begin flowing west from the Cascade Mountains on the southwest edge of Mt. Hood National Forest and soon are accompanied downstream by gravel and paved roads that become a network of arterials and highways on the lower river. On the upper river, bank anglers are more numerous and successful but, by the time the river flows past Molalla, drift boaters have joined the search for strikes and take the majority of steelhead from Molalla to Canby.

SALMON RIVER: A very successful summer-run hatchery program has been responsible for ballooning catches on the Salmon River, major tributary to the Sandy River. This short stream rises in Mt. Hood National Forest west of Wapanitia Pass and melds into the Sandy River at Brightwood.

Open to steelheading only between the late May opener and Dec. 31, the Salmon River has impassable waterfalls a dozen miles upstream from its mouth, so catches in 1983-85 seasons of from 1,500 to 6,400 steelhead are even more impressive. And, from Salmon River USFS Road No. 2618 bridge (trailhead) upstream to Final Falls, a hiking distance of about four miles, only fly angling is permitted.

Highway 26 is your major access route to the Salmon River and local information should be sought for public bank access.

SANDY RIVER: Glacial melt from the west shoulder of Mt. Hood and run-off from near Barlow Pass and the west side of the Pacific Crest Trail in Mt. Hood National Forest feed swiftly down through gorges and tree-lined canyons to become the Sandy River, one of Oregon's perennial Top 10 steelhead streams. The river follows Highway 26 from Brightwood to Sandy, then veers north to pour into the Columbia River north of Troutdale.

Open year-around to steelheading from mouth to the Brightwood Bridge and late May-Dec. 31 in mainstem and tributaries above Brightwood Bridge, the Sandy has special restrictions on hooks and weights and use of floating devices (see regs).

Sandy River steelheaders might catch from 5,600 to nearly 15,000 winter and summer steelhead each season within easy driving distance of Portland. Strong enhancement projects have boosted the winter fishery and planted summer-runs have achieved spawning populations on this extremely productive river that has yielded as high as 4,023 fish in one month (December 1984)!

Steelheaders may use motorized craft between Stark St. (Viking Bridge) and the mouth. Check current regulations for other boating/fishing regulations. There is good bank access on the lower river that can be reached from parks, picnic spots and road crossings from Sandy to Troutdale.

Baits work best in the silt-laden summer water after snowmelt begins to cloud the Sandy from late June to September. However, brightly colored spoons and throbbing spinners also will attract strikes from steelhead ranging between 5 and 18 pounds. Flies and tiny bobber/yarn lures may be used early in the cooler mornings. Winter anglers probe the Sandy with shrimp, cluster eggs, bobbers, spoons, spinners and plugs.

Frank Amato with a hatchery steelhead taken on a winged bobber from the Clackamas River, Oregon.

SANTIAM RIVER: Summer-run steelhead provide the largest fishery in the short mainstem of the Santiam River. However, in the approximately eight-mile flow from 1 1/4 miles south of Jefferson to the junction with the Willamette River two miles south of Buena Vista there is excellent angling for 300-1,400 steelhead.

Plunkers and boat fishermen share equal opportunities to hook incoming summer-runs bound for the North Fork Santiam and South Fork Santiam. There's a rough launch spot under Interstate 5 at the Santiam Rest Area that allows access to the Santiam's lower section for drifting to the Willamette and take-out at Buena Vista Park. The lower river is open all year around and will yield some winter fish, but the peak of its fishing is June and July.

NORTH FORK SANTIAM RIVER: Originating in National Forest highland creeks near Breitenbush Springs to Marion Forks, the North Fork Santiam River courses along the upper border of Linn County for nearly 60 miles before joining the South Fork below Jefferson on a brief jaunt to the Willamette.

Open year-around to steelheading from mouth to Big Cliff Dam, the North Fork and its major tributary, the Little North Fork, which enters the North Fork at Mehama, are capable of producing from 1,100 to over 7,000 summer steelhead. The prime time for North Fork fishing is from June through August. There are special regulations on the North Fork that must be followed.

Boat launch sites are spread along the river, which is followed on the north bank by Highway 22 from Stayton to Detroit Reservoir. South of the river, Highway 226 stretches from Albany to Lyons and county roads repeatedly tap or cross the North Fork.

Boat launch sites are well spaced on the North Fork Santiam from below Minto Dam to Mehama. Bank anglers also have ample access to the river. The North Fork offers excellent opportunities for steelhead fly-fishing.

SOUTH FORK SANTIAM RIVER: Highly popular and easy to reach, the South Fork Santiam River can deliver from 600 to over 5,300 steelhead annually, with the largest share of the fish being caught in late May through August.

Steelheaders may take fish year-around from its mouth to 1/4-mile below Foster Dam. Above Foster Reservoir, only catch-and-release steelheading is legal.

Highway 20 tracks the growth of the South Fork from tiny headwaters in the Willamette National Forest westward to Foster Reservoir, below which steelhead may be retained, and then to its junction with the North Fork Santiam below Jefferson. Much of the best steelheading is found from Lebanon to Foster. Good access is provided nearly the full length of the river by county paved and gravel roads.

Fly-fishermen, drift-rig casters and spinner and spoon users all tempt a fair share of South Fork Santiam River steelhead.

WILLAMETTE RIVER: The broad Willamette River rises in the central valley between Coast Range and Cascade Mountains, flowing north from Cottage Grove to meet the Columbia River around Sauvie Island north of Portland. This 150-mile-long flatland river is better known as a salmon producer, but steelheaders are fortunate enough to shortstop 1,000-3,000 anadromous winter 'bows headed for upstream tributaries in its year-around fishery. These fish are almost all caught from Meldrum Bar, near the mouth of the Clackamas River, upstream to Willamette Falls, near Oregon City.

Best fishing for steelhead occurs in December and January, with a flurry of good angling taking place again in April. The river's total catch is divided into mouth-to-Willamette Falls, Falls-to-Highway 34 Bridge and Highway 34 Bridge-Dexter Dam sections, as well as Middle Fork up to Dexter Dam.

Boat fishermen pulling Hot Shots or similar plugs, drifting with bait and/or bobber rigs and casting spoons and spinners take the lion's share of Willamette steelhead. Bank casters and plunkers do very well, however, fishing wing bobbers and baits in such spots as below the fishing deadline at Willamette Falls and off the mouths of tributaries.

Public access to Willamette River steelheading is never far from Interstate 5, which closely trails the big river from Cottage Grove to Portland and the Washington border. Highway 58 parallels the Middle Fork nearly to headwaters. To locate boat landings, public access sites and river crossings that might provide fishing opportunities, no Willamette River steelheader should be without the *WILLAMETTE RIVER RECREATIONAL GUIDE* pamphlet that is available free from the Oregon State Parks & Recreation Division, Willamette River Greenway Program, 525 Trade Street SE, Salem, OR 97310. It contains 16 detailed river section maps that point out boating, picnicking, wildlife study and overnight camping opportunities on public lands and advises river mile distances between major points. It is extremely well done, informative and invaluable for serious steelheaders.

CENTRAL ZONE

DESCHUTES RIVER: First draining south from the Lava Lakes in Deschutes National Forest, the Deschutes River flows through Crane Prairie and Wickiup reservoirs, then reverses direction to head north past Bend, Redmond and the Warms Springs Indian Reservation, to Maupin and then through miles of gorge to greet the Columbia River about 12 miles east of The Dalles.

A premier Oregon summer-run stream famous for its fine fly-fishing, the Deschutes is open to steelheading all year from mouth to Sherar Falls (about 43 miles) and late April-Dec. 31 from Sherar

Falls to Pelton Dam. Fishing peaks in August and September, although some years it can be excellent in late July and hold up strongly to early October.

Special regulations apply to Deschutes River steelheading, particularly in the use of non-barbed hooks, release of all fish not bearing healed hatchery fin-clip scars, and no fishing from buoyant devices (see regs). Catches recently recorded range from 6,000 in 1983 to over 7,300 Deschutes summer-runs taken in 1985.

The lower Deschutes is reached off Interstate Highway 84 near Celilo, site of the old Indian netting platforms now covered by a heightened Columbia, with public access available by foot and pedal bike for 12 miles upriver. From the end of that area upstream to Macks Canyon there are no roads. Fishermen use jet sleds to forge upriver or drift boats to fish down, selecting good bank spots or islands from which to cast. Mossy, flat rocktops in midstream also are utilized, with jet boats dropping fishermen off to perch on these solitary casting spots for a few hours. Much over-crowding of boats and fishermen is now occurring during the steelhead run from July to October, reducing the enjoyment of the fishing experience from the mouth upstream 50 miles to Maupin. Hordes of anglers and jet boats have drastically changed the serenity once treasured on the Deschutes.

Flies, spinners, bobbers and plugs all draw strikes from Deschutes steelhead and Columbia River fish that have temporarily entered the cold waters of the Deschutes for a breather before continuing upstream. Spinner fishermen generally do best in pockets near shore and behind boulder beds, while fly-fishermen sift the water of long, slow runs.

The Deschutes has many dangerous rapids that should not be tackled by novice rivermen. Guides are available, and it is wise to have several trips under the belt before tackling the Deschutes in your own boat.

HOOD RIVER: Hood River, a medium size stream, has twin tributaries that tumble and twist rapidly down from Lost Lake on the north face of Mt. Hood and from near Bennett Pass on the east flank. Fed by glacial melt, the East Fork and West Fork combine near the town of Dee, 12 miles above the Columbia River, then the Hood slides beneath Interstate 84 at the city of Hood River.

An average 3,000 to 4,000 steelhead are caught from the Hood River, mostly by bank anglers. A short, half-mile or so lower section of the river is boated by jet sleds at the mouth and drift boats working downriver from a boat site near the Interstate 84 bridge. Summer fisherman steadily take catches from May through September, while January and April are twinned peaks of production for winter runs.

The mainstem Hood River is open to steelheading all year around, as is the West Fork from mouth to Punchbowl fishway and East Fork to Middle Fork. There is a fly-fishing-only area open July 1-Oct. 31 on the West Fork above Dry Run Bridge on Lolo Pass Road.

Historic photo of Beavertail area on the Deschutes River in Oregon. This photo was taken about 1922 when the area was called Horseshoe Bend.

Irwin Brown, originally a midwest steelheader, caught this hatchery steelhead while fly fishing on Oregon's Deschutes River.

NORTHEAST ZONE

GRANDE RONDE RIVER: Summer steelheaders who derive pleasure from fishing unique, wilderness stretches of pools and riffles are keeping an eye on the Grande Ronde River, where a hatchery "wild fish" program appears to be revitalizing a fishery nearly extinct for decades.

Rising in the mountain edges near La Grande, the Grande Ronde wriggles and drops northeast to pass Troy, then crosses the state border into Washington and in another 35 miles reaches the Snake. The Grande Ronde's steelhead population has been bolstered to the point that it now is open for taking two hatchery steelhead per day. Only six steelhead may be retained in seven consecutive days.

Only adipose-clipped steelhead may be retained and all other steelhead must be released in the water. Steelheading on the Grande Ronde is split into two periods, Jan. 1-April 15 and Sept. 1-Dec. 31 and barbless hooks are required in both periods. Best access route is Highway 3 from Enterprise and then west on all-weather road to Troy, from which town anglers may reach downstream fishing via a gravelled road along the river. Excellent fly water.

JOHN DAY RIVER: The John Day River reaches slender fingers high into the Ochoco and Malheur national forest areas to drain strength into its watercourse. It flows more than 250 miles, first heading west from John Day to Kimberly, then (15 miles farther) turns sharply north and struggles more than 60 miles through roadless territory (designated a Scenic Waterway) to reach the Columbia River between Rufus and Quinton. Interstate Highway 84 crosses the mouth of the John Day.

The main John Day to the North Fork is open to steelheading all year. From Jan. 1-April 15 and Sept. 1-Dec. 31, steelheaders may fish the mainstem from North Fork to Indian Creek, Middle Fork to Highway 395 Bridge and North Fork to Highway 395 Bridge. One way to share the 1,500-2,400 summer-run catch is to raft the John Day from roads tapping the river at isolated spots. Best months are September and October.

SNAKE RIVER: Oregon anglers who reach the Snake River between the Washington border and Hells Canyon Dam take home a yearly catch of about 700 large, strong steelhead. The access from Oregon shores is difficult, as this portion of the Snake flows through the deep Grand Canyon of the Snake and is nearly roadless.

At the mouth of the Imnaha is one point of road approach; another route is to run a jet sled upstream from the mouth of the Grande Ronde. A determined angler might use the Wallowa-Whitman National Forest's mapped trail system to hike to the river from the Imnaha River Road.

COLUMBIA RIVER ZONE

COLUMBIA RIVER: Special regulations are listed in your regulations handbook for steelheading on the Columbia River, the huge aorta that annually pumps approximately 500,000 steelhead into Oregon, Washington and Idaho streams. These rules basically apply to time periods for releasing all steelhead having unclipped adipose fins, the means for differentiating between wild fish and hatchery fish. Heavy stocking programs and the mandatory release of wild fish appear to be reviving a vital fishery. The broad and powerful Columbia has been increasing its steelhead dividends in recent years to Oregon anglers, with catches rising from 2,600 in 1983 to nearly 8,000 in the late 1980s.

Access along, and to, the Columbia River is excellent from its mouth, where Highway 30 follows the river to Portland and Interstate 84 continues east along the Columbia's bank to Umatilla, where the Columbia swerves north into Washington. Boat launches at most river mouths and many points between permit trollers to waggle diving plugs and spoons in front of willing steelhead. Plunkers and drift-rig anglers line the popular bars on the river when steelhead schools are moving through. The Columbia once more is filling with steelhead available to Oregon anglers!

BR. COLUMBIA
WASHINGTON
MONTANA
WYOMING
OREGON
NEVADA
UTAH
IDAHO
Lewiston
Orofino
Grangeville
Boise
Pocatello
Clearwater River
N F
Lochsa River
Selway River
S F
Salmon River
Little Salmon River
SNAKE RIVER
M F Salmon R
Lemhi River
Salmon R
Pahsimeroi River
E F
Boise River
N F
S F
Snake River

Chapter 16

Idaho

Majestic mountain peaks shoulder into the cool, clean skies of Idaho, a scenically beautiful western state of 83,557 square miles, about 70 percent of which is in the public domain. Over 250 points of fishing and hunting public access are marked by "Sportsman's Access" and BLM signs.

An outdoorsman's paradise, Idaho also offers recreationists unparalleled skiing, hiking, riding, rockhounding, camping and photographic opportunities. More than 2,000 lakes and about 35,000 miles of streams qualify this state as a piscatorial paradise that's filled with bass, crappie, perch, bullhead and channel catfish, kokanee, sturgeon, salmon and steelhead. The Idaho Fish & Game Department currently is working on a list and map of public access areas for fishermen and hunters, but the project is not yet done.

Steelhead (and salmon) are considered the premier angling attractions for both resident and visiting fishermen. Anadromous fish mounting the Columbia River to reach the Snake, Salmon and Clearwater rivers furnish the only salt water-to-inland state fishery in the U.S. for these sea-going species. Idaho is, however, at the end of a long pipeline of water semi-blocked by long, slow pools between dams and juvenile steelhead and salmon smolts on their way to the ocean are drastically affected by high mortality due to disorientation, losses through power turbines and nitrogen illness. However, a strong and growing Idaho hatchery program is matched by an amenable amalgam of catch-and-release and harvest fishing regulations and seasons, resulting in an upswing in the numbers of steelhead catches in the last two or three years.

One of the keys to excellent steelhead fishing in Idaho is promulgation of two runs of fish..."A" run steelhead that predominantly spend only a year in the Pacific and return as 5- to 9-pounders, and "B" run steelhead that gorge on Pacific Ocean fare for two or more years, showing up in the Snake and Clearwater, especially, as fish ranging from 12 to 16 pounds and commonly boosting scale needles past the 20-pound mark. "A" fish are 60 to 80 percent one-salt steelhead and come over Bonneville Dam earlier than "B" run fish, which are 70 to 80 percent two-salt. There are wild "B" fish in the Salmon drainage too.

Management of steelhead fisheries is by the Idaho Department of Fish and Game, 600 S. Walnut St., P.O. Box 25, Boise, ID, phone 208-334-3700. Steelheading is covered in separate supplemental regulations booklets issued in both fall and spring for harvest seasons. It is essential for anglers to check the regulations booklet prior to fishing, as there are many seasonal and annual changes. First-time Idaho fishermen will find necessary the IDFG publication, *The Official Guide To Fishing In Idaho* available for 95 cents (1988 cost) from the department. (Steelheaders desiring float fishing trips might wish to obtain a copy of *Outdoor IDAHO Experiences* from the Idaho Outfitters and Guides Association, P.O. Box 95, Boise, ID 83701, which contains a list of float trip outfits that also provide fishing experiences.)

IDFG Anadromous Fishery Coordinator Steve Huffaker says of Idaho's "Big 3" steelheading rivers, "Fishing usually starts in the Snake River in September and continues through March... Both the Salmon and Clearwater rivers can be dynamite right after ice-out." Steelhead harvest, he noted, is estimated by a telephone survey after the season is over and consumptive catches recently have ranged from 25,000 steelhead harvested in 1984 to 32,000-35,000 in 1983, 1985 and 1986. Idaho's largest steelhead of record, as of this writing, is the 30-pound, 2-ounce fish taken from the Clearwater

River by Keith Powell on November 23, 1973.

Not exclusively a winter sport, steelheading on a catch-and-release basis may be enjoyed on ANY Idaho waters open to trout fishing during the general Saturday before Memorial Day through November season, EXCEPT the Middle and South forks of the Salmon River, their tributaries, and in the Salmon River from Lake Creek near Riggins to Long Tom Creek near the Middle Fork Salmon River.

"The Clearwater," Huffaker noted, for instance, "is managed as a 'catch-and-release' fishery until Oct. 15. Then the consumptive season begins and the 'aluminum hatch' is on."

Regulations require anyone 14 years of age or older to have a valid license or permit. Steelhead permits – for rainbow trout over 20 inches in length caught from the Salmon River drainage, Snake River drainage below Hell's Canyon, or Clearwater River drainage – must be held in addition to each angler's seasonal fishing license. It's important to note that each river drainage is managed separately and that each has a specific daily and seasonal bag limit. The steelhead permits (punch cards) must be held for three months past the close of a stipulated season so telephone surveys can be made to determine the success ratios of randomly selected anglers and to estimate the annual catch.

Residents pay $21 for combined fish and game licenses or $16 for a season's fishing license. Non-resident seasonal fishing licenses cost $41, with short-term fishing costs as follow: 1-day $6, 3-day $11 and 10-day $18. Anyone desiring to fish for steelhead must possess a season license and a $6 salmon/steelhead permit card on which each steelhead caught and kept must be recorded immediately after capture. These are all 1993 fees. (In addition, there now is available a 3-day non-resident license that costs $21 and entitles a visiting angler to try for steelhead.) Non-resident children under 14 years of age must be accompanied by a holder of a valid fishing license and their fish must be included in the license holder's limit. Idaho youths under 14 do not need a fishing license, but are required to obtain a steelhead permit in order to take their own catch limits.

Barbless hooks are mandatory for steelhead angling, whether during the general fishing season catch-and-release period or the fall and winter harvest season. Daily bag, possession and season limits are individually set for each fall and spring season according to dam counts and projected run estimates, which determine the anticipated number of returning, harvestable fish.

As this summer steelhead migrated up the Columbia River in August it ran into an Indian gill net and was almost caught. Each summer the Indian tribal fishery harvests about 100,000 to 150,000 summer steelhead in the Columbia River. The sport kill is about 50,000 to 70,000.

An angler may fish for steelhead at any hour of the day or night, except where specific regulations state otherwise. Also, artificial light restrictions of previous years have now been relaxed, allowing fishermen to employ to good advantage "glow-in- the-dark" luminescent, fluorescent and phosphorescent plug finishes as fished in neighboring states and to use lures lit up by tiny batteries.

It is essential steelheaders know and follow the detailed, fluctuating regulations on steelhead fishing in Idaho. Most rivers are open to general season fishing all year, but harvest and catch-and-release seasons on steelhead are shorter, and every angler seeking this widely-acclaimed sportfish should ensure they have, and understand, a current regulations booklet and steelhead season brochure from the ID-FG.

Here is where you will find Idaho's best steelheading:

BOISE RIVER: Open to steelheading ONLY when an excess number of hatchery-return fish can be trapped and hauled to the Boise, which permits (as in 1987) Boise regulations to allow a put and take harvest, with no barbless hook requirements. The area open to steelheading is from the mouth of the Boise upstream to Barber Dam, the lowest of three barriers that stem the Boise, forming Lucky Peak, Arrowrock and Anderson Ranch reservoirs.

Reached by City of Boise arterials, and by boat access points from near old Fort Boise, on the Snake River about eight miles west of Parma, to the city, the lower Boise River is hemmed by Highway 44 on the north and Highways 20/26 along its south shore. State Highway 21 leads upstream southeast of Boise toward the dam. Although a tamed river, the Boise nevertheless is a fine choice for plunking, pulling plugs, bait and/or bobber drift rigs and floating bobber/jig combinations.

CLEARWATER RIVER and MIDDLE FORK CLEARWATER: Steelhead catches may run as high as 20,000 fish in a banner year on the Clearwater River. Idaho's Number 1, the Clearwater tumbles down from the slopes of 10,000-foot-high peaks in the Selway-Bitterroot Wilderness mountain chain. It boasts excellent steelhead numbers, comprised of both hatchery and wild fish. Only steelhead with a missing adipose fin (healed scar) may be kept in any consumptive season. The world's largest steelhead rearing facility – Dworshak National Fish Hatchery – just above the North Fork Clearwater's mouth, between Ahsahka and Orofino, has doubled the numbers of steelhead smolts planted in Idaho streams since the 1970s and the resulting increase in steelhead catches is being reflected up the entire pipeline.

The main stem Clearwater and Middle Fork may be fished all year from mouth to the mouth of Clear Creek near Kooskia. Steelhead may be kept, during the two harvest seasons, from the Clearwater's mouth at Lewiston upstream to a posted line 150 yards downstream of the mouth of Clear Creek. All Clearwater River rainbow trout over 20 inches in length are considered steelhead.

Fishing access to the Clearwater is unparalleled. The City of Lewiston brackets the river mouth on south and north banks. Lewis and Clark Highway 12 follows the stream from Lewiston to Orofino, crossing the North Fork Clearwater River two miles below Orofino, then the highway drops southeast to Kamiah and Kooskia, a distance of about 70 miles, and next swings northeast along the Middle Fork and past the Selway River mouth to trace the Lochsa River before climbing over Lolo Pass into Montana. The lower 42 miles of river, Lewiston to Orofino, is the most heavily fished area, particularly below the North Fork, where the clear outflow from Dworshak Reservoir often permits fishing even when other sections of the river are muddy and silt-laden.

The Clearwater is a fine boat stream below the North Fork, but low flows often can drop the river level above Orofino to bones and boulders. There have been no motor regulations in past years between Kooskia and Orofino.

Because of heavy rapids below, this tailout is a good resting area for tired steelhead.

Summer fishermen enjoy catch-release Clearwater steelheading with flies, spoons and spinners cast from the bank, and plugs or drift gear fished from boats. In early winter and again in spring, bank anglers do very well with shrimp, cluster eggs, bobber/yarn rigs, or sliding float bobbers bearing small jigs or bait, while boaters best punch their fish on trolled Hot Shot, Tadpolly, Hawg Boss, Hot'N Tot, Flatfish and Wiggle Wart plugs, Jet Planers with bait, backtrolled shrimp and cluster eggs, Lil' Corky, Cutlass Drifter, Cheater, Fenton Fly, Sammy Special and Okie Drifter bobbers, or winged bobbers such as the Spin-N-Glo, Glo-Go and Birdie Drifter. The Clearwater is a fine steelhead fly-fishing river from September into November, weather allowing.

LOCHSA RIVER: Joins the Middle Fork Clearwater at Lowell, where U.S. Highway 12 climbs through the Wild and Scenic River Corridor toward Lolo Pass, following the Lochsa most of the way. A string of improved state campgrounds makes this an ideal summer vacation area. Currently, there is NO steelhead season on the Lochsa, as its fish are all naturally produced and are not harvested. In the past, it was managed under the Clearwater River drainage regs and anglers will have to check the supplemental brochures before each season to see if either catch-and-release or consumptive steelheading might in the future be permitted.

SELWAY RIVER: The conjunction of the Selway River and Lochsa at Lowell forms the Middle Fork Clearwater. From Lowell, a good gravel road leads east to Selway Falls, and summertime visitors may loop southwest on an unimproved road from the falls to Elk City, from which point Highway 14 tracks the South Fork Clearwater downstream to Grangeville. The Selway also is currently CLOSED to steelheading fishing and there are no hatchery plants. If seasons are allowed in the future, they will be shown in the supplementary management regulations.

NORTH FORK CLEARWATER: Open all year, the North Fork is perhaps the most heavily fished short section of river in the state. The area available to anglers during steelheading periods is on the west shoreline only, from the posted boundary 150 yards upstream from the mouth to the Ahsahka highway bridge. Outflow from Dworshak generally maintains the North Fork in clear, green, fishable condition.

Hardware – spinners and spoons – produces good numbers of prime, large Clearwater steelhead, as do bobbers, yarn or fly drift rigs, wing bobbers and plugs either cast and retrieved or fished with side planers. Because there usually are crowds of bank anglers, it's a good practice to match your tackle to the same type of rigging used by neighboring anglers. The speed of your drift is the criterion and a fisherman utilizing a slow angling method in a fast-fishing group or vice versa might quickly create enough line tangles to earn himself a whap upside the ear with an ugly stick!

SOUTH FORK CLEARWATER: Hatchery plants in the South Fork have added more miles of steelhead fishing to the Clearwater drainage. From Kooskia to Elk City, the South Fork is trailed by Highway 14. It receives good plants of hatchery fish and is becoming increasingly popular as a spring fishery. Fishing success varies with water clarity, as the south fork muddies with snow melt or rains, but if you catch it right it can be super.

SNAKE RIVER: The Snake River reaches thin fingers far into Wyoming's Teton peaks, then grows in power and size as it follows its convoluted pathway carved across southern Idaho to the Oregon border. At the state line, the Snake bears northward to plunge into ever-deeper gorges along the boundary of the two states until emerging from Hells Canyon to flow north between Idaho and Washington before reaching Lewiston. Winding westward, the Snake pours into the Columbia River near the Tri-Cities – Pasco, Kennewick and Richland – in southeast Washington.

Steelheading is almost exclusively limited to boat fishing on the Snake, due to minimal bank access. The Snake River is open to steelhead anglers from the Washington state line at the confluence of Snake and Clearwater rivers upstream to Oxbow Dam, including the slack-water pool between Hells Canyon and Oxbow dams. In the Oxbow between-dams section, barbless hooks are not required.

The Snake is big water, with many deep holes, and is best fished by trolling plugs, planer/bait rigs, or slow-drifting with bobber or bait/bobber set-ups. Anchoring up and using drop-back or backtrolling tactics also will yield fish. Some plunking is done in the lower river.

By far, most Idaho western border area fishermen will tackle the confluence of Snake and Clearwater rivers. In this area and to the Oregon border, harvestable steelhead must have a missing adipose fin, showing a healed scar, to be legally kept.

Idaho, Washington and Oregon have mutually reciprocal license agreements, whereby licensed BOAT fishermen of each state may angle, according to the fish and game laws of Idaho, the Snake River main flow where it forms the state boundaries but NOT from the neighbor state's shoreline, or in its sloughs or tributaries. Only ONE daily bag may be taken by an individual steelheader, no matter the number of different state licenses held.

SALMON RIVER: Longest river inside the state of Idaho, the Salmon river still is awesome in its bridled power and for its relatively untouched areas of primitive beauty. Only the lower and upper sections of river are heavily fished for steelhead, while a large portion of the Salmon is accessible only by float or powerboat trips through its deep canyons. Originating in the Sawtooth National Recreational Area, the Salmon River first swings east, then veers north, west across central Idaho to Riggins, north again, then finally loops west and south to join with the Snake River, thus flowing all directions of the compass.

Outfitters and guides at Riggins, on U.S. Highway 95, about 40 miles upstream from the junction of Salmon and Snake rivers, can arrange for boat fishing trips up or down the lower Salmon. Plugs, drift gear, planers and bait, flies and hardware all garner strikes from fall and spring steelhead. Best fishing is in the fall season, with ocean-fattened fish stacking in the river's deep holes and runs. Catches perk again in spring after the ice chill and turbidity of the flood-swollen river subsides.

At Riggins, there is a large recreation area that provides sportsmen with plenty of parking space and an opportunity for bank fishing, a rarity on this steep-sided stream. Called the "River of No Return" for its forbidding gorges and thunderous turbulence, the middle section of the Salmon runs through primitive, roadless wilderness. Intrepid fishermen can arrange steelheading trips that begin with airplane fly-ins and culminate in guided float trips to another airplane pick-up spot or to Riggins. Fishing is best from gravel and sand bars where fly-fishing, or casting spoons, bait or drift bobbers will deliver strikes.

The main Salmon River generally is open to steelheading from its mouth upstream to Red Fish Lake Creek in the spring harvest season and fall/winter harvest season. In 1988, a spring catch-release season was permitted from 100 yards above the Pahsimeroi River upstream to the mouth of the East Fork.

LITTLE SALMON RIVER: Steelheaders may harvest fish during the spring season from the mouth of the Little Salmon River to 100 yards upstream from the mouth of Rapid River. The highway follows the river from Riggins upstream to New Meadows and McCall. Fly-fishermen, as well as spinning gear users, do well with artificials on the Little Salmon.

SOUTH FORK, MIDDLE FORK, EAST FORK and NORTH FORK SALMON RIVER: These arms of the Salmon River flow mainly through wilderness areas and access is relatively difficult. The South Fork can be reached via Payette National Forest roads in a few spots, with hiking trails going upriver and down. Some access to the East Fork Salmon River from Challis, on Highway 93, is found by taking Highway 75 south, then along the lower East Fork on, first an oil road for 8 to 10 miles, then an unimproved road several miles more. The Middle Fork Salmon River tumbles through roadless territory and is designated as a Wild and Scenic Area. The North Fork Salmon is trailed by U.S. Highway 93 from the town of North Fork to the Montana border.

Each of the tributaries can produce catches of steelhead taken with a minimum of tackle, such as flies, spinners, spoons or drift bobber rigs. Steelheading normally is catch-and-release only in these tributaries, and anglers are cautioned to read the regulations very carefully as to specific season dates.

LEMHI RIVER: Paralleled and repeatedly crossed by State Highway 28 between Salmon and Leadore, the Lemhi River provides a share of the Salmon River's steelhead, but is closed to harvesting them once they have passed the big river's gauntlet of hooks and reached the home tributary. It yields some summer trout season sport with steelhead on a catch/release basis, however. Good choices of tackle on the Lemhi include hardware, drift gear and flies.

PAHSIMEROI RIVER: Another fine Salmon River tributary, the Pahsimeroi receives good hatchery plants of steelhead to help feed into the Salmon River, but only non-harvest steelhead fishing is allowed. Access is from U.S. Highway 93 near May, from which point all-weather roads lead upstream, the best of which is on the south shore. Summer season bait and bobber anglers, fly-fishermen, and spoon anglers tangle with the largest number of Pahsimeroi steelhead.

This hatchery winter steelhead took a weighted spinner.

OREGON
NEVADA
ARIZONA
MEXICO
CALIFORNIA
PACIFIC OCEAN
N
Smith R
Klamath R
Salmon R
S F Trinity R
reka
Mad R
Klamath R
Van Duzen R
Eel River
Mattole R
Russian R
Redding
Battle Cr
Red Bluff
Sacramento R
Feather R
Yuba R
American R
Sacramento
San Francisco
Colorado River
Los Angeles
San Diego

Chapter 17

Northern California

Third largest state in the United States of America, California has 158,693 square miles of land that varies from sand and cactus desert, some of which is below sea level, to mountains clad in fir, pine and redwood trees. There are 5,000 lakes, over 1,100 miles of Pacific Ocean shoreline and 30,000 miles of rivers in this most southern of the Pacific Coast states.

California's freshwater fish species include largemouth and smallmouth bass, crappie, perch, bluegill and sunfish, bullhead, catfish, kokanee and several species of trout. Anadromous fish are striped bass, sturgeon, salmon and steelhead.

Steelhead are found in regions where there is ample water, which generally limits these sportfish to areas which have more than 40 inches of rainfall each year...the north half of the Coast Ranges and upper Sierra Nevada watersheds feeding either into the Pacific Ocean or the top of the broad, central Sacramento Valley. Steelhead range from the Oregon border south to Monterey County.

California's largest steelhead of record is a 27-pound, 4-ounce fish caught from the Smith River in 1976 by Robert Halley of Crescent City.

Anyone 16 years of age or older must have a fishing license to take any kind of fish in California except for persons fishing from a public pier in ocean or bay waters. Only a basic fishing license is required for any fish except striped bass (special stamp needed) and for anglers fishing ocean waters south of Point Arguello, who also need an Ocean Enhancement Stamp. Steelhead rarely are caught in salt water and, in freshwater, are regulated as trout which may be fished for 24 hours a day, all year except where regulations specify otherwise.

Resident 1993 sport fishing licenses cost $23.65, and non- resident sport fishing licenses are $63.55. One-day sport fishing licenses for either resident or non-resident are $8.40. Management of sport fishing in California is by the Department of Fish and Game, 1416 Ninth Street, Box 944209, Sacramento, CA 94244-2090.

California's most popular steelhead rivers, according to Robert Reavis and Tim Curtis of the Inland Fisheries Division, DFG, are, Smith, main stem Klamath, Salmon, main stem Trinity, Mad, main stem Eel, south Fork Eel, Gualala, Russian, American, Feather and upper Sacramento Rivers. No catch counts are kept, but occasional creel censuses are made on specific rivers and an intensive smolt planting program adds millions of hatchery fish to streams each year. Low flow conditions may prompt stream closures to protect the resources (see regs).

Here are the major steelheading rivers of northern California:

SMITH RIVER: One of California's best-known steelhead streams, the Smith River bounces down the rocky ribs of the Siskiyou National Forest from Elk Valley, near the Oregon border, to pick up the North Fork Smith at Gasquet and the South Fork Smith River at the Six Rivers National Forest Recreation Area. It carries most of the water drained from the Six Rivers National Forest by the time it sweeps north west to enter the Pacific Ocean west of the town of Smith River.

Quick to clear, because of having a mostly rock and gravel watercourse, the Smith yields strong, and often large, steelhead. It produced the state record steelhead in 1976 and can be counted on for 20-pounders in each season's catches. The Smith River has a good, nearly self-sustaining population of wild-spawning steelhead, boosted every few years by enhancement hatchery plants. Plant records supplied us show no 1983-84-85 stocking, although a good plant of around 55,000 steelhead was made in 1982.

Bobber bodies – both round and winged versions – and cluster egg baits, spoons, spinners and metallic finish Hot Shot plugs all hold strong appeal for steelhead in the Smith River. Though the vodka-transparent water might tempt an angler to fish light lines and leaders, 10-pound test or stronger monofilament is recommended except for plunking, where 17- to 20-pound test mono should provide a happy medium between sporting catches and risking tackle loss to the occasional bruiser Chinook salmon that might gum your hook.

Access is excellent to the mainstem Smith River. Highway 101 crosses the stream a few miles inland from the mouth and Highway 197 follows the north bank of the Smith from Highway 101 to Jedediah Smith Redwoods State Park. At that point, Highway 199 from Crescent City meets 197 and follows the Smith River to the Oregon border, providing many angler approaches to the river. The lower river – the most popular stretch is from Highway 101 to the Highway 197 bridge – is easily fished from the bank via primitive roads on both of its shorelines and there is ample bank-fisherman access at Jedediah Smith Park and the Six Rivers National Forest Recreation Area a few miles upstream.

Boaters may launch at Jedediah Smith Park and take out near Tryon Corner or at Smith River. Outgoing tides are advised for fishing the lower river. Experienced Smith River guides should be contracted for the wild and woolly upper river and from Gasquet to the Six Rivers recreation site.

The short stretch of the North Fork Smith River open to fishing above Gasquet to Stony Creek is easily reached with 4WD vehicles, and the South Fork Road trails far upstream along the South Fork Smith River.

Two steelhead is the current daily limit that may be taken from the Smith in a year-around open season that sees its best steelheading from November into April. The mainstem Smith is open to angling from mouth to Patrick Creek, the North Fork Smith may be fished up to the mouth of Stony Creek and the South Fork is open to angling downstream from Jones Creek.

KLAMATH RIVER: The Klamath River originates in Oregon and crosses the California border in northern Siskiyou County, where it is twice penned by Copco Lake and Iron Gate Reservoir. Below Iron Gate, there's nearly 200 miles of excellent fishing in the state's second-largest river. Drift boats and bank anglers hold sway on the upper river to Weitchpec, then jet sleds and other powered boats generally garner the best fishing downstream to the broad river mouth at Requa.

From July through September, half-pounder steelhead (which may range from 1 to 4 pounds) appear by the thousands in the Klamath system. Heftier steelhead mount the river from October to March. Flies, spinners, spoons, plugs, bobbers and baits all trick strikes from the Klamath's sturdy and hard-fighting fish. A good spawning population of wild steelhead is abetted by hatchery plants such as the 200,000 smolts fed into the Klamath in 1984.

Highway 169 follows the lower Klamath River to Weitchpec and Highway 96 closely parallels the Klamath through Six Rivers and Klamath National Forests to Interstate 5 below the Iron Gate Reservoir. Access is excellent off both routes. There is quite a bit of private property along the Klamath, and permission is necessary to cross it to fish the banks. Also, some of the rugged topography prevents all but the most intrepid hiking-climbing anglers from reaching the upper river.

Generally, drift boats are required for reaching the best fishing on the upper three-quarters (about 140 miles) of the Klamath. Guides are strongly recommended, as this is not easy water to drift.

SALMON RIVER: The Salmon River and its North and South forks provide fair summer steelheading and good wintertime angling (see regs for mid-November-February 28 trout-only season). The North Fork curls down from high in the Marble Mountains and the South Fork drains the Salmon Mountains.

Access from Highway 96 at Somes Bar is via the Salmon River Road to Forks of Salmon, then up the North Fork on the Sawyers Bar Road or down the South Fork on the Cecilville Road, which goes through the mountains to Callahan, in the Scott River Valley.

Parts of the Salmon River system flow slowly over broad, boulder-filled gravel beds and other areas are in canyons where chains of deep pools and swift runs are best found when the road drops in elevation to within reach of the river. Spinners, spoons, bobber/yarn rigs and flies work well in front of, along and behind big boulders and in pockets of the shallow sections. Bait and spoon fishermen will take a large share of steelhead from the bottoms of the deep holes.

TRINITY RIVER: Excellent access and a plentitude of steelhead combine to make the Trinity River one of California's favorite fishing streams. Highway 96 from Weitchpec trails the lower river in the gorge area, and joins Highway 299 at Willow Creek, then 299 follows the mainstem Trinity River through the Trinity National Forest to Weaverville.

Heavily stocked, the Trinity receives from 300,000 small steelhead to over a million young fish annually. It is famed for its well-known fly-fishing drifts and riffles, but also yields well to spin-fished spoons, spinners and drift gear.

The main Trinity from old Lewiston Bridge downstream to mouth and South Fork Trinity below Hayampom Bridge are the popular fishing areas, but are no longer open year-round. Anglers must note current regulations and 1992-94 supplement changes to ensure they are fishing legally.

Footpaths, trails and overgrown log roads are your

best means of access to the canyon areas of the mainstem Trinity for about 10 miles above Weitchpec, while Highway 299 furnishes easy access at hundreds of angling spots along the river's edge upstream on the Trinity. The river is wadable in many areas. One of the keys to successful angling on the Trinity is to keep moving up or down Highway 299, searching for the runs or schools, then concentrating your efforts once a school has been located.

The Trinity has huge numbers of late summer and fall half-pounders which may weigh from that size to 3 pounds, then in winter produces bright steelhead that occasionally may push scale needles well into the teens.

MAD RIVER: Humboldt County's Mad River is a short coastal stream that can be very rewarding if anglers time their fishing to fall and winter periods when rain and tide conditions make it easier for steelhead to get past the sand bar at its lagoon mouth. The fish will move rapidly through the lower river, affording fine steelheading for short periods.

Open year-round downstream from the county road bridge at Maple Creek to its mouth above Arcata, the Mad River is productive for anglers fishing the lagoon/lower river area, and for fishermen who reach the river off frontage roads from Highway 299 and local roads on north and south banks below Blue Lake.

Best fishing on the Mad River is late fall and through the winter. Prolonged autumn dry spells will delay the runs until rains come. The Mad River is stocked with fairly hefty steelhead smolts from the Mad River Hatchery, near Blue Lake, such as the nearly 3,000 sturdy, 2.9 fish per pound plant made in 1985. Such fish have a very good, high rate of ocean survival. More commonly, smolt size will range between 4.5/lb. to 16.3/lb., as were the 1983 plants of 169,900 fall-run young steelhead and 58,000 winter steelhead smolts, the 181,300 winter smolts added in 1984 and 371,351 stocked in 1985. Returning steelhead may stack by the hundreds below the Mad River Hatchery deadline and can best be taken with roe/yarn and bobber/yarn drift rigs.

EEL RIVER: A very long coastal stream, the Eel River may be California's easiest to find and fish, since much of the South Fork Eel and mainstem is closely tracked by Highway 101, as well as the main Eel being readily accessible from state, county and local roads.

Stocked in Humboldt County with 95,250 large smolts in 1985, the lower Eel mainstem offers fine tidal area fishing, then scattered good periods of catches up to its junction with the South Fork Eel River. The mainstem Eel received a plant of 6,589 large smolts in 1985 at various Mendocino County sites, and the South Fork Eel had 3,200 sturdy young plants in 1984.

Generally, these planted steelhead will return, after two years in the ocean, as fish weighing 5 to 8 pounds, but a good number of Eel River fish come back as 10- to 20-pounders, which may indicate at least some Eel River steelhead will feed for an additional year or two in the Pacific.

Boaters can launch small boats from primitive launches found near salt water in the Cock Robin Island area of the Eel below Fernbridge. A network of soft gravel bars allows steelheaders access to the lower river, where chances are good that September fish can be stopped after each good rainfall. Upstream angling spots are readily located from Highway 101, or old Highway 254, which twines along the river and 101 past Humboldt Redwoods State Park and accompanies 101 a good distance down the South Fork. The park affords excellent access to the mainstem Eel below the forks and also a good base from which to fish the lower South Fork.

Steelheading is open all year from the Eel River mouth to the North Fork Eel River and specific opening/closing dates cover waters to Cape Horn Dam and Cape Horn Dam to Scott Dam (see regs). Anglers also should note artificial lure and barbless hook restrictions.

Joyce Herbst with a summer steelhead taken on a fly and a dry line.

Bridges and stream mouths are prime spots for steelheaders on the Eel River system. Good catches can be made on bait, bobbers, spinners, spoons, flies and, in the boating sections, on plugs fished by the hotshotting method. Good steelheading persists from late November through February.

VAN DUZEN RIVER: A major tributary to the Eel River, the Van Duzen River originates on the western side of Trinity County and is followed by Highway 36 across the county border and then the width of Humboldt County west to its junction with the Eel River a few miles south of Fortuna. It is open to fishing all year from mouth to Highway 36 bridge at Bridgeville, about midway across Humboldt County, but only steelhead (trout) may be retained in the winter season (see regs).

The Van Duzen has some fine, deep pools in the Chalk Bluffs area near Highway 101. However, much of the river is a series of shallow pools connected by shallow runs. Fly-fishermen will do very well fishing around large rocks and under brushy cutbanks, the best cover offered in the upper Van Duzen. Most of the bait and hardware angling is practiced on the lower river's deep holes and at the bridge spots, where abutments have allowed current to dredge out some very good, deep holes.

Grizzly Creek Redwoods State Park is a popular base for fishing up and down the Van Duzen.

MATTOLE RIVER: Humboldt County's Mattole River begins as tributary trickles high in the west edge of the Humboldt Redwoods State Park and gathers these into the mainstem by the time it reaches Honeydew, about 30 miles from entry into the Pacific Ocean at Mattole Point.

The Mattole main stem is open to fishing Jan. 1-Aug. 31 from Honeydew Creek downstream to its confluence with Bear Creek. Anglers must also review the artificial lures and barbless hooks restrictions on the Mattole.

Best fishing on the Mattole will be January, with the peak of steelheading in the cold months. Fly-fishermen can score good catches from the Mattole, fishing the riffles and shallow pools of the upper river and some of the deeper holes in the lower Mattole. Good bait/bobber drift-fishing and catches made on spoons and spinners can be had from the rocky, deep pools in the lower and middle mainstem.

Access is good along this out-of-the-way stream. Highway 211 (Mattole Road) crosses the river near Petrolia, local roads tap the downstream and upstream banks every few miles, and 211 tracks and crosses the river enroute to Honeydew.

NAVARRO RIVER: Rising in the Anderson Valley and coursing westward, the main Navarro picks up its North Fork at the foot of Flynn Hills and carries the increased flow to the Pacific Ocean, entering south of Navarro Point. Highway 1 crosses the mainstem above the mouth and Highway 128 trails the north bank of the mainstem to the forks and the North Fork Navarro past the town of Navarro. It is the best access for anglers, as there is private property along the south bank.

Dimmick State Park, at the junction of North Fork and Navarro, is a good base location for steelheaders and fish often "stack" here in the river below the North Fork mouth. Access from the North Fork to the upper fishing deadline at Hendy Woods State Park is difficult, due to private land, but the park road furnishes entry to some fair fishing.

Consistent water sources make the Navarro one of the best fall/winter steelheading prospects, and frequent plants of large smolts help enhance a much-diminished wild fishery. Nightcrawlers, roe clusters, bait shrimp, bobbers and small spinners and spoons fished in the deep holes will appeal to the Navarro's fish. Fly-fishermen also have some success fishing the pockets and boulder beds of the rocky little river. Steelheading is open all year on the Navarro, for two fish per day, from mouth upstream to the Greenwood Bridge.

GUALALA RIVER: The Gualala River is one of the better North Central District steelheading streams. The North Fork Gualala wriggles southwest down from the Squaw Rock area near Signal Ridge and the South Fork flows northwest from above Fort Ross to meet the Wheatfield Fork near Annapolis Road, then to the Pacific Ocean after combining with the North Fork inland from Highway 1, under which the mainstem courses to reach the sea.

Access at the mouth is fair, provided by a gravel road leading to tidewater, while county and local roads can be used to find upriver fishing spots.

Gualala steelheaders may fish below the junction of the Wheatfield and South Fork Gualala forks all year around to the Highway 1 bridge for two fish a day. Steelhead plants generally are composed of healthy fish 4.5 to the pound.

RUSSIAN RIVER: The Russian River drops through Sonoma County from southeastern Mendocino County, curling past Cloverdale, Healdsburg and Guerneville, dropping into salt water near Jenner. It is a long river system, but the best fishing for steelhead is near the mouth and in the lower area.

Open from mouth to confluence of its East Branch all year, the Russian once held a good wild run of steelhead now enhanced by plants such as the 10,000-plus 1984 smolt additions and 9,250 young fish stocked in 1985.

Highways 1, 116, 12, 101 and 128 and offroads from mouth to Healdsburg provide anglers access to the area on both sides of the river where private property does not bar entry. Good fishing can be found off gravel bars reached through Goat Rocks State Park near the mouth and other anglers fish the lagoon and lower tidewater from small boats.

The Russian River yields well to fly-fishermen, as well as to anglers using spinners, spoons, egg ties, bobbers, baits and plugs.

OTHER COASTAL STREAMS: Rainfall is the key to steelheading in California's coastal streams below the Mattole, which receives far more precipitation than more southerly rivers and creeks. Good steelheading – beginning with November rains – also can be found in Ten Mile River, Noyo River, Big River, Albion River and Garcia River.

Many rivers and creeks above and below San Francisco can provide sporadic runs of steelhead when Mother Nature turns on her water taps and flushes the sand and gravel bars from their mouths. Best for local fishing are Papermill Creek, Napa River, San Lorenzo River, Carmel River and Big Sur River. These are late fall and winter opportunities that must be immediately acted upon according to precipitation that allows steelhead to quickly slide into these small rivers and creeks on high water, with the fish rapidly moving upriver.

SACRAMENTO RIVER: Largest of California's rivers, the giant Sacramento is better known for its salmon fishing than steelhead catches. However, the big river from the City of Sacramento up to nearly Redding can be very productive for steelhead anglers who study its potential and peculiarities.

The Sacramento drains the Shasta National Forest rivers and creeks, is trapped in gigantic Shasta Lake, then snakes sinuously south through the Central Valley to join the San Joaquin River at Pittsburg, from where the combined waters flow west through Suisun Bay, San Pablo Bay and San Francisco Bay to mingle with the Pacific's salt water.

There is no closed season for steelheading on the Sacramento River, but there are specific areas that have closures (see regs). Daily bag limit is three per day.

Boat fishermen have the freedom of the river to fish anywhere within reach of the numerous public launch sites on the long Sacramento. Guides are available. There is bank fishing to be had off the gravel and sand bars and steelheaders will take fish on a variety of hardware, bobbers, baits and flies. The most popular type of fishing, however, is backtrolling plugs from boats and anchored drift-fishing or fly-casting.

Riffles, cutbanks, pools and runs below feeder stream mouths, heads of drifts and above tailouts are the most productive spots for fall and winter steelheaders. There are steelhead in the Sacramento almost every month of the year. Strong plants – such as the 406,700 in 1984 and 116,000 in 1985 – of large smolts – 6 to 7 fish per pound, continue to enhance the Sacramento's steelhead potential.

BATTLE CREEK: Edging down from the Cascades Range, Battle Creek tiptoes along the border between Shasta and Tehama counties, then pours into the Sacramento River a few miles below Balls Ferry. A small stream, Battle Creek is heavily stocked from the Coleman National Fish Hatchery, receiving steelhead numbers such as the following: 1983-1,108,000; 1984-625,500 and 1985-340,600.

Opened to steelheading only when 1,200 steelhead pass the Red Bluffs Diversion Dam between July 1 and Sept. 30, the fishing season from mouth to Coleman Hatchery generally is announced as Oct. 5 through January 1.

Access is via the Coleman Hatchery Road from Balls Ferry or Jelly's Ferry Road from the south. Boaters also drop downriver from Balls Ferry to fish outside the mouth of Battle Creek. The steelhead follow successive salmon runs up the creek and anglers must sort out non-keeper salmon from steelhead, of which three per day is the limit.

Artificial lures, such as bobbers, or pale color yarn ties and flies, reduce the number of salmon that might otherwise climb on baits or attack hardware offerings. There is limited camping in the area and the lower portion of Battle Creek is private property, so parking spots are at a premium.

FEATHER RIVER: The Feather River is one of the better inland California steelheading streams. It has excellent angling for steelhead in winter months and again in mid-summer. Daily limit is two steelhead. Generally open January 1, regulations for 1993-94 show scattered closing dates for specific river areas, so anglers must carefully read and follow their DFG booklet.

Access on the upper river is available through the Oroville Recreation Area and via frontage roads leading west from Highway 70 above Yuba City. Powered boats, drift boats and large rubber rafts are good choices for fishing the Feather, since there is much private property. A floating trip also can reach areas bank anglers may not have been able to touch, thus allowing you to test steelhead unspooked by other lines.

Flies, yarn egg ties, nightcrawlers, roe, tiny bobbers and small spinners work well on the upper Feather River, drawing sharp strikes from steelhead that generally range from 3 to 12 or 13 pounds. Larger fish are rare, but some are caught. The Feather is fed from the lower part of Oroville Dam, so its water remains clear in all but repeated, heavy rainfall, providing fishing when many other rivers are muddied.

Steelhead follow the fall runs of salmon into the Feather and best fishing is September through January. One good tactic is to fish below visible salmon stacking at the heads of runs or pools, working the middle of these waters and their tailouts. Cutbanks and overhanging willows or brush are other highly-suspect and often rewarding steelhead lies.

YUBA RIVER: Open all year (see regs) from its mouth to Englebright Dam, the Yuba River offers fair steelheading to late fall and winter anglers. Gaining its water from Plumas and Tahoe national forests, and from Middle and South Forks which straddle San Juan Ridge, the Yuba feeds into Englebright Lake, northeast of Smartville, before trundling southwest to its confluence with the Feather River at Yuba City.

Access to the upper Yuba River is off local roads from Highway 20 below Englebright Dam and from county roads above Yuba City. There is considerable private property, so bank spots must be carefully located. Boaters and floaters may have the best opportunities to fish flies, egg ties, baits, small hardware and plugs for steelhead weighing 3 to 10 pounds.

Don Roberts fly fishing for summer steelhead.

AMERICAN RIVER: A downtown delight of a stream, the American River's two forks begin high in the Sierra Nevadas above Folsom Lake, then press through Lake Natoma together to spill from Nimbus Dam as the mainstream American River for another 23 miles hemmed by outskirts, then the heart of Sacramento. The tamed stream meets the Sacramento River north of the center of the city.

State recreation areas, county and city parks and the huge American River Parkway, plus city arterials and offroads, provide unparalleled access along the American River. Boat launches on the lower river permit powered craft to fish from the mouth upstream, while drift boat fishermen can launch below Nimbus Dam for a leisurely float over good steelhead lies.

Backtrolling plugs or flies produces excellent catches of fall and winter steelhead. Early fish generally are of the Coleman Hatchery strain and weigh from 2 pounds to about 8 pounds, while late-runs can range from 5 to as much as 20 pounds. Popular gravel bar, beach and bank spots along the American also will yield fish taken on drift-rig baits, bobbers and egg ties. Fly-fishermen wading the shores do best on the riffles and around or below bottom obstructions such as rocks, current-moved stumps and large jetsam objects.

The American River is open to steelheading all year, except for specific area and salmon spawning time closures listed in the regulations booklet, and anglers may take two steelhead in their daily bag limit.

The following catch statistics for Oregon, Washington and British Columbia vary somewhat from year to year due to ocean and freshwater stream conditions. Use the following figures as a general indication of what streams to fish during what time period. For best fishing call ahead to see how run and weather conditions are.

Oregon – 1985 Estimated Steelhead Catch – Coastal Tributaries

STREAM	JAN	FEB	MAR	APR	MAY	JUN	JUL	AUG	SEP	OCT	NOV	DEC	TOTAL
ALSEA RIVER AND BAY 1/	2887	1072	241						17	21	207	2123	6568
DRIFT CREEK	59	55	8								4	8	134
FIVE RIVERS	38	30										8	76
LOBSTER CREEK	4	8											12
FALL CREEK	17	4											21
S FK ALSEA RIVER	17	38	4									4	63
N FK ALSEA RIVER 1/	490	481	59		4	4					17	152	1207
ALSEA BASIN TOTAL	3512	1688	312		4	4			17	21	228	2295	8081
BEAVER CREEK (LINC CO)	8	8										4	20
BIG CREEK (LANE CO)	17	8	13							4	4		46
BRUSH CREEK (CURRY CO)		13										4	17
CAPE CREEK (LANE CO)		17	4							4		8	33
CHETCO RIVER AND BAY	1950	2102	473				13	13	8	13	127	726	5425
COOS RIVER AND BAY	532	317	257	4							4	38	1152
MILLICOMA RIVER	72	25	30							4		8	139
W FK MILLICOMA RIVER	456	477	63									80	1076
E FK MILLICOMA RIVER	152	160	42								4	68	426
S FK COOS RIVER	684	173	203						4		13	190	1267
TIOGA CREEK	4	13	8										25
COOS BASIN TOTAL	1900	1165	603	4					4	4	21	384	4085
COQUILLE RIVER AND BAY	806	283	13								21	338	1461
N FK COQUILLE RIVER	393	933	241									55	1622
E FK COQUILLE RIVER	203	274	114									46	637
MIDDLE CREEK	25										4		29
S FK COQUILLE RIVER	1587	1351	397								38	325	3698
MID FK COQUILLE RIVER	38	38	13									25	114
COQUILLE BASIN TOTAL	3052	2879	778								63	789	7561
CUMMINS CREEK (LANE CO)		8											8
"D" RIVER AND DEVILS LAKE													0
ELK CREEK (CLATSOP CO)	4	4	4									8	20
ELK RIVER (CURRY CO)	241	257	152							4	46	89	789
FLORAS CR. LK & NEW RIVER	232	135	72								8	84	531
FOURMILE CREEK (COOS CO)		8											8
HUNTER CREEK (CURRY CO)	89	68	38								8	8	211
NECANICUM RIVER	675	772	144		8	8		8		25	93	283	2016
NEHALEM RIVER AND BAY	2085	950	498		4		34	21	4		42	587	4225
N FK NEHALEM RIVER	1380	916	241					4	13	8	38	350	2950
SALMONBERRY RIVER	4	17	25										46
COOK CREEK	363	131	8									68	570
ROCK CREEK	4	4	8										16
NEHALEM BASIN TOTAL	3836	2018	780		4		34	25	17	8	80	1005	7807
NESTUCCA RIVER AND BAY	2081	1051	675	468	523	1443	1000	409	886	481	637	1874	11528
THREE RIVERS	793	490	84								536	485	2388
BEAVER CREEK		13	8								4		25
LITTLE NESTUCCA RIVER	329	211	80			4		13	8	25	59	236	965
NESTUCCA BASIN TOTAL	3203	1765	847	468	523	1447	1000	422	894	506	1236	2595	14906
PISTOL RIVER	122	152	46							13	8	42	383
ROCK CREEK (LANE CO)													0
ROGUE RIVER & BAY, LOWER	1351	2169	1532	502	135	13	72	675	768	1654	1059	1270	11200
ILLINOIS RIVER	342	422	152	17							4	46	983
APPLEGATE RIVER	55	253	608										916
ROGUE RIVER, UPPER	148	245	549	253	21	8	46	215	110	295	249	165	2304
ROGUE BASIN TOTAL	1896	3089	2841	772	156	21	118	890	878	1949	1312	1481	15403
SALMON RIVER	848	523	215		4	46	25	63	148	51	131	393	2447
SAND LAKE	8										4		12
SILETZ RIVER AND BAY	1382	1469	793	224	350	1220	722	308	718	291	342	1228	9547
EUCHRE CREEK	4	30	8									4	46
ROCK CREEK										4	38	25	67
LITTLE ROCK CREEK	4		4									4	12
S FK SILETZ RIVER	38	42	30			8	17	21	34	17	42	21	270
N FK SILETZ RIVER	68	152	89			8	13	34	4	4	59	38	469
DRIFT CREEK	207	211	68							17	13	110	626
SCHOONER CREEK	8	4										8	20
SILETZ BASIN TOTAL	2211	1908	992	224	350	1236	752	363	756	333	494	1438	11057
SILTCOOS RIVER AND LAKE	13	4	4		8				4		17	8	58
SIUSLAW RIVER AND BAY	1194	587	203						21		148	840	2993
MUNSEL LAKE	4	4	4									4	16
N FK SIUSLAW RIVER	190	177	8								4	25	404
SWEET CREEK	4	8											12

STREAM	JAN	FEB	MAR	APR	MAY	JUN	JUL	AUG	SEP	OCT	NOV	DEC	TOTAL
LAKE CREEK	219	346	110								17	135	827
INDIAN CREEK	4	4	4										12
DEADWOOD CREEK	13	8	4										25
SIUSLAW BASIN TOTAL	1628	1134	333						21		169	1004	4289
SIXES RIVER	224	169	55								30	72	550
SUTTON CR, LK & MERCER LK	4		4										8
TAHKENITCH CREEK AND LAKE	4												4
TENMILE CREEK AND LAKES	532	325	89			8	4				72	308	1338
EEL LAKE													0
TENMILE BASIN TOTAL	532	325	89			8	4				72	308	1338
TENMILE CREEK (LANE CO)	42	42	51							4	4	21	164
TILLAMOOK BAY	17	8					8	25	8		4		70
TILLAMOOK RIVER	110	122	46					4			34	106	422
KILCHIS RIVER	160	122	152		13	42	46	25	38	38	89	173	898
MIAMI RIVER	122	139	106		8	17	8	8		8	55	110	581
TRASK RIVER	528	490	262	63	89	122	93	101	127	42	38	291	2246
S FK TRASK RIVER	30	13	21									13	77
N FK TRASK RIVER	38	42	25								4	38	147
TRASK BASIN TOTAL	596	545	308	63	89	122	93	101	127	42	42	342	2470
WILSON RIVER	912	587	329	148	122	422	279	181	346	186	300	920	4732
LITTLE NORTH FORK (WILSON		4	8										12
DEVILS LAKE FORK (WILSON)	8	4	4								4	4	24
WILSON BASIN TOTAL	920	595	341	148	122	422	279	181	346	186	304	924	4768
TILLAMOOK BASIN TOTAL	1925	1531	953	211	232	603	434	344	519	274	528	1655	9209
UMPQUA RIVER AND BAY	1448	739	270	122	42	101	114	135	160	89	203	1283	4706
SMITH RIVER	1005	612	144	8							17	663	2449
N FK SMITH RIVER	156	317	42								4	46	565
N UMPQUA RIVER, LOWER	177	165	122	42	38	25	89	110	181	84	42	72	1147
N UMPQUA RIVER, UPPER	135	177	177	59	84	274	1047	1828	1435	359	253	190	6018
S UMPQUA RIVER	933	371	266		4					8	13	93	1688
COW CREEK	55	17											72
UMPQUA BASIN TOTAL	3909	2398	1021	231	168	400	1250	2073	1776	540	532	2347	16645
WINCHUCK RIVER	511	114	25								8	80	738
WOAHINK LAKE	17	4	8										29
YACHATS RIVER	80	97	17							4		4	202
YAQUINA RIVER AND BAY	8	21							8	8		13	58
BIG ELK CREEK	447	241	46								21	63	818
YAQUINA BASIN TOTAL	455	262	46						8	8	21	76	876
TOTAL COASTAL TRIBUTARIES	33148	24667	10920	1910	1457	3773	3630	4201	5050	3765	5244	17211	114976

Columbia River System

STREAM	JAN	FEB	MAR	APR	MAY	JUN	JUL	AUG	SEP	OCT	NOV	DEC	TOTAL
ABERNATHY CREEK (WILL R)	4												4
BEAR CREEK (CLATSOP CO)	4	8											12
BEAVER CREEK (COL CO)	17	4									8		29
CLATSKANIE RIVER	279	152	97		30		4		4			42	608
BEAVER BASIN TOTAL	296	156	97		30		4		4		8	42	637
BIG CREEK (CLATSOP CO)	587	439	156		4	13	8	101	4	76	25	219	1632
CALAPOOIA RIVER		4	8	4	4								20
CLACKAMAS RIVER, LOWER 1/	1545	1064	1080	642	604	186	114	135	114	93	118	1110	6805
CLEAR CREEK	4	17	8										29
DEEP CREEK	4	4	4									4	16
EAGLE CREEK	110	595	692	156		4		4	8	4	4		1577
CLACK LOWER BASIN TOTAL	1663	1680	1784	798	604	190	114	139	122	97	122	1114	8427
CLACKAMAS RIVER, UPPER	114	76	186	46	80	485	988	629	810	401	97	144	4056
COLLOWASH RIVER	21	30	25		4		21	21	46	76	8	34	286
HOT SP FK COLLOWASH R			8				13	13	4	13	13	17	81
CLACK UPPER BASIN TOTAL	135	106	219	46	84	485	1022	663	860	490	118	195	4423
CLACKAMAS BASIN TOTAL	1798	1786	2003	844	688	675	1136	802	982	587	240	1309	12850
COLUMBIA RIVER, LOWER 1/	93	42	342			1220	1794	1739	515	13	8	68	5834
COLUMBIA RIVER, UPPER	110	30	4				266	464	245	443	203	291	2056
COLUMBIA BASIN TOTAL	203	72	346			1220	2060	2203	760	456	211	359	7890
DESCHUTES RIVER, LOWER				8	8	38	726	1764	2292	869	63	76	5844
DESCHUTES RIVER, UPPER						4	4	80	435	642	144	165	1474
DESCHUTES BASIN TOTAL				8	8	42	730	1844	2727	1511	207	241	7318
EAGLE CREEK (COLUMBIA R)		4	4	4	4	8	34	68	4	13	4	4	151
FIFTEENMILE CREEK					4								4
GNAT CREEK (CLATSOP CO)	156	72	72		8	42	17	8	25	8	42	21	471
HERMAN CREEK (COLUMBIA R)						4	8	4	17				33

STREAM	JAN	FEB	MAR	APR	MAY	JUN	JUL	AUG	SEP	OCT	NOV	DEC	TOTAL
HOOD RIVER	38	80	186	650	755	587	68	266	371	262	110	127	3500
W FK HOOD RIVER	8	4	8	13	4	13	106	51	38	30	21	4	300
E FK HOOD RIVER		4		4	4		8	34	38	8	4		104
HOOD BASIN TOTAL	46	88	194	667	763	600	182	351	447	300	135	131	3904
JOHN DAY RIVER	97	80	266		4	4		93	350	865	274		2033
N FK JOHN DAY RIVER	13	46	283							8			350
MID FK JOHN DAY RIVER		13	21							4	4	4	46
JOHN DAY BASIN TOTAL	110	139	570		4	4		93	350	877	278	4	2429
JOHNSON CREEK (WILL R)	30	8										4	42
KELLOGG LAKE (WILL R)	25	8	17	4									54
LUCKIAMUTE RIVER					4								4
MARYS RIVER		4									4		8
MCKENZIE RIVER, LOWER				13	55	279	257	122	152	114			992
MCKENZIE RIVER, UPPER				4	4	51	118	97	110	84			468
MCKENZIE BASIN TOTAL				17	59	330	375	219	262	198			1460
MILL CREEK (MARION CO)													0
MOLALLA RIVER	127	291	333	186	13		30	4	4	13	17	25	1043
PUDDING RIVER													0
BUTTE CREEK	4	4		13								4	25
ABIQUA CREEK		8	21	8									37
SILVER CREEK		4	13	13									30
MOLALLA BASIN TOTAL	131	307	367	220	13		30	4	4	13	17	29	1135
SANDY RIVER	2005	1735	1401	853	819	730	270	186	245	177	106	1064	9591
BULLRUN RIVER	8	4			4		21	4					41
SALMON RIVER						582	975	582	426	245	80	72	2962
SANDY BASIN TOTAL	2013	1739	1401	853	823	1312	1266	772	671	422	186	1136	12594
SANTIAM RIVER	55	63	224	118	131	270	241	135	55	72	13	42	1419
SOUTH SANTIAM RIVER	80	76	110	173	768	1587	1097	477	342	338	114	152	5314
THOMAS CREEK	17	8	30	17									72
CRABTREE CREEK	4	17	4	68	8	17	17		4	51	4	30	224
FOSTER RESERVOIR				8	4								12
S SANT BASIN TOTAL	101	101	144	266	780	1604	1114	477	346	389	118	182	5622
NORTH SANTIAM RIVER	148	106	397	431	582	1730	1270	498	274	409	156	350	6351
LITTLE N FK SANTIAM R	89	8	21	30	8	25	8		8	84	241	194	716
N SANT BASIN TOTAL	237	114	418	461	590	1755	1278	498	282	493	397	544	7067
SANTIAM BASIN TOTAL	393	278	786	845	1501	3629	2633	1110	683	954	528	768	14108
SCAPPOOSE BAY													
MILTON CREEK	8	13	8				4			4			37
SCAPPOOSE CREEK		8									4	4	16
N FK SCAPPOOSE CREEK	30	13	8										51
S FK SCAPPOOSE CREEK		8				8				8	4		28
SCAPPOOSE BASIN TOTAL	38	42	16			8	4			12	8	4	132
SNAKE RIVER	17	4	38						4	97	304	245	709
GRANDE RONDE RIVER													0
SUCKER CREEK (WILL R)											4		4
TANNER CREEK	13	4					8	4				4	33
TUALATIN RIVER	4	25	38		4								71
GALES CREEK	55	156	114	25	13	8							371
TUALATIN BASIN TOTAL	59	181	152	25	17	8							442
UMATILLA RIVER	42	25	46									38	151
WALLA WALLA RIVER		55	173	55								4	287
WILLAMETTE RIVER, LOWER 1/	384	114	181	388	397	68	21	21	4	8	34	338	1958
WILLAMETTE RIVER, UPPER	8	46	93	101	101	59	46	17	4			21	496
MID FK WILLAMETTE RIVER		4	55	21	42	59	89	38	4	25	51	4	392
FALL CREEK	21				4							4	29
WILLAMETTE BASIN TOTAL	413	164	329	510	544	186	156	76	12	33	85	367	2875
YAMHILL RIVER		4	13	4									21
S FK YAMHILL RIVER			4										4
MILL CREEK			4										4
WILLAMINA CREEK		8	30	17	8								63
N FK YAMHILL RIVER	4		8										12
YAMHILL BASIN TOTAL	4	12	59	21	8								104
YOUNGS RIVER AND BAY		8											8
LEWIS AND CLARK RIVER	156	118	55									38	367
KLASKANINE RIVER	93	160	25									42	320
S FK KLASKANINE RIVER	34	127	34										195
N FK KLASKANINE RIVER	549	490	215					8				25	1287
YOUNGS BASIN TOTAL	832	903	329					8				105	2177
TOTAL COLUMBIA RIVER	7214	6502	7163	4077	4486	8081	8651	7667	6956	5557	2286	5034	73674

Washington – Monthly Steelhead Catch

PROJECTED (FACTOR = 2.22)

NAME OF RIVER FISHED	SUMMER-RUN 1985 MAY	JUNE	JULY	AUG.	SEPT.	OCT.	WINTER-RUN 1985-86 NOV.	DEC.	JAN.	FEB.	MAR.	APR.	1985 SUMMER TOTAL	1985-86 WINTER TOTAL
BEAR RIVER	0	0	0	0	0	0	0	7	27	18	0	0	0	52
*BOGACHIEL/ QUILLAYUTE R.[1]	33	29	4	4	13	4	41	297	967	281	365	270	87	2221
*BURLEY CREEK	0	0	0	0	0	0	0	0	2	13	0	0	0	15
*CALAWAH RIVER[1]	40	42	38	33	62	49	16	98	377	114	90	26	264	721
*CANYON CREEK	11	24	4	7	7	4	2	4	53	31	0	0	57	90
*CARBON RIVER	0	0	0	0	2	4	4	9	4	0	0	0	6	17
*CASCADE RIVER[1]	13	9	11	49	18	2	3	11	18	3	0	0	102	35
CEDAR CREEK (CLARK CO)	0	2	0	0	4	0	4	4	2	4	0	0	6	14
*CEDAR CREEK (JEFFERSON CO)	0	0	0	0	0	0	0	0	7	4	0	0	0	11
*CEDAR RIVER	2	9	0	2	0	0	0	18	129	82	69	0	13	298
*CHEHALIS RIVER	0	0	0	2	0	0	2	2	67	306	282	29	2	688
*CHEHALIS RIVER, SOUTH FORK	0	0	0	0	0	0	0	0	0	2	2	0	0	4
*CLALLAM RIVER	2	0	0	0	0	0	0	0	13	16	0	0	2	29
*CLEARWATER RIVER	0	4	2	0	7	7	0	2	27	82	215	29	20	355
CLOQUALLAM CREEK	0	0	0	0	0	0	0	0	0	9	0	0	0	9
COAL CREEK	0	4	0	0	2	0	0	4	7	0	0	0	6	11
COL. R. BELOW BONNEVILLE DAM[2]	3	922	1474	1295	156	33	11	115	99	108	115	0	3883	448
COL. R. ABOVE BONNEVILLE DAM	2	0	31	164	49	2	0	0	0	0	0	0	248	0
COL. R. ABOVE DALLES DAM	0	0	13	7	4	62	27	33	62	71	0	0	279	0
COL. R. ABOVE JOHN DAY DAM	0	2	0	11	7	9	0	2	2	0	2	0	35	0
COL. R. McNARY DAM TO HWY 12	9	16	0	16	9	84	242	162	44	13	0	0	595	0
COL. R. HWY 12 TO PRIEST RAPIDS DAM	293	508	382	963	1578	675	95	69	75	36	31	11	4716	0
COL. R. ABOVE PRIEST RAPIDS DAM	4	2	13	31	44	24	2	2	13	2	0	4	141	0
COL. R. ABOVE WANAPUM DAM	2	0	4	4	20	27	7	13	22	20	4	0	123	0
COL. R. ABOVE ROCK ISLAND DAM	4	2	13	80	220	209	89	71	42	22	9	29	790	0
COL. R. ABOVE ROCKY REACH DAM	11	0	0	13	29	87	91	40	13	33	67	29	413	0
COL. R. ABOVE WELLS DAM	4	7	73	144	668	1895	915	577	246	149	258	36	4972	0
COWEEMAN RIVER	0	2	2	4	0	2	27	133	346	167	62	0	10	735
COWLITZ RIVER	58	138	451	357	202	80	637	3805	3572	1712	506	757	1286	10989
*CURLEY CREEK	0	0	0	0	0	0	0	7	18	16	0	0	0	41
*DAKOTA CREEK	0	0	0	0	0	0	0	0	11	7	0	0	0	18
*DEEP CREEK	0	0	0	2	0	0	0	4	36	9	0	0	2	49
DEEP RIVER	0	0	0	0	0	2	2	2	0	0	0	0	2	4
*DESCHUTES RIVER	0	0	2	0	0	0	2	2	115	80	42	0	2	241
*DEWATTO RIVER	0	0	0	0	0	0	0	40	53	9	0	0	0	102
*DICKEY RIVER[1]	4	11	0	0	0	0	0	0	30	18	24	2	15	74
*DOSEWALLIPS RIVER	0	2	0	2	0	0	0	13	78	40	36	0	4	167
*DUCKABUSH RIVER	0	2	0	0	2	0	0	36	111	38	16	0	4	201
*DUNGENESS RIVER	13	27	7	4	2	0	2	13	87	60	64	0	53	226
*EAST TWIN RIVER	0	0	0	0	0	0	0	2	4	4	0	0	0	10
*ELK RIVER	0	0	0	0	0	0	0	0	0	2	0	0	0	2
ELOCHOMAN RIVER	91	291	266	224	255	153	198	868	1374	278	140	0	1280	2858
*ELWHA RIVER	60	91	29	49	27	2	18	735	382	13	31	53	258	1232
ENTIAT RIVER	0	0	0	0	13	89	20	2	2	13	44	0	183	0
GERMANY CREEK	0	0	0	2	0	4	11	44	80	69	0	0	6	204
*GOLDSBOROUGH CREEK	0	0	0	0	0	4	2	0	22	9	0	0	4	33
*GOODMAN CREEK	0	0	2	0	2	0	0	2	64	66	0	0	4	132
GRANDE RONDE RIVER	0	0	0	0	4	18	0	0	0	0	2	0	24	0
GRAYS RIVER	0	0	0	7	13	7	4	95	186	60	62	0	27	407
*GREEN-DUWAMISH RIVER[1]	289	524	313	393	291	206	204	1039	2975	849	340	0	2016	5407
HAMILTON CREEK	0	0	0	0	0	0	0	0	2	0	2	0	4	0
*HAMMA HAMMA RIVER	0	0	0	0	0	0	0	16	18	4	0	0	0	38
*HOH RIVER	62	58	22	233	120	36	36	282	244	271	204	331	531	1368
*HOKO RIVER	0	0	7	0	0	0	13	47	104	89	0	0	7	253
*HOQUIAM RIVER	0	0	0	0	0	0	0	2	2	0	0	0	0	4
*HUMPTULIPS RIVER[3]	38	60	18	33	22	7	22	121	188	184	302	27	178	844
*HUMPTULIPS RIVER EAST FORK[3]	4	16	0	4	0	2	0	30	5	5	37	18	26	95
*HUMPTULIPS RIVER WEST FORK[3]	4	0	4	0	0	0	0	0	27	27	33	12	8	99
ICICLE RIVER	4	0	0	0	0	0	4	0	0	0	4	0	12	0
JOHNS RIVER	0	0	0	0	0	0	0	0	11	9	0	0	0	20
*KALALOCH CREEK	0	0	0	0	0	0	0	0	0	2	0	0	0	2
KALAMA RIVER	471	826	1152	824	650	448	260	664	579	322	380	240	4371	2445
*KENNEDY CREEK	0	0	0	0	0	0	2	4	49	22	13	0	0	90
KLICKITAT RIVER	7	53	60	373	289	93	11	0	0	0	0	0	886	0
LACAMAS CREEK	0	0	0	2	4	0	0	0	0	0	0	0	6	0
LEWIS RIVER	49	82	260	286	56	18	11	115	93	51	13	27	751	310
LEWIS RIVER, E. FORK	313	591	180	78	644	355	147	395	1001	508	375	115	2161	2541
LEWIS RIVER, N. FORK	164	471	857	899	304	69	33	331	355	213	87	275	2764	1294
LITTLE WHITE SALMON (DRANO LAKE)[4]	2	2	104	951	404	43	0	0	0	0	4	0	1510	0
*LYRE RIVER	20	9	4	4	40	11	18	251	255	111	0	0	88	635
*McDONALD CREEK	0	0	0	0	0	0	0	2	0	0	0	0	0	2
*McLANE CREEK	0	0	0	0	0	2	0	0	0	0	0	0	2	0

PROJECTED (FACTOR = 2.22)

NAME OF RIVER FISHED	SUMMER-RUN 1985 MAY	JUNE	JULY	AUG.	SEPT.	OCT.	WINTER-RUN 1985-86 NOV.	DEC.	JAN.	FEB.	MAR.	APR.	1985 SUMMER TOTAL	1985-86 WINTER TOTAL
METHOW RIVER	0	7	36	93	866	1598	440	20	47	178	1138	0	4423	0
MILL CREEK (COWLITZ CO)........	0	0	0	2	0	0	11	9	9	2	0	0	2	31
MILL CREEK (WALLA WALLA CO) ...	0	0	0	0	0	0	0	2	0	31	120	0	153	0
*MISSION CREEK	0	0	0	0	0	2	0	0	0	0	0	0	2	0
*MORSE CREEK	4	9	4	0	0	0	13	58	95	69	0	0	17	235
*MOSQUITO CREEK	0	0	0	0	0	0	0	0	27	13	0	0	0	40
NACHES RIVER	0	2	2	9	22	18	0	9	2	0	0	4	68	0
NASELLE RIVER	0	0	0	0	2	2	7	122	297	246	167	0	4	839
NEMAH R., NORTH	0	0	0	0	2	0	0	16	89	58	0	0	2	163
NEMAH R. MIDDLE	0	0	0	0	0	0	0	4	9	4	0	0	0	17
NEMAH R. SOUTH	0	0	0	0	0	0	0	0	0	7	0	0	0	7
*NEWAUKUM RIVER	0	0	0	0	0	0	0	2	9	9	160	0	0	180
*NISQUALLY RIVER......	13	31	40	13	2	0	2	40	71	486	544	817	99	1960
*NOOKSACK RIVER......	0	0	2	0	4	2	0	36	53	142	204	0	8	435
*NOOKSACK R. NORTH FK.	0	0	2	0	0	0	0	11	16	73	206	0	2	306
*NOOKSACK R. SOUTH FK.	0	0	0	0	0	0	0	2	0	7	7	0	0	16
NORTH RIVER	0	0	2	0	2	0	2	29	127	75	0	0	4	233
OKANOGAN RIVER	0	0	2	0	162	646	122	13	24	155	56	13	1193	0
OLEQUA CREEK	0	0	0	0	0	0	0	4	7	4	0	0	0	15
*OZETTE RIVER	0	0	0	0	0	0	0	0	2	0	0	0	0	2
PALIX RIVER	0	0	0	0	0	0	0	2	4	20	0	0	0	26
*PILCHUCK CREEK	0	0	2	4	2	2	2	9	9	36	0	0	10	56
*PILCHUCK RIVER[1]	0	0	0	0	0	0	2	78	154	77	0	0	0	311
*PUYALLUP RIVER[3]	2	2	2	0	13	0	46	964	925	381	123	0	19	2439
*PYSHT RIVER	0	0	0	0	0	0	0	7	100	24	0	0	0	131
*QUEETS RIVER	24	16	38	64	29	4	16	155	104	104	67	171	175	617
*QUILCENE RIVER.......	0	0	0	0	0	0	0	2	7	13	0	0	0	22
*QUINAULT R., LOWER ...	0	0	0	4	4	0	0	4	2	0	13	7	8	26
*QUINAULT R., UPPER ...	2	7	2	4	2	9	0	4	31	60	165	0	26	260
*RAFT RIVER	0	0	0	0	0	0	0	0	0	4	0	0	0	4
*RAGING RIVER[1]	0	0	0	0	0	2	0	3	22	21	0	0	2	46
ROCK CREEK (SKAMANIA CO)	0	0	0	0	0	4	11	0	0	0	0	0	4	11
SALMON CR. (CLARK CO)	0	2	0	0	0	0	0	4	27	29	26	0	2	86
*SALMON R. (JEFF CO) ..	7	2	11	0	2	9	0	18	62	29	0	0	31	109
*SALT CREEK	0	0	0	0	0	0	0	0	4	7	0	0	0	11
*SAMISH RIVER	2	0	0	2	7	4	22	204	382	69	73	0	15	750
*SAMMAMISH RIVER	0	0	0	0	0	0	0	42	135	78	64	0	0	319
*SATSOP RIVER	4	0	2	9	0	4	0	4	24	131	0	0	19	159
*SATSOP R., WEST FK. ..	4	7	0	4	0	0	0	11	0	0	0	0	15	11
*SAUK RIVER[1]	7	11	16	24	2	2	3	60	78	163	0	0	62	304
*SEKIU RIVER	0	0	0	0	0	0	0	0	16	26	0	0	0	42
*SHERWOOD CREEK	0	0	0	0	0	0	0	2	2	9	0	0	0	13
*SIEBERT CREEK	0	0	0	0	0	4	0	0	0	0	0	0	4	0
SIMILKAMEEN RIVER	0	0	0	0	31	80	16	2	11	11	595	0	746	0
*SKAGIT RIVER[1]	38	62	33	27	18	7	29	739	797	880	1687	0	185	4132
SKAMOKAWA CREEK....	0	0	0	0	0	0	4	2	4	2	7	0	0	19
*SKOKOMISH RIVER	9	22	0	0	2	9	4	75	164	56	27	0	42	326
*SKOOKUM CREEK	0	0	0	0	0	2	0	0	0	6	0	0	2	6
*SKOOKUMCHUCK R.	4	0	2	0	0	0	0	0	2	7	213	107	6	329
*SKYKOMISH RIVER[1]	182	730	757	542	382	284	213	1717	2271	576	227	0	2877	5004
*SKYKOMISH R., NO. FK.[1] .	9	36	69	47	62	24	12	20	84	20	13	0	247	149
*SKYKOMISH R., SO. FK.[1] .	0	16	18	58	11	2	6	12	8	11	17	0	105	54
SMITH CREEK	0	0	0	0	0	2	2	20	31	20	0	0	2	73
SNAKE R. BELOW ICE HARBOR DAM	0	0	0	0	69	42	24	31	9	0	2	0	177	0
SNAKE R. ABOVE ICE HARBOR DAM	0	0	0	0	33	9	111	87	27	4	4	0	275	0
SNAKE R. ABOVE L. MONUMENTAL DAM .	0	0	0	0	113	226	109	162	42	22	24	0	698	0
SNAKE R. ABOVE LOWER GOOSE DAM ..	0	0	0	0	9	47	51	317	133	109	4	0	670	0
SNAKE R. ABOVE LOWER GRANITE DAM .	0	0	0	0	151	730	619	573	448	557	62	13	3153	0
*SNOHOMISH RIVER[1]	44	184	36	13	31	13	82	846	486	139	46	0	321	1599
*SNOQUALMIE RIVER[1]....	42	275	335	167	151	111	47	431	564	154	64	0	1081	1260
*SOLEDUCK RIVER[1]	67	151	82	27	64	22	7	49	586	551	424	156	413	1773
*SOUTH PRAIRIE CREEK..	0	0	0	0	0	7	0	0	0	0	0	0	7	0
*SQUALICUM CREEK	0	0	0	0	0	0	0	0	0	7	0	0	0	7
*STILLAGUAMISH RIVER ..	7	18	4	2	2	0	2	411	224	173	36	0	33	846
*STILLAGUAMISH R., N. FK.	18	84	144	102	87	109	69	493	602	393	97	0	544	1654
*STILLAGUAMISH R., S. FK.	20	73	62	18	73	44	13	111	78	180	0	0	290	382
*SUEZ RIVER	0	0	0	0	0	0	0	0	0	11	0	0	0	11
*SUIATTLE RIVER	4	7	0	0	0	0	0	0	0	0	0	0	11	0
*SULTAN RIVER[1]	0	13	0	2	0	0	0	23	20	25	0	0	15	68
*TAHUYA RIVER	0	0	0	0	0	0	0	4	71	11	0	0	0	86
*TOKUL CREEK[1]	0	0	0	0	0	0	3	18	172	107	77	0	0	377
*TOLT RIVER[1]	33	42	51	18	40	29	18	57	128	44	0	0	213	247
TOUCHET R. (INCL. NORTH FK).....	0	0	0	0	2	0	2	0	2	7	451	0	464	0
TUCANNON RIVER	0	0	0	0	0	0	7	0	0	7	73	0	87	0
*UNION RIVER..........	0	0	0	0	0	0	2	9	78	47	7	0	0	143
*LAKE UNION SHIP CANAL	0	0	0	0	0	2	4	27	49	36	18	0	2	134
*VANCE CREEK.........	0	0	0	0	0	0	2	0	4	0	0	0	0	6
WALLA WALLA R.	0	0	0	0	7	218	160	82	104	331	597	329	1828	0
*WALLACE RIVER[1]	4	0	0	0	0	0	0	26	45	18	0	0	4	89
*WASHINGTON LAKE.....	7	0	0	13	2	0	0	0	4	2	0	2	22	8
WASHOUGAL RIVER	484	877	493	371	375	113	58	446	666	342	149	122	2713	1783
WASHOUGAL R. WEST FORK	16	31	27	53	209	111	67	16	31	4	0	0	447	118
WENATCHEE RIVER	0	0	0	0	0	0	0	360	215	191	0	0	766	0
*WEST TWIN RIVER	0	0	0	0	0	0	0	0	16	0	0	0	0	16

NAME OF RIVER FISHED	SUMMER-RUN 1985 MAY	JUNE	JULY	AUG.	SEPT.	OCT.	WINTER-RUN 1985-86 NOV.	DEC.	JAN.	FEB.	MAR.	APR.	1985 SUMMER TOTAL	1985-86 WINTER TOTAL
	PROJECTED (FACTOR = 2.22)													
*WHATCOM CREEK......	0	0	0	0	0	0	0	0	7	13	0	0	0	20
WHITE SALMON R.'.....	16	18	388	2672	347	15	2	8	34	29	4	4	3537	0
WILLAPA RIVER........	0	0	0	0	0	2	0	200	431	209	198	0	2	1038
WILLAPA R., SOUTH FK..	0	0	0	0	0	0	0	9	62	31	0	0	0	102
WIND RIVER	0	2	13	47	20	2	11	0	7	2	0	0	104	0
*WISHKAH RIVER	0	0	0	2	0	0	0	22	36	56	84	0	2	198
*WYNOOCHEE RIVER	89	111	109	122	75	58	9	58	40	182	393	0	564	682
YAKIMA RIVER.........	0	0	0	0	13	195	191	182	42	11	2	0	636	0
STATEWIDE														
SUMMER RUN TOTALS ..	3,252	7,710	8,614	12,133	9,782	9,668	3,368	2,819	1,670	2,004	3,559	472	65,051	—
WINTER RUN TOTALS ...	0	0	0	0	0	0	2,555	17,728	25,195	13,409	9,573	3,610	—	72,070
*BOLDT CASE AREA ONLY														
*SUMMER RUN TOTALS ..	1,245	2,848	2,301	2,131	1,715	1,120	0	0	0	0	0	0	11,360	—
*WINTER RUN TOTALS ...	0	0	0	0	0	0	1,044	10,245	15,636	8,822	7,286	2,074	—	45,107

British Columbia Angler Days and Catch Success – Wild and Hatchery 1986-87

Vancouver Island

STREAM NAME	DAYS FISHED REP	DAYS FISHED EST	NO. ANGLERS REP	NO. ANGLERS EST	WILD KEPT REP	WILD KEPT EST	WILD RELEASED REP	WILD RELEASED EST	HATCHERY KEPT REP	HATCHERY KEPT EST	HATCHERY RELEASED REP	HATCHERY RELEASED EST
ADAM RIVER	21	84	7	26	0	0	53	231	1	5	1	5
AMOR DE COSMOS RIVER	34	131	16	60	0	0	64	215	2	8	11	39
BEAR R.												
ASH RIVER	44	177	19	76	0	0	21	85	13	54	11	45
BENSON RIVER	2	8	1	4	0	0	2	8	0	0	0	0
BIG QUALICUM RIVER	931	3645	202	812	0	0	237	938	96	385	264	1018
QUALICUM R.												
BLACK CREEK	5	21	2	8	0	0	0	0	0	0	0	0
BROWNS RIVER	2	6	2	6	0	0	2	8	0	0	1	4
BURMAN RIVER	26	101	7	23	0	0	69	276	1	4	0	0
CAMPBELL RIVER	884	3380	198	693	1	2	263	1035	35	147	275	1110
CAYCUSE RIVER	35	146	7	29	0	0	38	160	0	0	0	0
CAYEGHLE CREEK	19	78	5	21	0	0	5	21	0	0	0	0
CHASE RIVER	5	21	1	4	0	0	4	16	0	0	0	0
CHEMAINUS RIVER	59	243	16	66	0	0	17	70	0	0	9	37
CHINA CREEK	63	262	13	55	6	25	94	390	1	4	0	0
CLUXEWE RIVER	100	402	28	110	0	0	118	463	7	27	28	114
COLEMAN CREEK	3	12	1	4	0	0	3	12	0	0	0	0
COLONIAL CREEK	8	33	3	12	0	0	5	21	0	0	0	0
CONUMA RIVER	5	20	4	16	0	0	5	21	0	0	0	0
COUS CREEK	12	45	5	19	1	2	11	45	0	0	0	0
COWICHAN RIVER	1555	6348	264	1073	2	8	702	2859	63	260	176	717
COTTONWOOD, SKUTZ FAL												
CYPRE RIVER	1	5	1	5	0	0	7	32	0	0	0	0
DAVIE RIVER	1	4	1	4	0	0	1	4	0	0	0	0
ENGLISHMAN RIVER	565	2265	127	517	1	4	228	944	62	257	125	525
ESPINOSA CREEK	2	8	2	8	0	0	2	8	0	0	0	0
EVE RIVER	28	115	15	60	0	0	27	115	1	5	1	4
FRENCH CREEK	14	55	5	18	0	0	1	4	0	0	0	0
GOLD RIVER	710	2749	180	669	2	8	1475	5568	9	27	72	280
UCONA R.												
GOLDSTREAM RIVER	6	25	5	21	0	0	1	4	0	0	0	0
GOODSPEED RIVER	3	12	2	8	0	0	0	0	0	0	0	0
GORDON RIVER	13	57	7	29	0	0	26	118	2	8	2	8
HARRIS CREEK	59	244	28	116	0	0	41	169	0	0	0	0
HASLAM CREEK	3	12	1	4	0	0	3	12	0	0	0	0
HEBER RIVER	9	34	6	22	0	0	6	27	0	0	0	0
JACKLAH RIVER	3	12	1	4	0	0	5	21	0	0	0	0
JORDAN RIVER	2	8	1	4	0	0	0	0	0	0	0	0
KAIPIT CREEK	6	25	2	8	0	0	10	41	0	0	0	0
KAKWEIKEN RIVER	2	9	1	5	0	0	0	0	0	0	0	0
KAOUK RIVER	13	54	3	12	0	0	10	41	0	0	0	0
ROWLAND CR.												
KEOGH RIVER	401	1621	67	270	0	0	400	1572	73	293	476	1865
KENNEDY RIVER	1	4	1	4	0	0	0	0	0	0	0	0
KITSUCKSUS CREEK	10	41	1	4	0	0	15	62	1	4	0	0
KLANAWA RIVER	9	38	2	9	0	0	16	66	0	0	0	0
KOKISH RIVER	16	64	9	35	0	0	24	99	1	4	0	0
KOKSILAH RIVER	33	136	11	45	0	0	8	33	0	0	0	0

STREAM NAME	DAYS FISHED REP	DAYS FISHED EST	NO. ANGLERS REP	NO. ANGLERS EST	WILD KEPT REP	WILD KEPT EST	WILD RELEASED REP	WILD RELEASED EST	HATCHERY KEPT REP	HATCHERY KEPT EST	HATCHERY RELEASED REP	HATCHERY RELEASED EST
KOOTOWIS CREEK	16	66	2	8	0	0	17	70	0	0	0	0
INDIAN R.												
LEINER RIVER	27	110	3	11	0	0	22	90	0	0	0	0
LITTLE QUALICUM RIVE	1034	4188	204	829	1	4	375	1520	123	511	263	1050
LITTLE ZEBALLOS RIVE	4	17	3	13	0	0	10	43	0	0	0	0
MACJACK RIVER	1	4	1	4	0	0	0	0	0	0	0	0
MAGGIE RIVER	6	25	1	4	0	0	0	0	0	0	0	0
DRAW CR.												
MAHATTA RIVER	12	52	7	29	0	0	17	70	0	0	0	0
MARBLE RIVER	109	421	24	87	4	16	70	281	0	0	1	3
AMAZON R., LINK CR.												
MEGIN RIVER	3	14	2	9	0	0	17	78	0	0	0	0
MILLSTREAM RIVER	6	25	1	4	0	0	8	33	1	4	0	0
MOHUN CREEK	8	33	3	12	0	0	11	45	0	0	4	16
TROUT CR.												
MOYEHA RIVER	2	8	2	8	0	0	8	33	0	0	0	0
MUCHALAT RIVER	2	8	1	4	0	0	1	4	0	0	0	0
MUIR CREEK	2	8	1	4	0	0	3	12	0	0	0	0
NAHMINT RIVER	30	125	13	55	0	0	64	264	0	0	0	0
NAHWITTI RIVER	24	97	12	49	0	0	52	216	0	0	0	0
NANAIMO RIVER	1010	4142	119	484	7	29	323	1334	52	215	162	669
NIMPKISH RIVER	127	522	40	161	0	0	128	533	0	0	2	8
NITINAT RIVER	21	87	12	50	0	0	7	29	0	0	0	0
LITTLE NITINAT R.												
OYSTER RIVER	326	1337	82	328	1	2	100	410	6	21	36	147
PUNTLEDGE RIVER	176	721	34	136	0	0	111	457	2	8	71	290
COURTENAY R.												
QUATSE RIVER	422	1759	65	269	1	4	85	346	51	213	290	1195
QUINSAM RIVER	960	3909	154	612	0	0	457	1862	60	234	302	1222
SALMON RIVER	105	409	42	157	0	0	98	402	0	0	4	18
BIGTREE CR.												
SAN JUAN RIVER	86	352	29	118	0	0	67	274	0	0	0	0
CLAPP, FLEET, GRANITE,												
SARITA RIVER	24	100	13	55	0	0	29	120	0	0	0	0
SOMASS RIVER	586	2353	94	367	1	2	142	556	147	579	413	1609
CHERRY CR.												
SOOKE RIVER	81	333	20	82	0	0	5	21	8	33	2	8
SPROAT RIVER	475	1922	79	314	6	17	146	587	98	394	431	1729
STAMP RIVER	2052	8156	409	1577	15	37	757	3100	362	1439	946	3890
SUCWOA RIVER	9	37	2	8	0	0	8	33	0	0	0	0
TAHSIS RIVER	41	169	4	16	0	0	25	103	0	0	0	0
TAHSISH RIVER	3	12	3	12	0	0	4	16	0	0	0	0
TAYLOR RIVER	7	29	3	12	0	0	5	21	1	4	2	8
TOQUART RIVER	12	45	5	19	0	0	24	99	0	0	0	0
TRENT RIVER	29	125	9	38	0	0	9	39	0	0	0	0
TSABLE RIVER	3	12	2	8	0	0	1	4	0	0	0	0
TSOLUM RIVER	9	37	2	8	0	0	0	0	0	0	0	0
TSOWWIN RIVER	4	17	2	8	0	0	8	33	0	0	0	0
TSULQUATE RIVER	10	41	3	12	0	0	11	45	0	0	0	0
WAKEMAN RIVER	10	21	3	6	0	0	7	14	0	0	0	0
WANOKANO CREEK	2	8	2	8	0	0	1	4	0	0	0	0
WAUKWASS CREEK	45	186	20	83	0	0	67	278	0	0	4	16
WHITE RIVER	15	56	9	31	0	0	11	41	0	0	0	0
WOSS RIVER	13	54	7	29	0	0	13	56	1	4	0	0
ZEBALLOS RIVER	123	501	10	37	0	0	32	123	3	12	0	0
ESCALANTE RIVER	1	4	1	4	0	0	0	0	0	0	0	0
COEUR D'ALENE CREEK	6	28	1	5	0	0	4	18	2	9	12	55
VILLAGE BAY CREEK	5	21	1	4	1	4	0	0	0	0	0	0
CAMBELL/QUINSAM RIVE	1	4	1	4	0	0	1	4	0	0	0	0
STAMP/SOMASS	77	323	15	64	0	0	13	58	19	82	458	1894
MILLSTONE RIVER	2	8	1	4	0	0	1	4	0	0	0	0
OUOUKINSH RIVER	1	4	1	4	1	4	1	4	0	0	0	0
AREA TOTALS:	13888	55806	2859	11262	51	168	7395	29602	1304	5254	4855	19598

Lower Mainland

STREAM NAME	DAYS FISHED REP	DAYS FISHED EST	NO. ANGLERS REP	NO. ANGLERS EST	WILD KEPT REP	WILD KEPT EST	WILD RELEASED REP	WILD RELEASED EST	HATCHERY KEPT REP	HATCHERY KEPT EST	HATCHERY RELEASED REP	HATCHERY RELEASED EST
ALOUETTE RIVER	2296	10557	240	1098	12	55	426	1966	195	890	486	2244
SOUTH ALOUETTE R.												
ASHLU CREEK	22	102	6	28	0	0	56	259	2	9	2	9
BEAR RIVER	6	28	1	5	0	0	0	0	0	0	0	0
BERTRAM CREEK	6	28	3	14	0	0	0	0	0	0	0	0
BIG SILVER CREEK	4	18	3	14	1	5	0	0	0	0	2	9
BIRKENHEAD RIVER	13	60	4	18	0	0	1	5	0	0	0	0

Lower Mainland Continued

STREAM NAME	DAYS FISHED REP	DAYS FISHED EST	NO. ANGLERS REP	NO. ANGLERS EST	WILD KEPT REP	WILD KEPT EST	WILD RELEASED REP	WILD RELEASED EST	HATCHERY KEPT REP	HATCHERY KEPT EST	HATCHERY RELEASED REP	HATCHERY RELEASED EST
BREM RIVER	4	17	3	13	0	0	5	22	0	0	0	0
BRITTAIN RIVER	1	5	1	5	0	0	0	0	0	0	0	0
BRUNETTE RIVER	24	111	8	37	0	0	4	18	0	0	8	37
CAPILANO RIVER	548	2511	86	391	0	0	80	369	21	96	43	199
BROTHERS CR.												
CHAPMAN CREEK	106	480	6	27	0	0	25	111	5	22	0	0
CHEAKAMUS RIVER	591	2694	106	473	0	0	376	1727	5	23	14	65
CHEEKYE R.												
CHEHALIS RIVER	1672	7664	324	1481	0	0	273	1247	186	849	497	2294
STATLU CR.												
CHILLIWACK RIVER	14909	67319	1437	6412	24	103	3448	15704	1199	5423	2281	10406
VEDDER R.												
COGBURN CREEK	14	63	8	36	0	0	6	27	3	14	4	17
COQUIHALLA RIVER	332	1493	84	368	0	0	122	548	3	14	30	134
COQUITLAM RIVER	138	635	34	156	0	0	63	290	0	0	3	14
DAKOTA CREEK	36	166	3	14	0	0	4	18	0	0	0	0
ELAHO CREEK	4	18	3	14	0	0	0	0	0	0	0	0
FRASER RIVER	2599	11730	239	1057	63	285	247	1115	11	49	21	97
GRAY CREEK	8	37	2	9	0	0	1	5	0	0	0	0
HARRISON RIVER	21	97	9	42	0	0	1	5	0	0	0	0
INDIAN RIVER	2	9	2	9	0	0	1	5	0	0	0	0
KANAKA CREEK	137	633	17	78	2	9	38	175	7	32	15	69
LANG CREEK	48	221	6	27	0	0	38	175	1	5	0	0
WOLFSOHN CR.												
LANGDALE CREEK	6	28	1	5	0	0	0	0	0	0	0	0
LILLOOET RIVER	9	40	4	18	0	0	2	9	0	0	0	0
LITTLE CAMPBELL RIVE	541	2495	72	330	1	5	52	240	19	88	17	78
LYNN CREEK	50	217	9	39	0	0	4	13	0	0	2	9
MCNAB CREEK	6	28	2	9	0	0	3	14	0	0	0	0
MAMQUAM RIVER	67	309	10	46	0	0	40	185	0	0	0	0
NAHATLATCH RIVER	24	99	9	37	0	0	18	69	0	0	0	0
NATHAN CREEK	5	23	1	5	0	0	0	0	0	0	0	0
BEAVER CR.												
NICOMEKL RIVER	200	923	29	134	0	0	14	65	2	9	3	14
NICOMEN SLOUGH	2	9	1	5	0	0	0	0	0	0	0	0
DEWDNEY SLOUGH												
NORRISH CREEK	7	32	6	27	0	0	0	0	1	5	0	0
SUICIDE CR.												
NORTH ALOUETTE RIVER	162	748	13	60	0	0	32	148	2	9	3	14
ORFORD RIVER	1	4	1	4	0	0	1	4	0	0	0	0
PHILLIPS RIVER	1	4	1	4	0	0	3	12	0	0	0	0
PITT RIVER	21	97	3	14	0	0	26	120	0	0	0	0
QUATAM RIVER	2	7	1	3	0	0	0	0	0	0	0	0
RAINY RIVER	38	171	5	23	0	0	6	26	0	0	0	0
ROBERTS CREEK	41	189	4	18	0	0	11	51	1	5	1	5
SALMON RIVER	57	263	8	37	0	0	7	32	0	0	0	0
SECHELT CREEK	1	5	1	5	0	0	0	0	0	0	0	0
SERPENTINE RIVER	17	78	4	18	0	0	1	5	1	5	0	0
SEYMOUR RIVER	1026	4594	154	692	0	0	240	1097	43	181	69	312
SILVERDALE CREEK	8	37	1	5	0	0	2	9	1	5	0	0
SILVERHOPE CREEK	127	585	24	110	0	0	51	233	0	0	17	78
SILVER CR.												
SQUAMISH RIVER	511	2291	150	662	6	28	275	1233	3	14	12	55
STAVE RIVER	46	212	11	51	0	0	4	18	1	5	2	9
SUMAS RIVER	90	398	9	33	0	0	16	73	3	11	1	4
TZOONIE RIVER	2	9	1	5	0	0	0	0	0	0	0	0
WEAVER CREEK	11	50	8	36	0	0	3	14	0	0	1	5
WHONOCK CREEK	4	18	2	9	0	0	4	18	0	0	0	0
WIDGEON CREEK	2	9	1	5	0	0	0	0	0	0	0	0
WILSON CREEK	4	18	2	9	0	0	0	0	0	0	0	0
MACNAIR CREEK	5	23	1	5	0	0	2	9	0	0	0	0
POTLATCH CREEK	13	30	3	9	0	0	13	30	0	0	0	0
AREA TOTALS:	26648	120739	3187	14298	109	490	6045	27518	1715	7763	3534	16177

Thompson – Nicola

STREAM NAME	DAYS FISHED REP	DAYS FISHED EST	NO. ANGLERS REP	NO. ANGLERS EST	WILD KEPT REP	WILD KEPT EST	WILD RELEASED REP	WILD RELEASED EST	HATCHERY KEPT REP	HATCHERY KEPT EST	HATCHERY RELEASED REP	HATCHERY RELEASED EST
CAYOOSH RIVER	51	179	3	12	0	0	4	18	0	0	0	0
DEADMAN RIVER	4	13	1	3	0	0	0	0	0	0	0	0
NICOLA RIVER	10	37	5	18	0	0	5	20	0	0	0	0
STEIN RIVER	1	4	1	4	0	0	1	4	0	0	0	0
THOMPSON RIVER	1800	6255	382	1362	9	32	1185	4038	1	5	41	129
COLDWATER RIVER	1	2	1	2	0	0	0	0	0	0	0	0
AREA TOTALS:	1867	6490	393	1401	9	32	1195	4080	1	5	41	129

Cariboo

STREAM NAME	DAYS FISHED REP	DAYS FISHED EST	NO. ANGLERS REP	NO. ANGLERS EST	WILD KEPT REP	WILD KEPT EST	WILD RELEASED REP	WILD RELEASED EST	HATCHERY KEPT REP	HATCHERY KEPT EST	HATCHERY RELEASED REP	HATCHERY RELEASED EST
ATNARKO RIVER	280	856	71	216	43	138	164	440	1	3	7	17
BELLA COOLA RIVER	1384	4398	248	777	201	625	802	2311	9	26	13	33
SNOOTLI CR.												
CHILCOTIN RIVER	91	314	32	108	5	17	98	346	0	0	0	0
ALEXIS CR, CHILANKO R												
CHILKO RIVER	2	7	1	3	0	0	2	7	0	0	0	0
CHUCKWALLA RIVER	100	256	29	71	36	90	160	441	0	0	0	0
CLYAK RIVER	3	14	1	5	0	0	1	5	0	0	0	0
DEAN RIVER	2023	5261	357	947	174	525	2878	7285	2	5	11	30
KILBELLA RIVER	40	128	13	33	12	38	77	272	0	0	0	0
KIMSQUIT RIVER	3	9	3	10	0	0	10	37	0	0	0	0
KWATNA RIVER	7	18	2	6	0	0	0	0	0	0	0	0
MACHMELL RIVER	3	12	1	4	0	0	0	0	0	0	0	0
NEKITE RIVER	12	50	4	16	1	5	14	63	0	0	0	0
NOEICK RIVER	4	18	1	5	0	0	1	5	0	0	0	0
QUESNEL RIVER	1	3	1	3	0	0	0	0	0	0	0	0
SALLOOMT RIVER	5	19	3	10	0	0	1	5	0	0	0	0
TALCHAKO RIVER	2	9	2	9	0	0	0	0	0	0	0	0
TALEOMEY RIVER	1	3	1	3	0	0	0	0	0	0	0	0
TASEKO RIVER	1	2	1	2	0	0	0	0	0	0	0	0
AREA TOTALS:	3962	11377	771	2228	472	1438	4208	11217	12	34	31	80

Skeena

STREAM NAME	DAYS FISHED REP	DAYS FISHED EST	NO. ANGLERS REP	NO. ANGLERS EST	WILD KEPT REP	WILD KEPT EST	WILD RELEASED REP	WILD RELEASED EST	HATCHERY KEPT REP	HATCHERY KEPT EST	HATCHERY RELEASED REP	HATCHERY RELEASED EST
BABINE RIVER	1224	3327	226	612	55	171	2093	5261	4	10	14	35
BISH CREEK	4	17	3	12	2	8	0	0	0	0	0	0
BULKLEY RIVER	4487	15635	705	2296	421	1514	2723	9208	4	9	62	166
BOULDER, CHICKEN, TOBO												
BULKLEY/MORICE RIVER	91	280	7	21	6	24	104	359	0	0	0	0
CANOONA RIVER	6	19	5	15	0	0	8	27	0	0	0	0
INDIAN R.												
CEDAR CREEK	18	71	8	31	1	4	20	61	0	0	0	0
CLORE RIVER	45	161	12	38	2	6	30	101	0	0	1	2
CRANBERRY RIVER	466	1528	125	415	81	250	224	790	2	4	3	12
DALA RIVER	1	4	1	4	0	0	0	0	0	0	0	0
DAMDOCHAX CREEK	71	172	13	32	1	4	211	459	0	0	0	0
BLACKWATER R.												
ECSTALL RIVER	4	18	2	9	0	0	0	0	0	0	0	0
FALLS R.												
EXCHAMSIKS RIVER	14	47	6	18	2	7	8	33	0	0	0	0
EXSTEW RIVER	23	93	3	10	2	8	9	37	0	0	0	0
GITNADOIX RIVER	15	49	6	20	3	11	3	12	0	0	0	0
INKLIN RIVER	5	21	2	8	0	0	5	21	0	0	0	0
ISHKEENICKH RIVER	102	394	29	111	18	73	127	489	0	0	0	0
KASIKS RIVER	9	35	5	20	0	0	0	0	0	0	0	0
KEMANO RIVER	4	17	2	8	2	8	1	4	0	0	0	0
KHYEX RIVER	5	21	4	17	1	4	8	33	0	0	0	0
KILDALA RIVER	1	4	1	4	1	4	0	0	0	0	0	0
KISPIOX RIVER	1247	3408	246	691	48	138	1186	3258	2	4	20	45
SWEETIN R.												
KITEEN RIVER	98	352	39	146	27	109	65	259	0	0	1	4
KITIMAT RIVER	1398	5591	201	769	160	652	391	1593	7	29	23	93
HIRSCH, LITTLE WEDEEN												
KITLOPE RIVER	10	41	1	4	0	0	9	37	0	0	0	0
KITSEQUECLA RIVER	9	33	3	11	4	15	2	7	0	0	0	0
KITSUMKALUM RIVER	1170	4625	236	908	118	478	555	2247	0	0	3	10
BEAVER R., KALUM R.												
KITWANGA RIVER	5	16	5	16	0	0	0	0	0	0	0	0
KLEANZA CREEK	12	46	2	6	0	0	0	0	0	0	0	0
KLOIYA RIVER	288	1191	25	103	8	33	114	471	2	8	0	0
KLUATANTAN RIVER	23	75	3	11	0	0	23	79	0	0	0	0
KWINAMASS RIVER	26	101	11	44	6	22	65	266	0	0	0	0
LAKELSE RIVER	925	3323	158	554	43	161	425	1636	2	6	7	28
COLDWATER, WILLIAMS C												
MEZIADIN RIVER	51	206	10	38	2	8	6	25	0	0	0	0
MORICE RIVER	2085	7196	339	1105	187	696	1380	4519	4	17	43	128
NAKINA RIVER	62	157	13	31	19	49	82	215	0	0	0	0
NANIKA RIVER	6	21	2	6	2	4	6	13	0	0	0	0
NASS RIVER	166	507	51	158	24	82	136	395	1	2	2	4
SKEENA RIVER	6469	21010	892	2790	869	2708	2408	7766	15	39	61	170
BOULDER, FIDDLER, KWIN												
STIKINE RIVER	21	72	11	35	1	2	7	21	0	0	0	0
SUSKWA RIVER	66	227	21	72	0	0	86	284	0	0	0	0

Angler days and catch success – wild and hatchery, 1986-87 (Skeena).

STREAM NAME	DAYS FISHED REP	DAYS FISHED EST	NO. ANGLERS REP	NO. ANGLERS EST	WILD KEPT REP	WILD KEPT EST	WILD RELEASED REP	WILD RELEASED EST	HATCHERY KEPT REP	HATCHERY KEPT EST	HATCHERY RELEASED REP	HATCHERY RELEASED EST
BEAR R.												
SUSTUT RIVER	301	801	59	162	42	108	217	557	2	4	1	2
BEAR R.												
TAHLTAN RIVER	54	205	16	58	18	69	21	70	0	0	0	0
TAKU RIVER	9	18	2	4	2	4	3	6	0	0	0	0
TATSAMENIE RIVER	25	47	4	8	1	2	1	2	0	0	0	0
TATSATUA R.												
TELKWA RIVER	59	225	16	57	4	16	8	33	0	0	0	0
TSEAX RIVER	195	671	71	244	32	118	156	601	0	0	0	0
TUYA RIVER	4	13	1	3	0	0	15	49	0	0	0	0
WEEWANIE CREEK	1	4	1	4	0	0	2	8	0	0	0	0
ZYMAGOTITZ RIVER	8	33	4	17	3	12	6	25	0	0	0	0
ZIMACOR R.												
ZYMOETZ RIVER	1527	5465	247	851	141	544	1059	3614	1	4	14	54
COPPER R.												
ENSHESHESE RIVER	1	4	1	4	0	0	1	4	0	0	0	0
KHUTZE RIVER	5	11	3	6	0	0	1	2	0	0	0	0
KINCOLITH RIVER	1	4	1	4	1	4	0	0	0	0	0	0
CHAMBERS CREEK	1	4	1	4	1	4	0	0	0	0	0	0
AREA TOTALS:	22923	77616	3862	12628	2361	8134	14010	44957	46	136	255	753

Queen Charlotte Islands

STREAM NAME	DAYS FISHED REP	DAYS FISHED EST	NO. ANGLERS REP	NO. ANGLERS EST	WILD KEPT REP	WILD KEPT EST	WILD RELEASED REP	WILD RELEASED EST	HATCHERY KEPT REP	HATCHERY KEPT EST	HATCHERY RELEASED REP	HATCHERY RELEASED EST
AIN RIVER	5	21	3	12	0	0	1	4	0	0	0	0
COPPER CREEK	169	677	31	119	21	82	182	734	0	0	0	0
DATLAMEN CREEK	6	25	2	8	0	0	15	62	0	0	0	0
DEENA CREEK	67	273	21	84	7	29	77	320	0	0	0	0
HIELLEN RIVER	33	135	6	24	2	8	23	95	0	0	0	0
HONNA RIVER	131	543	26	108	26	109	67	279	0	0	0	0
MAMIN RIVER	107	434	24	93	18	71	145	578	1	4	0	0
MATHERS CREEK	7	29	2	8	0	0	2	8	0	0	0	0
NADEN RIVER	6	28	1	5	1	5	2	9	0	0	0	0
PALLANT CREEK	57	221	19	73	6	18	87	347	0	0	1	5
MORESBY L.,MOSQUITO												
SANGAN RIVER	5	21	1	4	0	0	0	0	0	0	0	0
SKEDANS CREEK	20	83	2	8	1	4	12	50	0	0	0	0
TLELL RIVER	99	399	30	119	28	114	71	264	0	0	0	0
YAKOUN RIVER	991	4007	157	622	188	753	1574	6406	5	19	19	71
HAANS CREEK	5	21	2	8	0	0	12	50	0	0	0	0
LAGINS CREEK	1	4	1	4	0	0	0	0	0	0	0	0
SLATECHUCK CREEK	1	4	1	4	0	0	0	0	0	0	0	0
AREA TOTALS:	1710	6925	329	1303	298	1193	2270	9206	6	23	20	76

Steelhead licensees, active and successful anglers, catch and angling effort (1966-67 to 1986-87).

Year	Licencees	Active Anglers	Successful Anglers (%)	Total Catch	Days Fished	Catch/ Successful Angler	Days Fished/ Active Angler	Catch/ Angler Day
66-67*	44,100	32,077	4,208(40.9)		N/A			
67-68	39,388	22,289	8,167(37.0)		209,435		9.4	
68-69	39,775	19,789	7,820(41.7)		189,273		9.6	
69-70	45,824	24,515	8,338(36.7)		250,680		10.2	
70-71	43,750	23,533	8,131(35.2)	53,858	232,664	6.6	9.9	0.231
71-72**	26,253	18,270	7,934(44.5)	61,428	184,978	7.7	10.1	0.332
72-73	28,992	19,489	8,165(42.7)	61,452	203,393	7.5	10.4	0.302
73-74	31,315	20,291	8,282(41.1)	58,695	208,105	7.1	10.3	0.282
74-75**	24,399	16,469	7,296(46.5)	51,652	196,751	7.1	11.9	0.263
75-76	29,594	20,265	8,770(45.8)	58,036	219,797	6.6	10.8	0.264
76-77	25,539	18,356	6,998(40.3)	40,618	186,381	5.8	10.2	0.218
77-78	25,406	17,143	7,038(43.2)	45,201	174,721	6.4	10.2	0.259
78-79	24,600	15,788	6,746(44.2)	39,448	159,363	5.8	10.1	0.265
79-80	25,095	14,755	6,384(45.0)	39,569	134,569	6.2	9.1	0.314
80-81	22,276	12,894	6,388(50.7)	50,924	131,886	8.0	10.2	0.406
81-82	21,741	12,970	6,175(48.0)	57,704	126,145	9.3	9.7	0.463
82-83**	20,856	14,475	7,686(54.3)	74,109	148,892	9.6	10.3	0.517
83-84	20,576	14,918	8,547(57.7)	98,622	173,432	11.5	11.6	0.566
84-85	23,236	17,567	10,581(61.6)	147,838	207,370	14.0	11.8	0.730
85-86	25,619	19,397	11,150(58.7)	145,416	215,313	13.0	11.1	0.682
86-87	32,721	24,371	14,560(61.3)	188,417	279,505	12.9	11.5	0.707

* Estimated on the basis of incomplete licencing data.
** Increase in steelhead licence fees.

Estimated annual steelhead catch (1966-67 to 1986-87).

	Wild		Hatchery		Combined Catch		
Year	Kept	Released	Kept	Released	Kept	Released	Total
66-67					77,513	?	
67-68					48,508	?	
68-69					41,403	?	
69-70					37,092	?	
70-71					33,919	19,939	53,858
71-72					36,704	24,724	61,428
72-73					35,782	25,670	61,452
73-74					32,482	26,213	58,695
74-75					27,807	23,845	51,652
75-76					31,490	26,546	58,036
76-77					20,168	20,450	40,618
77-78					18,246	27,093	45,201
78-79					14,700	24,748	39,448
79-80					12,663	26,906	39,569
80-81					10,941	39,983	50,924
81-82	8,604	43,139	1,361	4,600	9,965	47,739	57,704
82-83	10,849	54,259	2,634	6,367	13,483	60,626	74,109
83-84	10,578	68,926	4,506	13,612	15,084	83,538	98,662
84-85	11,648	107,301	7,261	21,628	18,909	128,929	147,838
85-86	10,978	95,745	8,442	30,251	19,420	125,996	145,416
86-87	11,554	126,791	13,223	36,849	24,777	163,640	188,417

INDEX

IF HE'S WILD . . .
LET HIM GO!

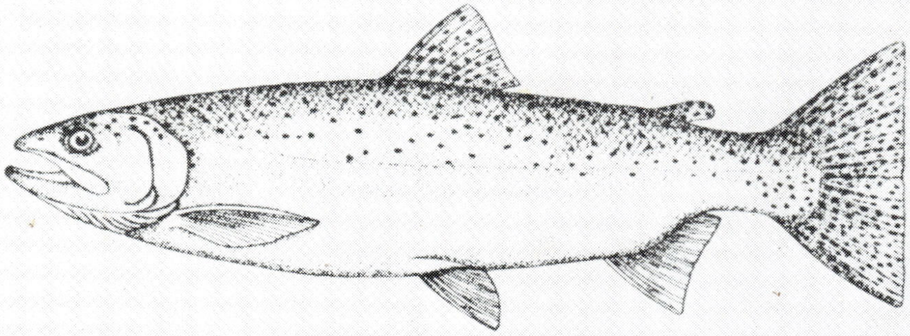

STEELHEAD TROUT
. . .CAN YOU TELL THE DIFFERENCE?

BENT or CROOKED RAYS IN DORSAL FIN

DORSAL FIN MAY BE COMPLETELY DUBBED OFF, GIVING 'CLIPPED' APPEARANCE

Pectoral (side) or Pelvic (belly) fins may also contain crooked rays or have 'clipped' appearance

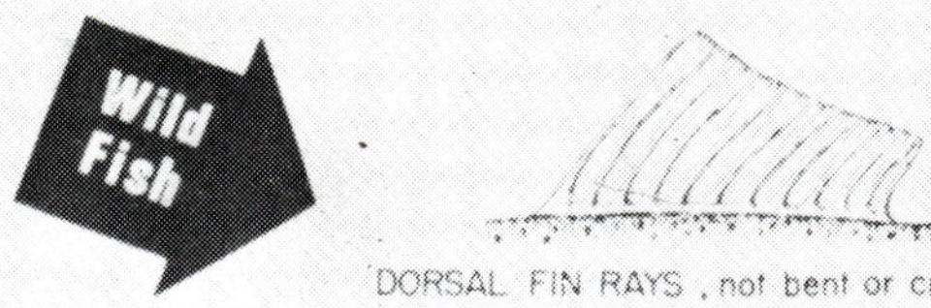

DORSAL FIN RAYS, not bent or crooked

- KEEP WILD FISH IN THE RIVER!
- KILL YOUR FISH, KILL YOUR FISHING!
- DEAD FISH DON'T SPAWN!
- YOUR FISH COUNT!

NORTHWEST STEELHEADERS COUNCIL
OF TROUT UNLIMITED